THE TRIALBOOK
A TOTAL SYSTEM FOR THE PREPARATION AND PRESENTATION OF A CASE

THE TRIALBOOK
A TOTAL SYSTEM FOR THE PREPARATION AND PRESENTATION OF A CASE

JOHN O. SONSTENG
Professor of Law, William Mitchell College of Law
Member, Minnesota Bar

ROGER S. HAYDOCK
Professor of Law, William Mitchell College of Law
Member, Minnesota Bar

JAMES J. BOYD
Trial Instructor, William Mitchell College of Law
Member, Minnesota Bar

With the assistance of
DONALD W. NILES

STUDENT EDITION

WEST GROUP

Bancroft-Whitney • Clark Boardman Callaghan
Lawyers Cooperative Publishing • WESTLAW® • West Publishing

COPYRIGHT © 1984 By WEST PUBLISHING CO.
　　　　　　610 Opperman Drive
　　　　　　P.O. Box 64526
　　　　　　St. Paul, MN 55164–0526
　　　　　　1–800–328–9352

ISBN 0–314–85865–2

TEXT IS PRINTED ON 10% POST
CONSUMER RECYCLED PAPER

6th Reprint — 2002

To
Our
Families

*

INTRODUCTION

The TRIALBOOK presents an innovative system and a thorough approach to the preparation and presentation of a case for trial. This book is designed to be a trial advocacy text and a resource manual of trial theories and techniques. Tactics, ideas, approaches, concepts, strategies, and considerations will be presented in a systematic format to better prepare you for your trials. This system will provide you with a structure and analytical approach to trial advocacy that will both increase your understanding of trial advocacy and improve your trial performance.

We consider you to be an attorney for purposes of this book, and we ask you to also consider yourself to be a trial advocate. This perspective will significantly increase your grasp of the materials. The more you view yourself as a trial lawyer the more effective will be your learning experience. We believe this book will provide you with the materials to become an organized and prepared litigator and a more confident and skilled advocate.

This TRIALBOOK has been designed to be used in all civil and criminal, jury and court trials. Each major facet of a trial appears in a separate chapter. A general description of the purposes of each respective litigation stage begins each chapter. A presentation of the applicable rules, procedures, and case law and an explanation of recognized strategies, tactics, and techniques follow in a summary format. An analysis of ethical guidelines and standards is included to provide depth and balance. Each chapter concludes with a bibliography and a set of forms.

This integrated system attempts to present a comprehensive approach to the preparation and presentation of the trial of a case. The tactics and theories have been selected for inclusion based upon their effectiveness in current trial practice, the advice of experienced trial lawyers, the limited empirical research available, and our trial and teaching experience. Current editions of other trial advocacy books do cover all aspects of trial advocacy. This TRIALBOOK adds a new dimension to the trial literature by providing a comprehensive approach and creative system for trial advocacy.

No one book can claim to be an all-inclusive source on why, how, and when to do it. The presentation of a case depends upon many variables including the available legal theories, the facts, the witnesses, and the individual advocate's abilities. A book which aspires to be a thorough coverage of all the available alternative approaches would be enormous. For this book to pretend to be all things to all advocates would make us similar to Bullwinkle Moose's Mr. Know-It-All. This TRIALBOOK does, however, attempt to address all major facets of trial practice in a systemized format.

Too many lawyers ineffectively and inefficiently try cases. These less than competent presentations deny litigants justice, cost enormous amounts of money, waste substantial time, and demean our profession. The primary cause for poor trial advocacy is the failure or inability of trial lawyers to prepare and plan the trial presentation. Novice trial advocates need a comprehensive set of materials which does not over-complicate the trial process and a simplified system to effectively try a case. This TRIALBOOK has been designed to meet those needs and to promote efficient and economic trial presentations. The approaches and strategies listed in this book detail the factors that need to be considered in trial advocacy and provide an orderly system for implementing trial tactics and techniques.

The format of this notebook has been designed to be flexible. Space has been provided for ideas and insights that you gain from other sources and that you will have as you use and apply the materials. This space may also be used to include notes regarding local practice, procedure and case law which affect trial advocacy. Forms have been provided which provide a guide to the organization of a case. The forms have been designed to guide you through the analytical process necessary to thoroughly and effectively plan a case. The three hole punch, soft cover format allows you to place these materials in a ring binder and to three-hole punch copies of the rules, statutes, cases, and other materials and create one source for all your trial information.

Lawyers have professional obligations to be orderly, systematic, analytical, and thorough. Our clients expect this; our system of justice requires it; our internal standards of ethics and excellence should demand it. We hope this manual will assist you in fulfilling those professional goals. We view trial practice—like law school—as an exciting, challenging, intense, anxious, frustrating and depressing experience. We believe this notebook will make your trial advocacy education and your trial preparation, planning, and presentation more rewarding and enriching.

John O. Sonsteng
Roger S. Haydock
James J. Boyd

ACKNOWLEDGEMENTS

This TRIALBOOK represents a joint effort by many individuals who suggested ideas, made revisions, prodded us on, and assisted us in a variety of ways.

The initial concept of the trial notebook approach to the preparation and presentation of a case came in part from THOMAS VAN HORN to whom we owe much more than an acknowledgement.

This project lay dormant for some time until some William Mitchell students provided the needed research, assistance and editing. We have singled out DONALD W. NILES and listed him on the title page because of his dedicated work. CAROL ECKERSEN also provided significant work in the latter stages of the project. SEANEEN BRENNAN initially researched the law regarding the ethical and malpractice standards applicable to trial lawyers. Other individuals who deserve our thanks are DAVID MEYERS, BRIAN THYSELL, and BEVERLY ANDERSON.

ALBERTA DOWLIN and STEPHANIE ANDERSON ably word processed many of the drafts while LINDA VOLLBRECHT helped with the forms. CONSTANCE BOYD assisted in the preparation of an original draft of some of these materials. DEAN GEOFFREY PETERS, DEAN ROBERT OLIPHANT, and DEAN MELVIN GOLDBERG provided us with the resources to make this book a reality.

Our clients afforded us the opportunities to develop our approach to trial practice and our colleagues provided their ideas and suggestions regarding this venture.

Our families, who provided much more than support and to whom we owe the most, deserve much more than the tribute that comes from the dedication of this book to them.

Without all of these individuals this TRIALBOOK could not exist.

*

Table of Contents

Chapter 1
TRIAL PREPARATION

Few things are brought to a successful issue by impetuous desire, but most by calm and prudent forethought.

—Thucydides

Let us watch well our beginnings, and results will manage themselves.

—Alexander Clark

1.1 The Science, The Art, and The System

The presentation of a case is both a science and an art. An attorney's adherence to and application of rules, procedure, and practice constitute the science. The attorney's adaption of strategies, tactics, and techniques constitute the art. The effectiveness of preparation and presentation will be significantly enchanced by the attorney's use of a "system".

This *Trialbook* presents a systematic and effective, yet economical, approach to the planning, preparation, and presentation of a case. This system is the product of years of experience and teaching. Generally, the best trial systems share several characteristics: rational development, professional approach, practical orientation, derivation from experience, and continual evolution. This *Trialbook* has been designed so that trial lawyers of all levels of experience will be able to use, apply, and adapt its ideas to their own system.

The system advanced in this book, like all other systems, will continue to evolve. Advances in technology are continually changing the shape of the legal profession and the way lawyers prepare to try cases. Word processing systems and computers are now common in law offices. The ideas contained in this manual may be adapted for use with word processing or computer systems thereby making the attorney's preparation efforts more efficient.

The systematic and analytical approach presented in this *Trialbook* has limitations. The trial presentation of a truly effective litigator will be the product of both preparation and experience. Although this book provides most of the concepts necessary for adequate preparation, experience is an essential ingredient. In the final analysis, the effective presentation of a case by a trial lawyer will be the product of many factors including experience, preparation, devotion to the client's case, an understanding of professional ethics, and an internal standard of excellence.

1.2 Trial Notebooks

A. General Notebooks

This *Trialbook* will serve as the basis for a generalized trial notebook for all cases. This base can be expanded by the inclusion of notes, the addition of case law, the insertion of new sections, and the revision of suggested ideas. This notebook can become the primary structural framework for compiling ideas, theories, tactics, and strategies regarding trial practice.

The *Trialbook* should become a constant companion during the preparation, planning, and presentation of the case. This notebook can provide a vital source of information, a checklist of ideas and theories, a compendium of rules and procedures, a place for notes and ideas that would otherwise be forgotten, and a singular source of advice. This book allows the attorney to create and maintain an effective, efficient, and economical system for organizing trial work.

B. Specific Trial Notebooks

Many cases will require an attorney to prepare a specific trial notebook for a particular case. The trial-specific notebook enables the attorney to:
1. Plan and prepare a case in an organized uncluttered manner.
2. Have ready access to pertinent and relevant information.
3. Work on many cases at one time and be involved in other office business.
4. Set aside the case for a period of time, pick it up later, and understand what the case is about.
5. Refer the case to another attorney who can become familiar with it in a short time.

This Trialbook provides a structure for the creation of a specific trial notebook. The forms that appear at the end of each section permit an attorney to prepare and present an individual case for trial.

CASE LAW—LOCAL PRACTICE & PROCEDURE—IDEAS

Outline   Notes

1.3 Case Analysis

A. Initial Analysis

The client interview provides the trial lawyer with the first source of facts and legal theories to initiate analysis of the case. The attorney needs to begin a systemized approach to trial preparation with the first client contact. See Form 1-1 Client Information.

B. Evaluating Facts and the Law

The theories supporting recovery or defenses need to be tested against the facts and law of the case. The legal elements of a prima facie case need to be ascertained. Facts consistent with the claims or defenses need to be obtained. Information that bolsters the persuasive weight of the evidence needs to be gathered. Arguments for and against the various positions should be reviewed to determine their strengths and weaknesses. Theories lacking factual or legal support will need to be revised or abandoned depending on the circumstances of that case. See Form 1-2 Case Evaluation Worksheet.

C. Procedural Rules

The procedural posture of a case must be analyzed to determine timing and notice requirements. A tentative calendar scheduling the service of pleadings, taking of discovery, hearing of motions, and date of trial will provide the initial structure for a case. See Form 1-3 Tentative Trial Schedule.

D. Proof

The elements and requirements of proof should be outlined and matched with the facts to determine which facts support the claims or defenses and whether additional facts need to be gathered. Considerations include:

1. Which facts are necessary to prove the prima facie elements of the case?
2. Which facts will bolster the persuasive weight of the evidence?
3. Which facts will corroborate evidence?
4. How will a fact be proved? If a fact will be proved using testimony, who will prove it? If a fact will be proven using a document or exhibit, which document or exhibit will prove it?
5. When during the trial should a fact be proved?

See Form 1-4 Proof of Facts Worksheet.

E. The Theme

The theme is the central unifying concept of a case. It may be made up of one or more major concepts and several consistent sub-themes. The themes of a case may be likened to strands of thread that are repeatedly used to sew the evidence together into a pattern the jury can easily understand. Common examples of themes for a plaintiff in a personal injury case include the payment of an obligation, the value of human life, and the importance of public safety. Common examples of themes for the defendant in a criminal case include the motivation of vengence, mistaken identify, and the need for fairness. Adequate preparation will aid in the selection of themes, will shape these concepts as the case progresses, and will help mold the entire trial presentation into the themes.

An effective theme must be a concept that the jurors can identify with and believe in. A theme should motivate the jury to decide a case favorably. The persuasive value of a theme will depend in part upon the relationship the theme has with the values of the fact finder. The more the fact finder shares the values espoused by a theme the more likely the fact finder will accept the concept and render a decision consistent with the theme. For example, in a personal injury action, a theme based upon the notion that the injured plaintiff should recover because it is fair is usually not as effective a theme as the concept that the plaintiff has a right to recover damages because the defendant owed a duty to the plaintiff which obligation the defendant breached. More jurors and judges will be persuaded by the later concept because they share a community belief that someone should not be forced to pay for another person's suffering unless that someone has deprived a person of a right and should pay that debt. In a criminal case, a defense theme based on the notion that a prosecution witness is lying is usually not as effective as the concept that the witness is mistaken. Most fact finders share a community belief that most people do not lie under oath but that many people make mistakes because of poor perception or memory.

The theme needs to be presented and reinforced throughout the trial through the use of key words, phrases, images or evidence. Each witness' testimony and each exhibit should be presented in a way that is consistent with the theme of the case. By using a combination of evidence, some directly supporting the themes and some subtlely reinforcing the themes, the attorney will lay a solid foundation for the closing argument. During the closing argument, the attorney will show the jury how each element of the case matches neatly and consistently with the themes. See Form 1-5 Theme Selection Worksheet.

Of course, the need to select a theme early in the trial preparation process should not preclude the refinement of the themes as the trial progresses. In fact, sometimes the discovery of new information may require that the themes be completely changed. Consistent themes are important in presenting a credible case, but the attorney must retain enough flexibility to adapt to the changing circumstances of the case.

F. Theories   Every case needs to be analyzed to determine the most appropriate legal theories and the most effective factual theories.

1. *Legal Theories.* Case law and statutory law will provide the elements for the available legal theories. In most cases, the appro-

priate legal precedent will be obvious. In other cases, the legal theories may need to be modified, analyzed, or created from analogous precedent. See Form 1-6 Legal Theories Worksheet.

2. *Factual Theories.* The facts of a case will usually be susceptible to various interpretations. One or more reasonable inferences may be drawn from the direct and circumstantial evidence. Factual theories must be selected from among these interpretations and inferences. These factual theories must be consistent with the themes of a case, appropriate to the legal theories, and supported by the evidence. As the case develops the factual theories may need to be revised to reflect the most reasonable factual interpretations and favorable evidentiary inferences. See Form 1-7 Factual Theories Worksheet.

G. Alternative Theories   Each case will have available alternative legal and factual theories. The attorney will need to review the alternatives and select the most appropriate theories. It is not uncommon for several sequential theories to be selected. For example, in a contract case, the defense might be: there was no acceptance. If there was, the consideration was inadequate. There was no signed contract. If there was the defendant did not sign the contract. If the defendant did sign the plaintiff defrauded the defendant.

CASE LAW—LOCAL PRACTICE & PROCEDURE—IDEAS

Outline   Notes

1.4 Case Planning

A. Legal Research

Legal research and investigation in a case will initially help develop the theory of the case, uncover new theories, suggest possible theories of the opponent, and set the parameters of the case. See Form 1-8 Legal Investigation Worksheet. Legal research during later stages of the case will aid in discovery, assist in negotiations, and formulate the basis for jury instructions.

B. Fact Gathering

Facts will need to be obtained from a variety of sources, including the client, witnesses, documents, public records, private records, photographs, recordings, personal property, real property, illustrations, and the scene of the event. See Chapter 3 on Discovery.

C. Pleadings

An analysis of the law and facts will form the basis for the pleadings of a case. The complaint and answer provide the framework for constructing the case for trial. See Form 1-9 Summons and Complaint Worksheet and Form 1-10 Answer Worksheet.

D. Support Staff

Part of the case preparation requires the attorney to determine which members of the support staff should become involved in the case. Legal research and fact gathering responsibilities may be delegated to paralegals, investigators, law clerks, clerical staff, or other attorneys. While the clerical staffs' role is usually limited to preparation of documents and correspondence, the opportunity to gain these person's ideas and insights on a case should not be overlooked. The client and other third persons may also be of assistance when gathering and reviewing information.

E. Systemized Approach

The planning of a case should occur in a logical, rational, and systematized way and not in a haphazard manner. Files should be arranged to maintain the pleadings, correspondence, and documents in an orderly manner. Research memos need to be maintained in a central location. Computerized law office equipment readily permits an attorney to create research data banks which may prevent the needless repetition of legal research in later cases.

F. Evidence

The facts which will constitute evidence in the case need to be documented and preserved for use at trial. Potential testimony may need to be recorded. Documents may need to be authenticated, and exhibits may need to be prepared.

G. Trial Memos

A specific trial memo will provide the court and opposing attorney with a concise legal analysis supporting a specific position taken in a case. Questions regarding the validity of theories, the propriety of a certain procedure, and the admissibility of evidence can be addressed in a trial memo to persuade the court. A trial memo should be simple and concise. A one to two-page memo, which focuses on one issue, will usually suffice. The presentation of these memos at a time when the issue is argued will often make the difference between success and failure on particularly close questions. Trial memos, when thoroughly prepared and neatly presented, show that the attorney is well prepared to try the case.

H. Trial Briefs

Some courts require the attorneys to prepare a general trial brief covering a case. These briefs explain the facts, the law, and the evidence involved in the case, identify the trial witnesses, detail any stipulations, describe any pre-trial motions, and include references to other trial matters such as the anticipated length of the trial. The primary purpose of these briefs is to inform and persuade the judge regarding the claims and theories. These briefs may be submitted to a court even though not requested in an attempt to persuade the judge in a case.

A general trial brief may consist in part of concise memos regarding various issues in the case; these memos may be separated from the main brief and submitted to the court as individual issue-oriented trial memos. The preparation of a general trial brief may assist the attorney in planning a case even if a general brief will not be required by the court.

I. Memo and Brief Banks

Trial memo and brief banks can be developed in a law office and updated, when necessary, as the same issues arise in different cases. This research bank is particularly useful as a law firm develops specialties and there is a recurrence of similar issues and problems.

CASE LAW—LOCAL PRACTICE & PROCEDURE—IDEAS

Outline   Notes

1.5 Analysis of Self   *" 'Know Thyself' means this, that you get acquainted with what you know and what you can do."*

—Meander of Athens.

A. *Verbal Analysis*   Diction, pace, tone, and volume will affect the ability of the fact finder to understand what an attorney says. The eloquence as well as the vocabulary of an attorney will also influence the message. Poor grammar, stammers, and fillers, (i.e. "OK, uhuh, uh, and I see") reduce the lawyer's effectiveness. Word choice will likewise affect the jurors' ability to understand the case. Legalese and complex terms may create confusion. Words should be selected that are simple and easy to understand.

B. *Mental Analysis*   An attorney's mental assets and liabilities will shape the parameters of case presentation. Mental strengths need to be taken advantage of while methods are developed to compensate for weaknesses. For example, many attorneys overly rely on written notes for trial presentations because they believe they need memory aids. Practice, concentration, confidence, and a memory outline will usually suffice to overcome this or other perceived inabilities.

C. *Physical Analysis*   The appearance of an attorney and the image an attorney wishes to convey must be consistent for optimum persuasiveness. An attorney who wishes to be perceived as a professional, organized, and orderly advocate must be and appear that way.

Whether or not it is an appropriate consideration, the fact finder will be influenced to some degree by the dress and physical comportment of an attorney. The degree of impression will depend upon many variables including the awareness of the fact finder and whether the appearance of the attorney meets the expectations of the fact finder. The attorney should not become overly concerned about "dressing" for the fact finder but, rather, should attempt to match physical appearance and dress with the image and message that will be communicated to the fact finder.

Posture, mannerisms, and habits may also have an effect on the attorney's ability to communicate and persuade. Twitches, scratching, toe-tapping, swaying, knee-jerking, eyeglass jabbing, hand waving, scribbling, doodling, and paper games may detract from a presentation.

Body language may also affect what the fact finder perceives. The more consistent the content of the message is with the attorney's body language, the more credible the attorney will be. Various postures may signal different messages to different individuals. The attorney should assume a posture that is comfortable, yet professional in appearance.

D. Credibility Analysis

The honesty and sincerity of an advocate will significantly affect that advocate. During all stages of the trial, the jury will be assessing the integrity of the attorney. It is critical for an attorney to appear to believe in the case and client during trial.

It is also critical for the attorney to believe in the case and client during pre-trial preparation. This attitude will prevent the attorney from unconsciously under preparing for trial because of a belief that the case or client is not worth the effort.

E. Coping with Stress

All trial attorneys will suffer stress from one or more sources including unrealistic expectations, money, fatigue, ego, physical discomfort, anxieties, tension, peer pressure, unpleasant feelings, neglect of personal affairs, emotional withdrawal, neglect of spouse and family, and preoccupation with a trial. The unconscious motivation an attorney has to take a case may intensify the stress. Attorneys may take cases for financial rewards but may also unconsciously take them to accept a difficult challenge, to pursue a relationship with a client, to obtain publicity, to achieve fame, to satisfy a rescue fantasy, to change the law, to protect a client's rights, and to promote justice. To maintain a proper and balanced attitude toward trial work it is necessary for such attorney to cope with the stress of being an advocate. Suggestions that help many lawyers handle or reduce stress include.

1. Before accepting a trial, reflect on the reasons why you are taking the case and what your expectations are.
2. During the preparation of a case, involve the client in making decisions and avoid over-controlling the case.
3. Do not worry about events or matters that cannot be controlled. Learn to let go and accept what cannot be changed.
4. Expect that relationships with family, friends, and colleagues will be disrupted.
5. Advise family and friends of the upcoming disruption of time, the resulting stress, and problems that might arise.
6. Anticipate that some family members or friends may emotionally withdraw or be resentful.
7. Maintain a balanced relationship with the client throughout the trial.
8. Discuss feelings and attitudes with family and friends.
9. Monitor the trial workload to avoid becoming overworked.
10. Delegate appropriate responsibility and tasks to support staff.
11. Learn not to unnecessarily interfere and second guess decisions.
12. Avoid excess alcohol, pills, and drugs and other sources of escape.
13. Discuss a case thoroughly after a verdict or decision with the client.

14. Celebrate victories and accept losses.
15. Plan a break after a major trial.

CASE LAW—LOCAL PRACTICE & PROCEDURE—IDEAS

Outline   Notes

1.6 Analysis of
Opponent
A. Strengths and Weaknesses

The persuasive assets and liabilities of an opponent will affect the presentation and effectiveness of a case. Factors that need to be considered concerning the opposing lawyer include:

1. Level of experience.
2. Talent.
3. Presence and demeanor.
4. Reputation.
5. Relationship with the judge.
6. Habits and preferences.
7. How that attorney will be perceived by the jury.

It might be helpful to maintain records of various experiences with different lawyers, especially for attorneys who are encountered infrequently or intermittantly. The log book which appears in Form 1-11 provides a method of maintaining these records. Information about an opposing lawyer may need to be obtained from other sources, especially if the attorney has not opposed that lawyer before. Colleagues, law clerks, bailiffs, and other individuals who know the lawyer may be helpful in providing needed information.

CASE LAW—LOCAL PRACTICE & PROCEDURE—IDEAS

Outline   Notes

1.7 Analysis of the Judge

A. Strengths and Weaknesses

Familiarity with the judge's strengths and weaknesses will help the attorney guide the case. Factors which an attorney needs to consider about the judge include:

1. What are the strengths of the judge as a judge?
2. What are the weaknesses of the judge as a judge?
3. How does the judge handle evidentiary rulings?
4. How does the judge run the courtroom?
5. What special demands may the judge place on lawyers?
6. Has the judge heard any similar cases?
7. What is the educational and professional background of the judge?
8. What is the judicial philosophy of the judge?

It may be helpful to maintain some of this information about judges in a written format. The log book which appears in Form 1-12 provides a method of recording this information. The retained information may be useful in future cases and for other lawyers in the office who have not appeared before a particular judge. Information about a new judge or a judge who has not presided over one of the attorney's cases may be obtained by talking with the law clerk, court reporter, clerk, bailiff, or by asking the judge.

CASE LAW—LOCAL PRACTICE & PROCEDURE—IDEAS

Outline   Notes

1.8 Analysis of the Courtroom

The physical setting established by the courtroom will influence the presentation of the case. An attorney needs to learn the physical setting and become comfortable and familiar with the acoustics, distances, spaces, and general layout of the courtroom. What can and cannot be done in the courtroom will affect how and where the attorney stands during examination and argument and how the attorney presents exhibits. The jury and judge need to have unobstructed and unimpaired views of the attorney, the witness, and exhibits. Some courtrooms have interferences, such as traffic, fan noise, uncomfortable jury chairs, and other problems that the attorney needs to be aware of before proceeding with a case.

The log book appearing in Form 1-14 allows an attorney to build a record of the various courtrooms the attorney attends as a reminder of what can and cannot be done in that room.

CASE LAW—LOCAL PRACTICE & PROCEDURE—IDEAS

Outline   Notes

1.9 Obtaining Information About Court Personnel

Court personnel will also influence the presentation of a case. Careful planning requires the trial attorney to take into consideration the influence that the court reporter, clerk, and bailiff may have on a case. A court reporter will record the trial proceeding, usually on a steno machine and sometimes backed up with an audio recording system, and will mark exhibits. The clerk will usually provide the oath to the witnesses, perform general clerical duties during the trial, and may mark and handle exhibits. The bailiff will usually be responsible for maintaining order in the courtroom and will be responsible for the jury during selection and deliberation. The preferences, characteristics, and practices of these individuals may affect the manner in which a case proceeds. It is necessary for the trial attorney to know what they will do. The log books contained in Forms 1-15 and 1-16 provide a means to record some helpful information.

CASE LAW—LOCAL PRACTICE & PROCEDURE—IDEAS

Outline   Notes

1.10 Preparation of Witnesses

A. Proper Preparation

An attorney needs to develop a system to assure that all witnesses have been contacted and subpoenaed if necessary. It is generally advisable to subpoena all witnesses, even favorable witnesses, to make certain they attend and to make the witness appear more neutral. A subpoena must be accompanied by a witness fee and mileage in most jurisdictions. State statutes determine the amount of these fees.

B. Witness Satisfaction

A satisfied and informed witness may be more effective and persuasive at the trial. Initial and subsequent contacts that an attorney has with a witness will affect the witness's impression of the attorney and of the case. Factors which will influence the witness' perceptions include:

1. Who conducts the preparation? Does the witness feel important because the attorney conducts the preparation?
2. When does preparation occur? Will the witness be more comfortable if the preparation takes place at a time convenient to the witness?
3. Where does the preparation occur? The location, the office, furniture, and physical layout will also affect the impression of the witness.
4. Why does the preparation take place? Do the witnesses understand their role in the trial and the issues in the case to the extent necessary to be an effective witness?

C. Preparation for Direct and Cross Examination

A witness must know what is expected and what will happen at trial. The lawyer must know how the witness will perform. Areas to be covered with a witness before the trial include:

1. The application of the oath and the need to tell the truth.
2. The facts the witness knows.
3. A review of the exhibits the witness will identify.
4. Appropriate demeanor at the trial.
5. The need for the witness to answer questions in a conversational style using their own vocabulary.
6. The role of the lawyers, the judge, the court reporter, the clerk, and the bailiff.
7. When to appear in court.
8. Whether the witness should sit in the courtroom before being called and remain after testifying.
9. Areas of likely cross-examination.
10. Objections and the witness' possible response.

An attorney may need to or wish to provide witnesses with additional information. If the witness is a client, obviously that person will need to be involved in all aspects of the case and know everything about the case. An attorney may decide to explain to some witnesses the theory of the case, the purpose of the witness' testimony in the case, and other information about the case. This knowledge may help the witness be more effective and credible at trial, but may also provide additional areas that can be explored on cross-examination. Preparation must be coordinated to avoid the appearance of having overly influenced the testimony of the witness.

The type and extent of preparation will vary from case to case and attorney to attorney. Some attorneys prefer to conduct a complete dress rehearsal of a planned direct examination and a probable cross-examination complete with questions and answers. Other attorneys prefer to prepare a witness by outlining the structure of the examination without rehearsing specific answers to specific questions. Whatever the approach taken, the witness must be properly prepared to testify in an effective way that does not appear memorized and in a credible way that does not appear manufactured.

Witnesses may be prepared individually, in sets, during one interview or during several interviews. These decisions will depend upon the type of case, the ability of the witnesses, and the time available. Some witnesses may have problems which require special consideration before trial. A child witness, a person with a communication, physical, or mental handicap, the extremely nervous witness, the obnoxious witness, and other types of witnesses may need special care during preparation. Additional resources may assist in dealing with these problems, such as a doctor, linguist, therapist, or interpreter. Some problems may be impossible to solve, and some might not be solved without destroying the integrity of the witness.

D. Witness Integrity

The goal of witness preparation is to have the witness testify truthfully and be believed by the fact finder. Some attorneys overprepare a witness by "sandpapering" and "sanitizing" their testimony. All witnesses will have some weaknesses and problems. These must be dealt with in an open and honest way throughout the trial.

E. Flexible Preparation

An attorney should adjust the approach to a witness depending upon the experience that witness has in testifying, the importance of the testimony, the witness' ability to testify, and the witness' effectiveness in communicating information. Different approaches will need to be taken with different witnesses, particularly if the witness is an expert or professional witness.

F. Experts

Witnesses such as doctors, economists, engineers, appraisers, and other professional witnesses all have strengths and weaknesses. The Logs contained in Form 1-17 will assist in recording and maintaining information about these experts.

G. Explanation of Witness' Obligations   After preparation and before the trial, the attorney should instruct the witness to keep the attorney informed concerning the witness's whereabouts and any new information or ideas concerning the case.

H. Client Guidelines   A client who sits as a party through a trial at counsel table may need to be advised about certain procedures. The client should be told that:

1. The party will be periodically watched by the jurors and the judge and should always be conscious of being observed.
2. The party should periodically maintain eye contact with the jurors and the judge. This helps personalize the client.
3. It is preferable that the client not interupt the attorney during trial unless necessary or when the attorney seeks advice. It may be preferable for the client to write a note to the attorney.
4. It is advisable for the client to pay attention throughout the trial and concentrate on the evidence and arguments and to watch the judge and jury. The client may be able to catch something the attorney missed.

CASE LAW—LOCAL PRACTICE & PROCEDURE—IDEAS

Outline   Notes

1.11 Considering Settlement   Over 90% of all civil and criminal cases are settled or plea bargained. The negotiation process, replete with its tactics and strategies, comprises a substantial and complex area of practice, beyond the scope of this *Trialbook*. One of the most important factors which affects both the decision regarding settlement and the results of a negotiation is the attorney's trial skills. The willingness of the attorney to try a case, the experience of that attorney, the preparation of the case for trial, and the skills of the trial attorney, all significantly influence the negotiation process. A trial attorney must carefully plan and prepare to negotiate, as carefully as preparing for trial. See Form 1-18 Negotiation Worksheet.

CASE LAW—LOCAL PRACTICE & PROCEDURE—IDEAS

Outline   Notes

1.12 Presentation of the Case

The preparation of a case for trial requires the attorney to systematically plan the presentation of the evidence. Form 1-19 Trial Facts Worksheet and Form 1-20 Trial Proof Worksheet provide a structure for such preparation.

The preparation of a case also requires an understanding that the presentation of evidence is a reenactment of an historical event. An attorney directs this play using actors and actresses as witnesses who perform for an audience composed of the jury and judge. Many trials are presented in a boring, uninteresting, and unpersuasive way because the attorneys fail to understand the importance of this perspective. The presentation of a case resembles the presentation of information in the realm of theatre, literature, movies, television, education, and other communication situations. The elements of drama, interest, humanism, excitement, suspense, and other factors that comprise a great work of art will also influence the success of a trial.

CASE LAW—LOCAL PRACTICE & PROCEDURE—IDEAS

Outline	Notes

1.13 Planning the Case Around the Closing Argument

The closing argument is the destination point of the case. Preparing the closing argument is also the beginning point of a trial. The content of a closing argument provides a form and structure for the presentation of the case. The closing argument contains an explanation of the facts, inferences, and arguments that will be necessary to secure a verdict for a party. Planning for such facts, inferences, and arguments at the beginning of the trial preparation process provides a means to present an effective, persuasive, and complete case.

The preparation of a closing argument should precede the preparation of all other facets of a case, including the opening statement. The other parts of the trial may then be planned around the content of the prepared summation. If a fact must be established to support a statement during closing argument, the attorney can plan to introduce the fact through direct or cross-examination. If a closing argument omits certain unnecessary facts, the attorney need not plan to present that evidence during trial. Form 1-21 provides a format to establish an outline for an initial closing argument.

A closing argument that is prepared early in a case will undoubtedly change as case preparation proceeds. The actual jury instructions and evidence presentation may require that alterations be made in the closing argument. The initial closing argument will evolve to some degree as the attorney finalizes trial preparations and the trial progresses.

CASE LAW—LOCAL PRACTICE & PROCEDURE—IDEAS

Outline   Notes

1.14 Court or Jury Trial   There exist many theories concerning whether a judge or jury is more desirable in a particular case. Some considerations include:

1. Whether the case can be presented more effectively to a jury or a judge.
2. Whether it is the type of case that has some sympathetic or emotional aspect that might be more advantageous if a jury considers the case.
3. Whether the case involves technical issues or other complexities that may be better understood by a judge.
4. How effective an advocate the opposing lawyer is before a jury or judge.
5. Whether the witnesses or evidence will be better perceived by judge or jury.
6. The preferences of the client.

The attorney may want to initially demand a jury trial because the demand can be waived later if, as the case develops, it appears that a bench trial would be better. The timing of the waiver of the right to a jury trial may affect which judge is assigned to hear the case. If the attorney would like to have a certain judge or would like to avoid a certain judge, the timing of the decision to waive the jury trial may be crucial. One last consideration is the effect of this decision on a potential appeal. Appellate courts are usually less likely to overturn the factual findings of a jury than those of a trial judge.

CASE LAW—LOCAL PRACTICE & PROCEDURE—IDEAS

Outline   Notes

1.15 Preparation and Presentation of Court Trial

A trial before a judge will require different forms of preparation and presentation than a jury trial. These differences include the following considerations.

A. Opening Statement

There may be no need to make an opening statement in a court trial if the judge appears familiar with the case. Often the trial judge will discuss the case in chambers with the attorneys to determine the issues and attempt to mediate a settlement. This discussion may be a sufficient substitute for an opening statement.

An opening statement presented before a judge may include more than just a recitation of the facts. An explanation of the legal principles, particularly in a complex or technical case, may be advisable.

B. Evidentiary Rulings

The judge who must both decide the admissibility of evidence and the facts may have a difficult time avoiding the influence of inadmissible evidence. When deciding whether to admit or deny the introduction of certain evidence, a judge must understand what the evidence is and may have to accept an offer of proof. Judges may not rely on inadmissible evidence in reaching their decision but it may be difficult for them to disregard the impact of such evidence.

Judges in a court trial will be more inclined to admit evidence than exclude it. Trial judges realize that appellate courts are more likely to overturn a court decision if key evidence is omitted than if the evidence is admitted. The exclusionary rules of evidence have been primarily designed to restrict the introduction of evidence in jury trials.

C. Introduction of Evidence

The presentation of the evidence of a case through witnesses and documents must be addressed to the one person audience—the judge. Strategies and tactics that present information in a persuasive and effective way should be employed. Some attorneys, when presenting evidence, will be less formal and less careful when a jury is not present.

D. Arguments

Objections, arguments, statements, and motions may be brought without regard to having those matters heard outside the presence of a non-existent jury.

E. Closing Argument

The attorney needs to fashion a closing argument which will have the most impact on a judge. Many parts of a closing argument that are designed for a jury will be unnecessary, inappropriate, or ineffective if directed to a judge.

F. Overall Approach

Some attorneys assume that a judge will be more influenced by a rational, logical presentation and do not present information or arguments that would have been presented to a jury. Judges may be influenced and persuaded by some of the same tactics and techniques that affect jurors. For example, the use of demonstrative evidence may be as helpful to a judge in understanding a case as it is to a jury. Case themes and impact phrases may be equally persuasive with a judge. Most judges will be influenced by factors other than pure rationality and cold logic. Many trial lawyers believe that it is easier to present a case and persuade one person (a judge) than it is to persuade six or twelve jurors.

CASE LAW—LOCAL PRACTICE & PROCEDURE—IDEAS

Outline   Notes

1.16 Avoiding Mistrials and Reversals
A. Generally

The American Bar Association Code of Professional Responsibility (Code) and the Model Rules of Professional Conduct (Model Rules) establish standards and impose restraints on a lawyer's behavior. Case law also regulates the conduct of a trial lawyer. The final section of each chapter in this Trialbook will summarize applicable sections of the code and model rules that codify ethical standards and will cite cases that develop practice standards for mistrials and reversals. These latter cases will provide an indication of how a variety of courts have dealt with particular trial conduct.

The Code and Model Rules can be viewed as an external set of regulations that should be followed and not broken. A trial lawyer must also develop a strong, internal personal code of ethics. This Trialbook provides space to record local customs, rules and cases, along with any special considerations involving particular judges, opposing attorneys, or practices peculiar to individual jurisdictions. In the arena of the trial and in the course of litigation, the trial lawyer is constantly judged by peers, the court, and even the community through clients, witnesses, juries, and court personnel. If the lawyer is perceived as dishonest or one who commits "sharp practice" in the courtroom, the lawyer will lose credibility with the court and the bar.

B. Interpreting the Code and Model Rules

While Canon 7 of the Code and Rules 3.1–3.9 of the Model Rules set out guidelines for trial ethics, they can only do so in a broad sense. Consequently, many words and phrases require subjective interpretations (i.e. "zealously," "harass," "vexatious"). The application of the Code and Model Rules is subject to the varying interpretations by the courts and the bar.

C. The Consequences of Misconduct

The most outrageous conduct will be handled by the trial court through the contempt citation and by the appellate court through a reversal. Lesser misconduct elicits a reprimand or other sanction imposed by local Ethics Committees. But local Ethics Committees deal with very few cases of trial misconduct. Surveys by the American Bar Association which rank incidents of lawyer misconduct do not even list trial misconduct. Yet the fact that external sanctions are few and far between should not be taken as unlimited license to do anything that will win the case. The true sanctions are self-inflicted through the loss of reputation, credibility, and ultimately cases and clients.

CASE LAW—LOCAL PRACTICE & PROCEDURE—IDEAS

Outline   Notes

1.17 Bibliography

TEXTS

G. Bellow & Moulton, *The Lawyering Process* 124–598 (Foundation Press, Mineola, NY, 1978).

P. Bergman, *Trial Advocacy in a Nutshell* 374–84 (West Pub. Co., St. Paul, MN, 1979).

S. Goldberg, *The First Trial in a Nutshell* 71–179 (West Pub. Co., St. Paul, MN, 1982).

K. Hegland, *Trial and Practice Skills in a Nutshell* 133–43, 192–250, 275–301 (West Pub. Co., St. Paul, MN, 1978).

J. Jeans, *Trial Advocacy* Chs. 3, 6, 17–18 (West Pub. Co., St. Paul, MN, 1975).

R. Keeton, *Trial Tactics and Methods* 303–50 (Little, Brown & Co., Boston, MA, 1973).

J. Kelner & F. McGovern, *Successful Litigation Techniques* Chs. 2, 4, 6–7 (Matthew Bender, New York, 1981).

T. Mauet, *Fundamentals of Trial Techniques* 1–22 (Little, Brown & Co., Boston, MA, 1980).

J. McElhaney, *Effective Litigation* 270–78 (West Pub. Co., St. Paul, MN, 1974).

A. Morrill, *Trial Diplomacy* 148–77 (Court Practice Inst., Chicago, IL, 1972).

CLIENT INFORMATION   **Form 1-1**

Client _____   File _____

Date   Attorney of Record

Office File   Interviewer

Name

Address

Phone: Home   Business

Social Security No.

Occupation

Employer

Address

Age   Birthdate

Marital Status   Spouse

Income   Gross Pay   Annual   Monthly
                                         Weekly   Hourly

                  Net Pay   Annual   Monthly
                                                         Hourly

                  Pay Period From   To

Children — Names — Addresses

Education   Military

Past Employment

Member of Business, Civic, Fraternal, Social Organizations/Clubs

Criminal/Traffic Record

CLIENT INFORMATION
CLAIMS OR DEFENSES   **Form 1-1 (continued)**

WHO — Names & Addresses of Parties Involved

WHEN — Date of Incident

WHERE It Happened

HOW It Happened

WHY It Happened

WHAT did Client say or do

Has Client given a statement?   To Whom   When

Does Client have copy of statement?

CLIENT INFORMATION
WITNESSES

Name	Address	Phone Home	Business

What can witness prove?

Exhibits

Comments

CLIENT INFORMATION
DAMAGES

Form 1-1 (continued)

Types

Medical Bills   Loss of Income
  Doctor   Gross Pay From   To
  Hospital   Net Pay From   To
  Ambulance   Total
Drugs   Property Damage: Market Value
                                   Before   After
Appliances   Collision
Other   Deductible
Total   Other Damages—Specify
Other Bills
Total   Total

Strengths/Weaknesses

Mitigating Factors

INSURANCE DATA

Policy Provisions

Client's Insurance Company
Address
Phone   Policy No.   Adjuster

Opponent's Insurance Company
Address
Phone   Policy No.   Adjuster

PRIOR LAWSUITS/INCIDENTS/CLAIMS/OFFENSES

Explain

CLIENT INFORMATION
ADVICE

Advice Provided Client

Fee Arrangement

Action to Be Taken

Additional Information/Documents to Be Provided by Client

Need Client compose written summary of facts or event?
A diary of past, present, and future damages or incidents?
Need Client obtain documentation (bills, receipts, checks, estimates)
 for damages?

Has Client executed:
 1. Retainer Agreement
 2. Medical Authorization
 3. Employment Authorization

 4. Income Tax Authorization
 5. Accident Report Authorization
 6. Other Authorizations

Attorney's impressions of client's case

Liability

Damages

Client as a witness

Appearance

Demeanor

Speech

Eye Contact

Other Considerations

Next scheduled appointment   Did Client receive business card?

CASE EVALUATION WORKSHEET
LIABILITY ANALYSIS

Form 1-2

Client _____   File _____

1. Facts of Case

2. Theory(ies) of Liability

3. Analysis of Liability:

    A. Facts

    B. Law

4. Chances/Probability Proving Liability on a 1 to 10 Scale.
    (1 = Poor − 10 = Excellent)

        Rating

    Why/Reasons

CASE EVALUATION WORKSHEET
DAMAGE ANALYSIS

Client _____   File _____

1. Damages

2. Strengths & Weaknesses

3. Mitigating Factors

4. Basis of Recovery for Damages

5. Basis of Non-Recovery Against Damages

6. Analysis of Damages:

   A. Facts

   B. Law

7. Amount of Probable Damage Recovery $

   Why/Reasons

CASE EVALUATION WORKSHEET
ADDITIONAL FACTORS

Form 1-2 (continued)

Client _____   File _____

1. How will Plaintiff appear as a credible witness?

2. How will Defendant appear as a credible witness?

3. How will non-party witnesses appear:

    A. Plaintiff

    B. Defendant

4. What other factors affect case such as bias, sympathy, prejudice, status of parties?

TENTATIVE TRIAL SCHEDULE
Form 1-3

Case _____ File _____

Timing or Notice Requirement	Deadline	Date Completed

Statute of Limitations

Complaint

Answer

Discovery:

  Interrogatories

  Depositions:
      (1)
      (2)
      (3)
      (4)

  Requests for Production

  Examinations

  Requests for Admission

Motions

Trial

Other

PROOF OF FACTS WORKSHEET   Form 1-4

Case _____   File _____

Prima Facie Facts to Be Proved	Persuasive Weight Facts to Be Proved	Corroboration Evidence	Facts Through Testimony	Facts Through Exhibits	Timing of Introduction of Facts

THEME SELECTION WORKSHEET

Form 1-5

Case _____   File _____

What is the central unifying theme of the case?

What sub-themes appear in the case?

What key words, phrases, images, or evidence will highlight the theme and sub-themes?

LEGAL THEORIES WORKSHEET

Form 1-6

Case _____   File _____

What are the most appropriate legal theories to support the client's claims or defenses?

What are alternative legal theories?

What statutory or case precedent supports the legal theories?

FACTUAL THEORIES WORKSHEET

Form 1-7

Case _____   File _____

Facts   Reasonable Interpretation

Facts   Favorable Interpretation

LEGAL INVESTIGATION WORKSHEET　　Form 1-8

Case _____　　　　File _____

Table of Authorities

Applicable Statutes

Controlling Case Law

Secondary Authorities

Legal Conclusion

LEGAL INVESTIGATION
WORKSHEET

Form 1-8 (continued)

Case _____   File _____

Trial Outline

Legal Elements Necessary to Prove a Prima Facie Case

Methods of Proof for Supporting Facts

Evidence to Increase Persuasive Weight of Facts

SUMMONS AND COMPLAINT WORKSHEET   Form 1-9

Case _____   File _____

Plaintiff(s)

Court   Jurisdiction   Venue

Name of Defendant(s)   Address for Service

Plaintiff's Claims:

I.

II.

III.

IV.

V.

VI.

VII.

Addendum Clause $

Date of Service on Defendants

Note of Issue to Be Served and Filed

Trial Calendar Situation   Months

Anticipated Date of Trial

All Affidavits of Service Attached to Original Summons and Complaint

ANSWER WORKSHEET   **Form 1-10**

Case _____   File _____

Defendant

Denials: General

                      Specifically denies paragraphs of plaintiff's complaint.

                      Is without sufficient information on which to form a belief as to the
                          truth of the allegations of paragraphs

Affirmative Defenses:

        Accord & satisfaction   Arbitration & award
        Assumption of risk   Contributory negligence
        Discharge in bankruptcy   Duress
        Estoppel   Failure of consideration
        Fraud   Illegality
        Injury by fellow servant   Laches
        Statute of limitations   Waiver
        Other

Procedural Defenses:

        Lack of jurisdiction   Lack of jurisdiction over
            over subject matter   the person
        Improper venue   Insufficiency of process
        Insufficiency of service   Failure to state a claim
            of process   upon which relief can
        Failure to join a party   be granted
            under Rule 19   Other

Counterclaim

Cross claim for contribution and/or indemnity

Other cross claim

Third party claim for contribution and/or indemnity

Other third party claim

Note of Issue to be served/filed

Third party Note of Issue to be served/filed

Anticipated date of trial

Insurance policy limits

Excess notice letter sent to client

OPPOSING LAWYER LOG   Form 1-11

_____
                    (name)

1. Strong points

2. Weak points

3. Idiosyncrasies
   a) That might allow flexibility

   b) That might limit flexibility

4. Proficiency, Competency
   a) Generally

   b) Evidence

   c) Procedure

5. Negotiation
   a) Strengths

   b) Weaknesses

OPPOSING LAWYER LOG   Form 1-11 (continued)

6. Settle or go to trial

7. Discovery
   a) Prepared or
           not prepared

   b) Harass client?

   c) Tough to deal with
           or cooperative

8. Prepare trial brief

9. Trial Skills
   a) Experience

   b) Preparation

   c) Presentation

10. Other thoughts

JUDGE LOG

_____
                (name)

1. Idiosyncrasies

2. Special court rules

3. Evidence, rulings
   a) Strong points

   b) Weak points

   c) Special considerations

4. Procedure, rulings
   a) Strong points

   b) Weak points

   c) Special considerations

5. Special Ethical Requirements

6. Other thoughts

LOCAL CONSIDERATIONS LOG

(Location)

1. Case law

2. Court Rules

3. Other Rules that may
   limit or restrain
   conduct

COURTROOM LOG

_____

(Location)

1. Acoustics

2. Dimensions

3. Furnishings
   a) Lecturn

   b) Tables
      i) Counsel

      ii) Other

   c) Arrangement

4. Technical capabilities
   a) Outlets

   b) Overhead projector

COURTROOM LOG   Form 1-14 (continued)

c) Screen

d) Shadowbox for X-rays

e) Chalkboard or
   white board

f) Easels

g) Microphones

h) Lighting

i) Interference
   i) Traffic

   ii) Other noise

j) Air conditioning,
   heating

COURT REPORTER LOG

Form 1-15

_____
            (name)

1. Strong points

2. Weak points

3. Efficiency

4. Accuracy

5. Feedback to attorney
   a) Reliability

   b) Accuracy

6. Helpfulness:

7. Idiosyncrasies:

8. Other thoughts:

CLERK/BAILIFF LOG

_____
                (name)

1. Strong points

2. Weak points

3. Idiosyncrasies

4. Helpfulness

5. Expectations of
   lawyer behavior

6. Other thoughts

PROFESSIONAL/EXPERT WITNESS LOG   Form 1-17

_____

(name)

_____

(title or profession)

1. Strong points

2. Weak points

3. Idiosyncrasies

4. Qualifications
   a) Education

   b) Honors

   c) Experience
      i) Generally

      ii) This case

   d) Specialty

   e) Academic appointments

   f) Publications

   g) Continuing professional education

   h) Other background

PROFESSIONAL/EXPERT
WITNESS LOG

5. Testimony
   a) Previous testimony

   i) What side

   ii) How helpful or damaging

   b) Style, presentation, appearance

   c) Quality of content

   d) Prepared

   e) Credibility

   f) Honesty

   g) Cost/expense

   h) Availability

   i) Cross-examination

   j) Other

NEGOTIATION WORKSHEET   Form 1-18

Case _____   File _____

1. Preliminary considerations

    Anticipated litigation/trial cost equal $

    Advantages of settling now include

    Disadvantages of settling now include

    Will client's interests best be met by settling now?
    Why?

2. Preparation

    What needs to be done to prepare for negotiations?

    What should be included in the negotiation agenda? What topics, issues, facts, law and positions need to be discussed?

    What information needs to be obtained from opposing lawyer? What questions need to be asked?

    How should the negotiation process proceed? By telephone, letter, face to face discussions?

    What authority has the client provided for settlement? What settlement range has the client approved?

NEGOTIATION WORKSHEET   Form 1-18 (continued

3. Positions
    What interests, needs, wants, and positions of the client complement the interests, needs, wants, and positions of the opponent?

    Which conflict?

    What reasons/explanations support negotiation positions:

        Facts

        Law

        Prior Verdicts

        Economic Data

        Tax Consequences

        Business Concerns

        Principles

        Tradition

        Fairness

        Reciprocity

        Satisfaction

        Objective Factors

NEGOTIATION WORKSHEET   Form 1-18 (continued)

4. Concession Positions

    Initial Offer/Demand   Supportive Reasons

    Subsequent Offers/Demands

    Final Offer/Demand

    Prediction of Opponent's Offers/Demands

    Reaction to Opponent's Positions

5. Settlement

    Case settled for $

    Client approved

    Settlement check sent   Received

    Release of claims executed

    Stipulation of dismissal executed

TRIAL FACTS WORKSHEET

Form 1-19

Case _____   File _____

1. What facts establish and corroborate the client's version of the case?

2. What facts weaken or contradict the client's version of the case?

3. What facts establish and corroborate the opposing party's version of the case?

4. What facts weaken or contradict the opposing party's version of the case?

TRIAL PROOF WORKSHEET   **Form 1-20**

Case _____   File _____

Elements to be Proved	Key Facts to be Established	Methods of Proof

CLOSING ARGUMENT
PLANNING WORKSHEET   **Form 1-21**

Case _____   File _____

1. Introduction:

2. Theories of the case:

3. Legal Theories:

4. Facts/Witnesses/Documents:

CLOSING ARGUMENT
PLANNING WORKSHEET

Form 1-21 (continued)

5. Factual Theories/Inferences:

6. Law/Instructions:

7. Conclusion and Verdict:

Chapter 2
TRIAL RULES AND MOTIONS

I have only one life, and it is short enough. Why waste it on things I don't want most?

—Louis Dembitz Brandeis

A calm inquiry conducted among those who have their main principles of judgement in common, leads, if not to an approximation of views, yet, at least, to an increase of sympathy.

—Thomas Arnold

2.1 Introduction

Many rules, motions, rulings, standing orders, customs, traditions, and procedures govern the conduct of a trial. Some jurisdictions have committed these practices to writing through local or statewide rules. Many jurisdictions rely on the experience of lawyers and unwritten customs to govern trial procedures. An effective trial lawyer must learn the rules, available motions, likely rulings, and customs applicable in a local forum.

This section summarizes various rules and practices which a trial lawyer must consider to effectively prepare strategy for a case.

2.2 Scheduling a Case

A. Trial Calendar

1. *Civil.* Civil rules of procedure will govern how an attorney places a case on the trial calendar. Typically, a written demand for a jury or court trial or a note of issue is required. After such notification has been served upon the parties and filed with the court, the clerk will place the case on the trial calendar. The attorneys should always know the period of time that will elapse before the case will be called for trial. Each jurisdiction varies, and many jurisdictions will vary from year to year depending upon how many cases have been docketed. The clerk can be contacted and asked how much time will elapse before the case will be called to trial.

2. *Criminal.* Criminal cases are scheduled by the clerk's office without the need for the lawyers to file notes of issue or certificates of readiness. The Constitution, state law, and the defendant's right to a speedy trial govern the scheduling of these cases for trial.

B. *Attorney Readiness*   Many facets of trial preparation should be conducted as soon as possible after the event. The facts will be fresh in the minds of witnesses and documents will be available for preservation. Early discovery is usually more productive than later efforts. The schedule for discovery, however, will be influenced by many factors including how soon a case will be called for trial.

Some jurisdictions require the attorneys to notify each other and the court when they are prepared for trial by filing a certificate of readiness. This notification may terminate discovery unless opposed by one of the parties. This notification may also be a prerequisite to placing the case on the trial calendar.

CASE LAW—LOCAL PRACTICE & PROCEDURE—IDEAS

Outline   Notes

2.3 Selecting a Judge   Some attorneys will attempt to schedule a trial or a hearing so that a certain judge may be appointed. These attorneys reason that certain judges will be more inclined to rule in a particular way that will be favorable to the client's cause. Most jurisdictions limit the choice an attorney has in selecting a judge and appoint judges on a random or set schedule.

A. Removing a Judge   All jurisdictions allow an attorney an opportunity to request that a judge be removed from a case for cause. A judge will ordinarily remove himself or herself from a case in which a conflict of interest or an appearance of impropriety exists. The attorney who believes a judge should be disqualified for good cause will usually have to bring a motion requesting such removal. These situations will arise infrequently and such motions will rarely be granted.

Many jurisdictions allow lawyers a limited opportunity to remove a judge without having to submit a motion and without having to show good cause. These jurisdictions usually permit a lawyer to file a certificate of removal or similar form document which requests that another judge be appointed to hear a case. This procedure does not allow an attorney to select a judge but does permit the removal of the initial judge assigned to the case. The hope of the attorney is that the second judge appointed will be more favorable to the particular case.

The decision by an attorney to submit such a certificate and request can be a tactically difficult decision. In some jurisdictions such requests are made routinely and the judges do not know whether a request for replacement has been made. In these situations, the strategic judgment may be easy. In other jurisdictions such requests are viewed with disdain by the judges. In these situations, it may be better to stay with the intitial judge rather than offend the other judges.

B. Disqualification of Judge   A judge may become unable to hear a case because of illness, disability, or death. Federal Rule of Civil Procedure 63 and similar state rules provide a procedure to replace the judge.

CASE LAW—LOCAL PRACTICE & PROCEDURE—IDEAS

Outline   Notes

2.4 Pretrial Case Summary

Some courts require the trial lawyers, as part of pretrial preparation, to exchange written statements which summarize aspects of the case. These statements assist the lawyers in preparing, highlighting, or narrowing disputed areas, facilitate settlement discussions, and help the court understand the case. These statements may typically include the following information:

1. Name and address of the client.
2. Name and address of the attorney who will try the case.
3. The identity of any insurance carriers.
4. A summary of the pleadings, issues, claims or defenses.
5. A description of the discovery that has been completed and that remains to be completed.
6. A list of any pretrial motions to be brought.
7. The names and addresses of all witnesses who will testify at trial, including expert witnesses and the areas of their expertise.
8. A concise statement of the party's version of the facts of the case.
9. A listing of all exhibits to be offered as evidence.
10. Stipulations the parties have entered into regarding facts, procedures, or evidence.
11. The elements of law that will need to be proved in the case.
12. Citations to relevant statutes, ordinances, or cases that act as authority.
13. An itemized list of special damages if involved.
14. The estimated length of the trial.

See Form 2-1 Pretrial Summary Worksheet.

CASE LAW—LOCAL PRACTICE & PROCEDURE—IDEAS

Outline   Notes

2.5 Pretrial Conferences

A. Chamber Discussions

Immediately prior to a trial or before a jury panel has been summoned, the court may order or a party may request a pretrial conference. See Fed. R. Civ. P. 16. These conferences may serve many purposes and permit the trial judge to:

1. Discuss settlement possibilities or other dispute-resolving opportunities with the attorneys.
2. Determine whether settlement possibilities have been exhausted.
3. Determine all the issues in the case and whether any pleadings need to be amended.
4. Attempt to simplify issues by inquiring whether:
   a) Any issues in the case may be eliminated, narrowed or modified by stipulation, motion, or dismissal;
   b) Admissions of facts exist;
   c) Undisputed facts can be presented by stipulation or in a summary fashion;
   d) Stipulations regarding the waiver of foundation and other objections concerning certain evidence or exhibits may be reached;
   e) Any motions in limine will be made or evidentiary problems will arise during the trial; and
   f) Any critical or unusual legal or factual issues will be presented or arise.
5. Determine the advisability of refering issues to a master or referee.
6. Inquire whether the number of witnesses, including experts, may be reduced.
7. Estimate the time required for testimony and arguments.
8. Determine whether any scheduling problems may occur during trial because of other commitments or conflicts the attorneys, witnesses, or the court may have.
9. Advise counsel of the hours and days scheduled for the trial.
10. Inquire whether counsel plan to use any visual aids or exhibits during opening statements or final arguments.
11. Certify that a jury has been demanded or has been waived.
12. Review the procedures for proposed jury selection interrogation.
13. Summarize the introductory statement the trial judge plans to make to the prospective jurors explaining the case, issues, and law.
14. Determine the number of alternate jurors and peremptory challenges.
15. Begin preliminary consideration of jury instructions.

See Form 2-1 Pretrial Summary Worksheet.

B. Court Rulings   On some matters, the court will make final or provisional rulings during the pretrial conference. See Fed. R. Civ. P. 16. On other matters, a judge will prefer not to make an immediate ruling. The court may reserve a decision until trial in order to consider how the issues are presented or how the evidence is offered.

C. Record   Motions, objections, stipulations, and rulings must be preserved on the record. If a court reporter is present during pretrial discussions, a record is being made. If a court reporter is not present, a record can be made at the end of the conference by summarizing all unwritten matters that need to be preserved in the presence of the court reporter.

CASE LAW—LOCAL PRACTICE & PROCEDURE—IDEAS

Outline   Notes

2.6 Court Personnel   Court personnel may influence the presentation of a case. The court reporter may have some preferences regarding the taking of testimony. The court reporter or clerk may have a system for the premarking of exhibits. The bailiff will have some information about jury procedures. The law clerk may prefer briefs to be in a certain form or length. The trial attorney should become familiar with the preferences and practices of the various court personnel.

CASE LAW—LOCAL PRACTICE & PROCEDURE—IDEAS

Outline   Notes

2.7 Attorney's Trial Conduct   The attorney's conduct is important during every phase of the case. The attorney's conduct will affect the way that persons react to that attorney and, more importantly, to that attorney's client. Below are some general guidelines for attorney conduct. More specific examples appear in the final section in each chapter entitled "Avoiding Mistrials and Reversals."

A. Avoiding Familiarity   During trial the attorney should not display familiarity with the judge, jurors, parties, witnesses or other counsel. The expression of familiarity in the advocacy setting may be viewed as improper.

B. Names   The judge should never be addressed by first name in the courtroom but rather as "Your Honor" or "the Court." It is improper for counsel to address the attorneys or jurors by their first name during trial. It is advisable, and required in some jurisdictions, to refrain from addressing witnesses by their first name to avoid any suggestion of improper familiarity. Some witnesses, such as children, may be appropriately referred to by their first name. Some attorneys will prefer to call witnesses by their first name in an attempt to personalize the witness or for other strategic reasons. It is advisable to seek permission from the court to use first names if the practice of the judge is unknown.

C. Interruptions   An attorney should not interrupt an argument, question, or response unless patently objectionable or prejudicial. It is a matter of professional courtesy to permit opposing counsel to speak without interruption. An examining attorney should wait until a witness has completed an answer before asking another question and should not repeat the witness' answer to a prior question before asking another question.

D. Approaching the Witness/Bench   An attorney should not wander around the courtroom, approach a witness, or approach the bench without first requesting permission from the judge. This procedure is unnecessary if the attorney knows the judge does not require such a request. Some judges will require the attorneys to sit at counsel table or to stand at a lectern during direct and cross-examination. Other judges will require the attorneys to stand at certain positions for a bench or sidebar conference.

E. To Stand or Sit   Courts vary in their requirements regarding whether counsel should stand or sit during various stages of the trial. It is universally common for counsel to stand during opening statement and closing argument. Where counsel stands in relation to the jury and whether counsel must stand behind a lectern may depend upon local rules. Some jurisdictions require counsel to stand during examination and the making of objections. Other jurisdictions allow the attorneys to remain seated. The effective trial lawyer considers the courtroom a stage and seeks permission from the court to stand or sit in order to enhance the attorney's persuasiveness. The decision where to stand or where to sit should be based upon an analysis of where in the courtroom the attorney will be most effective in presenting information or making an argument.

F. "Off the Record"

Any request by counsel to read or mark an exhibit or to go "off the record" should be addressed to the court and not the reporter or clerk. Usually the reporter will only stop recording if the judge so indicates.

G. Demeanor

Counsel should at all times act with respect for the court and all participants in the trial. This professional demeanor should not prevent counsel from becoming assertive, insistent, or aggressive in appropriate situations. Displays of anger, rudeness, and other inappropriate conduct, however, should not occur during the trial.

Counsel should not indicate by facial expressions, body language, head shaking, gesturing, shouts, or other conduct any disagreement or approval of evidence, rulings, or events that happen during the trial. During the time the opposing lawyer makes a presentation or conducts questioning, the other attorney should refrain from reacting, either verbally or non-verbally, to statements and responses.

H. Dress

Counsel should dress appropriately according to the rules or customs of decorum in a jurisdiction. Many attorneys dress according to a standard they believe is expected of them by the judge and jury. Attorneys may have to conform their dress to the standards of a particular jurisdiction or judge to safeguard and promote the best interests of a client. The dress of an attorney should not become an issue which detracts attention from the client's case. Some attorneys prefer to wear a distinctive piece of clothing during a trial to help the jurors remember and identify the attorney.

CASE LAW—LOCAL PRACTICE & PROCEDURE—IDEAS

Outline   Notes

2.8 The Taking of Evidence

A. Witnesses

Counsel should attempt to schedule witnesses in an efficient manner to avoid unnecessary delays. Attorneys should exchange good faith estimates regarding the length of witness examinations. The examining attorney has a responsibility to make certain that the next witness is present in court when needed. Usually a witness' testimony should be pursued until it is concluded and should not be interrupted by the taking of other evidence.

B. Sequestering Witnesses

An attorney may request that the court exclude future witnesses from the courtroom to prevent them from hearing testimony of other witnesses. This strategy may prevent one witness from being influenced by another witness. However, during the preparation of that witness by opposing counsel, that witness may have been informed about the full facts of the case. If so, exploring this area on cross-examination will show the jury that the witness has been thoroughly informed about the case by opposing counsel.

The rules of evidence may also affect the opportunity to exclude witnesses from the trial. Federal Rule of Evidence 615 prohibits the exclusion of a party or of a person whose presence is essential to the presentation of a case, such as an expert witness.

C. Use of Interpreters

A witness may need an interpreter in order to testify. The party calling that witness should advise the court in advance of the need for an interpreter. An interpreter provided by the examining attorney may be sufficient if that person is reliable; otherwise, the court will select an interpreter to ensure that the testimony is interpreted fairly and completely.

The rules of evidence may also regulate the use of an interpreter. Federal Rule of Evidence 604 provides that an interpreter must be qualified as an expert and must be administered an oath or affirmation that the translation will be true.

D. Issuance of Warrants

A witness who fails to abide by a subpoena may be subject to a contempt citation and arrest. See Fed. R. Civ. P. 45(j). Such a warrant may be issued if the service of the subpoena and attendant fees were proper or if no reasonable excuse exists for the witness' failure to attend. The attorney who subpoenaed the witness should make diligent efforts to obtain the witness' appearance or to determine the reasonableness of the witness' failure to appear.

CASE LAW—LOCAL PRACTICE & PROCEDURE—IDEAS

Outline   Notes

2.9 Court Intervention

A. Court-Appointed Experts

A court on its own motion or on the motion of any party may appoint an expert witness to testify in a case. The rules of civil procedure or evidence in a jurisdiction will usually cover the specifics of the appointment. Federal Rule of Evidence 706 governs the appointment of court experts. A judge may perceive the need for an expert to clarify confusing points or assist the fact finder in determining certain issues.

B. Court Witnesses

The court may on its own motion or on the motion of any party call a witness who has not been called by a party. This situation will not occur very often. All parties will be entitled to cross-examine the witness. Federal Rule of Evidence 614(a) authorizes the court to call any person as a witness.

C. Questioning by Court

A judge may interrogate witnesses whether they are called by the court or by a party. See Fed. R. Evid. 614(b). Questioning by a judge will rarely occur in a jury trial and will more often occur in a court trial. The judge will usually not examine a witness until the parties have completed their questions. Most judges limit their questioning to those areas that need clarification. After the judge has finished, the attorneys have the opportunity to further examine the witness on the matters covered by the judge.

D. Right to Object

An attorney has a right to object to the court's appointing an expert, calling a witness, or questioning a witness. See Fed. R. Evid. 614(c). The attorney should make an objection on the record outside the hearing of the jury and ask for a curative instruction.

E. Master/Referee

A judge in certain cases may appoint a master or a referee to assist with the factual or legal matters in a case. Some jurisdictions will have full time masters or referees (or magistrates) who assist the judge with preliminary discovery and pre-trial matters. Federal Rule of Civil Procedure 53 permits federal district courts to appoint standing masters or special masters for cases involving complicated issues, complex damages, or matters of account. Usually, any reference by a judge to a referee will be the exception and not the rule. The judge may allocate the costs in appointing a master or referee between the parties.

CASE LAW—LOCAL PRACTICE & PROCEDURE—IDEAS

Outline   Notes

2.10 Matters to be Heard Outside the Presence of the Jury

Several events that occur during a trial should occur outside the hearing of the jury because of their potential prejudicial impact. See Fed. R. Evid. 103(c) and 104(c). For example:

1. Evidentiary arguments. Concise evidentiary objections may be made within the hearing of the jury, but arguments should be made outside their hearing.
2. Offers of proof and supporting arguments.
3. Stipulations and offers to stipulate.
4. Motions and oral argument.
5. Sensitive areas of evidence. Questions, answers, exhibits, statements, or arguments that may be prejudicial, inflammatory, or inadmissible should be brought to the attention of opposing counsel and the trial judge outside the hearing of the jurors before they occur. An attorney may need to frame a question or an initial argument in such a way as to avoid the suggestion or use of inadmissable information.

CASE LAW—LOCAL PRACTICE & PROCEDURE—IDEAS

Outline   Notes

2.11 Admissions and Stipulations

A. Offer and Use

Facts that have been admitted or stipulated to before or during the trial must be presented to the fact finder in an affirmative way. The attorney who wishes to introduce such evidence must offer the evidence and request that the fact finder be informed in one of a variety of ways.

Fact stipulations may be read to the jury by the attorney offering the evidence or by a neutral person, such as a clerk. Deposition testimony may be presented to the jury with the offering attorney reading the questions and an associate or a neutral person sitting in the witness box reading the answers. Deposition testimony may also be entered in a summary fashion by reading a summary of the testimony to the jury in narrative form. Stipulated exhibits may be explained or provided to the jury in any one of the ways described in Chapter 7 on Exhibits.

B. Evidence Summaries

Lengthy, complex, or factually complicated cases may necessitate the introduction of time-saving evidence summaries. The court may order or the parties may stipulate to several types of summaries including a summary of the testimony of a witness based upon a deposition, a summary list of exhibits and their contents, summary outlines of information, or any other summary which makes the evidence more understandable to the jury.

C. Judicial Notice

Adjudicative facts generally known within the territorial jurisdiction of the court or capable of accurate and ready determination by highly reliable sources may be judicially noticed by a court. See Fed. R. Evid. 201. A party may supply such facts to the court and request the admittance of such evidence, or the court on its own motion may take notice. A judge may take judicial notice of a fact at any time during a proceeding and will ordinarily explain to the jury the fact or facts which have been judicially noticed and their effect in a case. In a civil case, judicially noticed facts shall be deemed to be conclusive; in a criminal case the fact finder may disregard the facts. See Fed. R. Evid. 201.

CASE LAW—LOCAL PRACTICE & PROCEDURE—IDEAS

Outline   Notes

2.12 Trial Motions

A. Generally   Many different types of motions may be made during a trial depending upon what occurs. See Form 2-2 Motion Worksheet. The more common motions include the following motions.

B. Motion in Limine   A motion in limine seeks to exclude from the trial the introduction of certain evidence which is objectionable. This motion may be made before the trial begins in anticipation of certain evidence or during the trial when such evidence is offered.

C. Motion to Strike   A motion to strike is usually made during trial to strike some objectionable matter from the record. Such matter is never actually stricken from the record and this motion serves no useful purpose. A curative instruction from the judge is what should be requested.

D. Motion for Curative Instruction   A motion for curative instruction is a request for the judge to advise the jury to disregard some objectionable matter.

E. Motion for Summary Judgment: FRCP 56   A motion for summary judgment may be brought under Federal Rule of Civil Procedure 56 or a similar state rule. A motion for summary judgment is usually made before the trial begins, but may be brought whenever there exists no genuine issue of material fact and a party is entitled to a judgment as a matter of law. A summary judgment motion may seek a partial judgment on some matter regarding which no genuine issue of material fact exists.

F. Motion for Involuntary Dismissal: FRCP 41   This motion, which is brought pursuant to Federal Rule of Civil Procedure 41 or a similar state rule, requests the judge to dismiss the case for failure by the opposing party to show any right to relief.

G. Motion for Directed Verdict or Motion to Dismiss: FRCP 50(a)   After the close of an opponent's case in chief, an attorney may assert a motion for a directed verdict under Federal Rule of Civil Procedure 50 or similar state rule. A judge will grant such a motion if the evidence that has been introduced is insufficient to support a verdict for the opposing party. In civil cases the proper motion is for a directed verdict. In criminal cases, the proper defense motion may be a motion to dismiss for failure to prove a prima facie case.

H. Post Trial Motions   These motions are explained in Section 11.6.

CASE LAW—LOCAL PRACTICE & PROCEDURE—IDEAS

Outline   Notes

2.13 Motion Argument Preparation

The preparation of an argument in support of or in opposition to a motion requires the same degree of preparation that any other facet of trial advocacy requires. The judge will expect an attorney to be prepared. An opposing attorney will evaluate a lawyer's performance during motion argument and assess that lawyer's trial skills and capabilities.

A. Time

Whether a specific time limit will be set for a motion argument depends upon the court and the judge. Some courts will schedule motions for a specific and limited amount of time; other courts will schedule motions in sequence and allow attorneys a reasonable time for argument. The attorney needs to decide how much time is necessary and how the available time should be used. If more time for argument is needed than is allocated by a court, the clerk may be contacted and more time arranged.

B. Court Proceedings

In some jurisdictions it may be an expedient practice, prior to the motion argument or upon arriving at the court, to check with the clerk to make certain that the motion has been scheduled, that the file is in the courtroom, and that the file contains all moving papers. Occasionally, calendars may become confused and files may be routed to the wrong courtroom.

C. Preparation of the Judge

An attorney needs to ascertain whether the judge has read or is familiar with the motion, the case, and the applicable law. Some judges will review the file before the hearing; others will not have time to do so. The extent of the judge's familiarity with the motion will affect the beginning and content of the motion argument. The judge who is not familiar with the case may spend the first few minutes looking through the file and not actually listening to the beginning attorney's argument. The judge who is familiar with the case may not need much information about the background of the case. The extent of the preparation by the judge may be learned by the attorney by contacting the clerk or law clerk and inquiring about the judge's knowledge about the case.

D. Assignment of Judge

Some jurisdictions have a judge retain a case and hear all motions and matters relating to it. Other jurisdictions rotate judges and the same judge who resolved the motion may not be the same judge who presides over the trial. A judge may or may not prefer to stay with a case from the initial motion hearing through the trial. If a case is complex or presents interesting issues, a judge may be inclined to retain the case. Whether a judge will only hear the motion or whether the judge will later be involved with the case may or may not make a difference in how the attorney presents a motion argument.

E. Sequence of Argument

The moving party will usually argue first with the opposing attorney then having an opportunity to speak in opposition to the motion. Judges will usually permit rebuttal arguments by both lawyers as long as the statements appear necessary and relevant to the motion.

F. Memoranda

Many judges will require some written legal authority supporting or opposing the granting of the motion. Some jurisdictions will require a brief or citation of authorities to be submitted in support of a motion. Some other jurisdictions will also require a memorandum from the lawyer who opposes the motion.

A memorandum should be short in length and contain a summary of the vital facts and the legal authorities supporting the position asserted by the attorney. A lengthy, detailed memorandum is usually not necessary for a motion argument because most trial judges for reasons of efficiency and crowded calendars will not be able to devote the time to thoroughly read such a memo. A one or two page memo that lists the issues and supporting legal authorities and citations may be sufficient.

A memorandum may also be submitted to the court after a motion argument if some issues have been brought up during argument which were not briefed and which need briefing to assist the judge in making a decision. An attorney may suggest that a memorandum and a reply memorandum be submitted to the court, or a judge may request such submissions from the attorneys.

G. Proposed Order

It is good practice to submit to the court a proposed written order which contains the relief sought in a motion. Such a proposed order will make clear to the judge the specific relief requested and will make it easier for the judge to grant such relief.

During argument, some judges will make their ruling on the record or indicate which way they will most likely decide the motion. If a written order is necessary, the successful attorney in these situations should offer to submit an order consistent with the decision by the judge. This practice maintains an active, direct role by an attorney in the decision-making process.

CASE LAW—LOCAL PRACTICE & PROCEDURE—IDEAS

Outline   Notes

2.14 Motion Argument Presentation

An effective, efficient, and economic presentation in support of or in opposition to a motion must address the following question: What information does the judge need to decide the motion in favor of the client?

A. The Facts

Many motions revolve around questions of law and the facts of the case may not make a significant difference in the outcome of the motion. Many other motions will depend upon the development of the facts. The presentation of facts in a motion hearing will often occur by the submission of affidavits which contain the relevant, necessary information. Some motion hearings will involve the presentation of live testimony through witnesses and the introduction of exhibits. Such evidence offered during a motion hearing will usually mirror the direct and cross examinations of the witnesses in a trial.

When affidavits are submitted in support of or in opposition to a motion, there may be no need for the client or any witness to attend the hearing. When an attorney believes that additional evidence or live testimony is necessary or may be preferable, the party or the witnesses with such information should attend the hearing. When a judge believes that the granting or denial of a motion will turn on a fact which neither party has submitted to the court, it may be necessary to continue the motion hearing or to present the information by way of affidavit after the motion hearing terminates.

B. Chambers Argument

Arguments on some motions may occur in chambers rather than in the courtroom. Some judges may prefer to discuss the merits of the motion on an informal basis in the chambers rather than in a formal argument in the courtroom. If an attorney believes that the determination by the judge regarding the motion would more likely result in a favorable ruling if the argument were presented in the courtroom, then the attorney should request the matter not be heard in chambers but rather in the courtroom.

C. Courtroom Argument

The courtroom presentation of a motion will usually involve the attorney standing and arguing before the judge. These arguments will usually not be recorded unless such proceedings are routinely recorded in a jurisdiction or unless an attorney requests and a judge approves that such matters be recorded.

CASE LAW—LOCAL PRACTICE & PROCEDURE—IDEAS

Outline   Notes

2.15 Motion Argument Techniques

The techniques of motion hearing argument do not significantly differ from other oral argument situations. The appropriate techniques to be employed will depend upon the judge's familiarity with a motion, the type of motion presented, the position asserted by the opposing lawyer, and the time available.

A. Conversational Approach

Many lawyers will present a closing argument in a formal way as if they were in a debate. This approach may not be as effective as a conversational approach in which the attorney converses with the judge instead of arguing with an opponent in front of a judge.

An attorney, to be an effective "conversationalist" in this setting needs to adopt a persuasive style, to display familiarity with the facts of the law, to exude confidence, and to persist when necessary. Rapport, eye contact, voice tone, diction, pace, gestures, and other facets will influence the effectiveness of a presentation.

B. Preface

An attorney should preface the substance of an argument with a brief outline of what will be covered. It will be easier for a judge to follow an argument when the judge knows what points the attorney will argue. The judge may then suggest to the attorney certain matters that need not be covered because the judge may be familiar with them or may have already resolved them. A judge may also be inclined to postpone asking questions about a matter until that point is reached during the argument.

The moving attorney who speaks first may also want to include as a preface a short description of the motion, its grounds, and the relief sought to remind the judge about why the attorneys are in court. The moving attorney may also wish to provide the court with some background regarding the nature and history of the case to put the motion in perspective for the judge. An opposing lawyer may inform the court of such information if a moving party fails to do so.

C. Structure

The argument that follows the prefatory remarks an attorney makes during a motion hearing must be structured in an effective, persuasive manner. The optimum order for an argument will depend significantly on the type of motion presented. Any lengthy argument must be carefully structured so that it can be easily followed by a judge. The motion, memorandum, proposed order, affidavits, or other moving papers may provide an attorney with an outline for a structure.

D. Substance of Argument

What an attorney will say and what relief will be requested will depend upon the type of motion presented. An explanation of the facts and the law mixed with reason, logic, emotion, and equity will comprise the content of a presentation. Some techniques that may increase the persuasive value of an argument include the following considerations:

1. Should the strongest position be asserted first, with the second strongest position last, with other weaker positions explained in between?
2. Should key words, phrases, or positions be emphasized and repeated throughout the argument?
3. Should who or what brought about the need for the motion be mentioned?
4. Is the motion a routine request, an unusual request, or a common request?
5. Should the failure or refusal of the opposing attorney to cooperate with the moving lawyer in resolving or compromising the issues of the motion be mentioned?

E. The Law

Legal explanations should be accurate and understandable. Many arguments lose their effectiveness because the attorney exaggerates the applicable law and explains it in a confusing way. An attorney should carefully select references to the law to be explained during argument. Leading cases, supporting statutes, and persuasive quotations should be referred to as necessary. Cases from other jurisdictions, peripheral legal authorities, and overly technical explanations should be minimized. Legal matters should be argued if they can be explained more effectively in oral argument rather than in a brief. Legal matters that can be effectively presented in a memo need not be repeated orally, unless the attorney anticipates the judge will not read the memo.

References to the law should also be concise. Quotations from cases or statutes should be woven into an argument and should not be read in detail. Long quotes and specific citations should be provided the judge in a memo, brief, or outline of authorities. An attorney should be able to explain the legal positions without having to bore a judge by reading from some authority.

F. Factual Descriptions

A description of the facts should include a complete and accurate recitation of the relevant evidence. Some attorneys will ramble during motion argument and provide the court with some factual information which does not appear in an affidavit, in the file, or on the record. The opposing attorney should point out to the judge the inadequacy of this information and the inappropriateness of the attorney attempting to testify or provide evidence in an improper manner. Other attorneys may exaggerate or stretch the facts to match a point of law. These tactics will usually backfire because the inherent weakness of such a position will be readily apparent to the opposing lawyer and to the judge.

G. Notes   An argument should not be read to a judge. A set of notes outlining the essential points of an argument may be used during a presentation as a guide. The failure to use notes may indicate the lack of preparation of an attorney and may make a complete and logical presentation difficult. Whatever notes an attorney uses should not detract from the presentation of an argument.

H. Visual Aids   Visual aids such as diagrams, charts, graphs, exhibits, or other devices may help an attorney present an argument and may assist a judge in understanding an argument. The use of visual aids may seem inappropriate to a judge or an opposing attorney during argument. However, if visual aids will enhance the persuasiveness of an argument, then a lawyer may wish to consider their use. An opposing lawyer may be advised and permission of the judge may be sought prior to the hearing to avoid problems at the hearing and to prevent any waste of time in preparing visual aids.

I. Interruptions   Interruptions of the opposing attorney and of the judge should be avoided. It is unprofessional and discourteous to interrupt opposing counsel unless the statements are prejudicial, bear no relation to the motion, or mischaracterize something that requires immediate correction. Many judges will admonish an attorney who unnecessarily interrupts. It may be more effective for a lawyer to note any misstatements of fact or law and comment on any inappropriate statement after the opposing lawyer has completed an argument.

A lawyer should direct all statements to the judge and should avoid directly arguing with the opposing attorney. It may be necessary in some situations for a lawyer to request that the court direct the opposing counsel to apologize for a remark or to admonish that counsel for making disparaging statements.

J. Opposition Weaknesses   An argument should contain references to the weaknesses of the other side's case or to the inappropriateness of a position taken by the opposition. It will be necessary sometimes to anticipate positions taken by an opposing lawyer and counter those points during argument. If this is not possible or appropriate, rebuttal will afford an opportunity to expose the weakness in the opponent's case. An argument will sound more persuasive if it is directed in a positive, constructive manner. A defensive argument that merely attacks the opposition may appear to be weak. A lawyer opposing a motion must be careful not to present such an appearance.

K. Candor and Compromise

An attorney must be candid during arugment. If the facts and supporting law provide the judge with the discretion to grant or deny a motion, a moving party should not argue that the judge has only one option and that is to grant the motion. If the facts and supporting law provide a moving party with a reasonable position, an opposing lawyer should not unnecessarily castigate the position or pretend that precedent requires the judge to deny the motion.

An attorney may also have to compromise during a motion hearing. Many judges will view the hearing as an opportunity to force the attorneys to negotiate a resolution to the problem. Attorneys who argue set positions during a motion hearing must be prepared to propose or accept alternative positions to resolve a matter. A motion hearing may provide a forum for a judge to mediate a solution to a problem the attorneys were unable to solve on their own.

L. Questions by the Judge

Questions asked by the judge should always be answered at the time asked and should rarely be postponed until later. The judge will expect an answer to a question when asked and may not listen to the continuing argument until the question has been answered.

An attorney should directly and completely answer a question and should avoid hedging or qualifying a response. An attorney should also attempt to provide an answer in a light most favorable to a position. An attorney must be prepared to, if necessary, concede a point in a response and avoid arguing an issue with a judge. The attorney should attempt to place a concession in perspective and continue on with another point.

M. Involving the Judge

The attorney should prepare and present an argument that seeks to involve the judge in the motion. Some judges will be more inclined to be active and others will be more inclined to be passive during oral argument. An effective presentation by an attorney will be an approach that develops an interchange between that attorney and the judge. The more the judge participates in a discussion regarding the motion, the better the judge may understand the case and the more likely it may be that the judge will properly decide the motion. The attorney may want to invite questions from the judge to involve the judge as much as possible.

N. Summary

The primary purposes of motion argument include acquainting the judge with the merits of a position, answering questions the judge may have, and persuading the judge that the client is entitled to the relief sought.

CASE LAW—LOCAL PRACTICE & PROCEDURE—IDEAS

Outline   Notes

2.16 Trial Problems

A. Problem Witnesses
An attorney who examines a witness on direct examination must be prepared to direct and control the testimony of the witness. Likewise, a cross-examiner must control the responses of an unfavorable witness. An attorney may need to admonish a witness who is not responsive by politely and firmly insisting upon a response to a question or by seeking assistance from the judge, who may or may not agree to admonish the witness. An attorney should initially make one or more attempts to control the responses of a witness before seeking the intervention of a judge, and should know ahead of time whether the judge will intervene or force the attorney to control the interrogation.

B. Problem Judges
A trial attorney who has difficulties caused by a judge who makes inappropriate comments, improper remarks regarding evidence or objections, unfair comments on the testimony or credibility of a witness, incorrectly prohibits an attorney from presenting the case, or engages in facial grimaces, body language, or non-verbal conduct that disrupts the presentation of that attorney should place all these matters on the record denoting what has happened and objecting to the behavior. This can be a delicate and difficult task but may be necessary to correct the judge's behavior and preserve the client's best interests. The attorney who is objecting to this behavior may prefer to initially approach the bench and, out of the hearing of the jury, request the judge to refrain from such conduct.

C. Attorney Problems
If the opposing counsel creates problems for the attorney by making improper statements, behaving in a distracting manner, or engaging in any other inappropriate behavior detrimental to the case, the attorney should object on the record. The court should be requested to intervene and admonish opposing counsel. An attorney should avoid arguing with opposing counsel. Some lawyers may attempt to "bait" another attorney into an argument but such situations should be avoided.

CASE LAW—LOCAL PRACTICE & PROCEDURE—IDEAS

Outline   Notes

2.17 Avoiding   Various courts and jurisdictions may have local rules and prac-
Mistrials and   tices which must be followed. In many instances, local rules of de-
Reversals   corum and standing practice orders will be just as important as state
and federal procedures. In order to avoid mistrials, reversals, and
allegations of attorney malpractice, the attorney must become familiar with these local rules and practices.

It would be impossible to include every local rule and practice
in this *Trialbook*. Each of the other chapters contains a section on
avoiding mistrials and reversals. With other chapters, it is possible
to draw some general conclusions regarding specific trial conduct.
With local rules and practice, the most that can be said with any
accuracy is that each jurisdiction will vary. The best advice is to
become familiar with the local rules and practice of the court and
jurisdiction where the trial will take place.

CASE LAW—LOCAL PRACTICE & PROCEDURE—IDEAS

Outline   Notes

2.18 Bibliography

TEXTS

P. Bergman, *Trial Advocacy in a Nutshell* 333–45 (West Pub. Co., St. Paul, MN, 1979).

S. Goldberg, *The First Trial in a Nutshell* 1–60 (West Pub. Co., St. Paul, MN, 1982).

R. Haydock & J. Sonsteng, *Negotiation Manual for Demonstration Videotapes* (Nat'l Inst. for Trial Advocacy, St. Paul, MN 1982).

K. Hegland, *Trial and Practice Skills in a Nutshell* 83–85 (West Pub. Co., St. Paul, MN, 1978).

J. Jeans, *Trial Advocacy* Ch. 4–5 (West Pub. Co., St. Paul, MN, 1975).

R. Keeton, *Trial Tactics and Methods* 216–36, 354–89 (Little, Brown & Co., Boston, MA, 1973).

J. Kelner & F. McGovern, *Successful Litigation Techniques* Chs. 3, 9 (Matthew Bender, New York, 1981).

J. McElhaney, *Effective Litigation* 279 (West Pub. Co., St. Paul, MN, 1974).

A. Morrill, *Trial Diplomacy* 4–7, 39–42, 56–59, 212–25 (Court Practice Inst., Chicago, IL, 1972).

PRETRIAL SUMMARY WORKSHEET

Form 2-1

Case _____   File _____

1. Summary description of case

2. Description of discovery that remains to be completed

3. Reasons why case has not been settled

4. List of pretrial motions

5. Description of motions in limine or prospective evidentiary problems

6. Identity of all trial witnesses, including experts

7. List of all trial exhibits

PRETRIAL SUMMARY
WORKSHEET

Form 2-1 (continued)

8. Concise statement of party's version of facts, including damages

9. Concise summary of party's claims or defenses

10. Stipulations of facts or undisputed facts

11. Elements of law that need to be proved

12. Citations to specific statutes or case law

13. Case to be tried by: Court   (   )   Jury   (   )

     If jury, number of jurors _____

     Number of alternate jurors _____

     Number of peremptory challenges _____

     Estimated time for trial _____

14. Other problems to be considered by trial court

MOTION WORKSHEET

Form 2-2

Case _____   File _____

Date   Judge

Time   Courtroom

Purpose of motion

Supporting affidavits

Legal memorandum of law in support or opposition to motion

Notice of motion, motion supporting affidavits and legal memorandum of law, and proposed order for granting motion

Served   Filed

Chapter 3
DISCOVERY

Through every rift of discovery some seeming anomaly drops out of the darkness, and falls, as a golden link, into the great chain of order.

—Edwin Hubbel Chapin

If I have ever made any valuable discoveries, it has been owing more to patient attention, than to any other talent.

—Isaac Newton

3.1 Purposes
A. Fact Gathering

The investigation and discovery of facts serve many purposes in the trial system. The gathering and exchange of information:
1. Establishes the various versions of what happened.
2. Provides for the mutual disclosure of information.
3. Explores the perceptions and approaches of the opposition.
4. Documents data and preserves facts and exhibits.
5. Narrows issues and isolates disputed facts.
6. Promotes settlements based upon accurate and complete information.
7. Fosters verdicts based upon accurate and complete information.

CASE LAW—LOCAL PRACTICE & PROCEDURE—IDEAS

Outline   Notes

A. Information From the Client

Initial and subsequent client interviews will reveal information and sources of information. See Form 1-1 Client Information in Chapter 1.

B. Information From Documents

Every case will involve written materials or data which provide additional information. Form 3-1 provides a listing of common documentary sources.

C. Information From Witnesses

Witnesses will have vital knowledge and information. See Form 3-1 Factual Investigation Worksheet. These individuals may have firsthand or hearsay information. Several considerations affect the fact gathering process:

1. *Who should be contacted?* All persons with information need to be contacted. This includes persons who can confirm, add to, fill in, corroborate as well as contradict and challenge the client's version.

2. *When should they be contacted?* A witness who is contacted soon after the event will usually have more accurate and worthwhile responses than a witness who is contacted long after the event. It may be advisable to contact witnesses before the opposition in an attempt to gain untainted or even favorable responses from the witnesses.

3. *How should the witnesses be contacted?* Friendly witnesses will usually cooperate. Neutral witnesses may need a reason to tell what they know. Unfriendly witnesses may disclose little or no information unless deposed. Most witnesses will cooperate if they understand why they are being questioned. Reasons investigators use to persuade a witness to cooperate include:
   a) The client's crucial need for the information;
   b) The importance of the witness and the information to the case;
   c) The cooperation of the witness now may prevent further involvement in the future;
   d) The witness's responsibility as a citizen to cooperate;
   e) A sense of fairness and justice on the part of the witness;
   f) The witness need only listen to the investigator relate what happened and then correct the story; and
   g) A threat to subpoena the witness later.

4. *What approach should be taken?* The two extremes of witness interviewing are (1) the narrative, open ended approach where the witness tells the story, and (2) the leading question, controlled approach where the witness corrects or confirms a story told by the investigator. Most interviews will involve a series of

narrative questions followed by specific, clarifying, and probing questions. This method usually provides a complete and accurate account of the witness's perceptions.

5. *What should the statement include?* The contents of a statement should include:
   a) Name, address, home phone, business phone of witness;
   b) Witness' occupation and employer's name;
   c) Brief background of the witness;
   d) Date, time, location of event from the perspective of the witness;
   e) Description of the event, including all details and documents;
   f) Presence of any other witnesses; and
   g) Agreement of witness to sign, initial, or affirm statement.

6. *How should the information be preserved?* It may or may not be advisable to permanently preserve the information through a statement, memo or tape recording. The need to make a record, the concerns about discoverability of such information, and the potential use of a record at trial are factors which need to be considered.

7. *Types of witness statements.* Witnesses may provide information in a variety of ways:
   a) Handwritten statements;
   b) Investigator handwritten or typed statements signed, initialed, or approved by the witness;
   c) Court reporter transcripts of the interview; and
   d) Contemporaneous tape recording of the person-to-person or telephone interview.

D. *Summary*   See Form 3-2 Investigation Worksheet

CASE LAW—LOCAL PRACTICE & PROCEDURE—IDEAS

Outline   Notes

3.3 Scope of Civil Discovery

A. Relevance: Federal Rule of Civil Procedure 26(b)(1)

Information is discoverable if it:
1. Bears on the subject matter of the case or could lead to other matters that bear on any issue;
2. Relates to any claim or defense of any party; or
3. Is reasonably calculated to lead to admissible evidence.

B. Privileged Status: FRCP 26(b)(1)

A privilege may be conferred by constitutional provisions, statutory enactments, or common law. Courts interpret and apply privileges in light of reason and experience. Information will be privileged if it was intended to be and remains a confidential communication. Some privileges will be absolute; others will be qualified. Protective orders will sometimes permit selective disclosure of information.

C. Trial Preparation Materials: FRCP 26(b)(3)

Trial preparation materials are writings prepared in anticipation of litigation or for trial. Factors that influence their discoverability include:
1. Why were the materials gathered?
2. Who prepared the materials?
3. When were they prepared?

Trial preparation materials will be discoverable only if the party seeking discovery has substantial need of the materials and is unable to otherwise secure the information.

D. Witness Statements: FRCP 26(b)(3)

A party or witness may obtain a copy of the statement if the statement was signed, approved or contemporaneously recorded.

E. Attorney's Mental Impressions: FRCP 26(b)(3)

Creative legal efforts, opinions, and work product will be exempt from disclosure. The efforts by an attorney in thinking about, analyzing, reviewing options, considering applicable legal theories and similar efforts will be protected even if reduced to writing and recorded in a file.

F. Expert Information: FRCP 26(b)(4)

There are four categories of expert information:
1. Experts who testify at trial must reveal through interrogatories their identity, subject matter of proposed testimony, facts, opinions, and bases for opinions.
2. The identity of retained or specifically employed experts may be discoverable, but other information will only be available under exceptional circumstances.
3. No discovery is available from experts informally consulted.
4. Full discovery is available from experts who are employees or agents of the party.

G. Protective Orders: Reasonable restrictions may be placed on disclosure of infor-
    FRCP 26(c)   mation including terms, conditions, timing and method of disclosure.
              A court may also prescribe who will have access to information. Rule
              26(c) details the various types of potential orders available.

CASE LAW—LOCAL PRACTICE & PROCEDURE—IDEAS

Outline   Notes

3.4 Scope of Criminal Discovery

Discovery in criminal matters is not as broad as discovery in civil cases. Federal rules of criminal procedure limit the discovery that is available to both the government and the defendant. State law or local rule may also limit the discovery by the government and the defendant of information in either of the parties possession. In addition, the constitutional requirement of a speedy trial for the defendant may drastically limit the availability of discovery because of the lack of time.

The government usually has the capability to have law enforcement officials take complete statements from witnesses and victims of criminal offenses. The government also has the ability to obtain information through the grand jury. Most of this information is generally discoverable by the defense.

The obligation of the defendant to provide information to the prosecution is not only constitutionally restricted but is limited in most cases by the fact that most of the information about the case is in the hands of the prosecution with the exception of alibi, mental illness or mental defect defenses. Generally, the provisions in Sections 3.1, 3.2, 3.5 and 3.11 are applicable to criminal as well as civil matters.

A. Government Required to Disclose: Fed. R. Crim. P. 16

Certain evidence in criminal cases is required to be disclosed by the government.

1. *The Statement of the Defendant.* On request of the defendant the government must disclose to the defendant relevant written or recorded statements made by the defendant in the control of the government which is known or should be known by the government. At the request of the defendant, the government must also disclose oral statements made by the defendant, the substance of any oral statement made by the defendant that the government intends to offer at trial, and any recorded testimony of the defendant before a grand jury which relates to the offense charged. Fed. R. Crim. P. 16(a)(1)(A).

2. *Defendant's Prior Record.* On the request of the defendant the government must furnish to the defendant a copy of the defendant's prior criminal record which the government has or becomes known to the government. Fed. R. Crim. P. 16(a)(1)(B).

3. *Documents and Tangible Objects.* Upon the request of the defendant the government must disclose to the defendant books, papers, documents, photographs, tangible objects, buildings, or places in the possession of the government which are material to the preparation of the defense or are intended for use by the government as evidence in chief at the trial or which were obtained from or belong to the defendant. Fed. R. Crim. P. 16(a)(1)(C).

4. *Reports of Examinations and Tests.* On request of the defendant the government must disclose to the defendant the results or reports of physical or mental examinations and of scientific tests or experiments in the control of the government or which may become known to the government which are material for the preparation of the defense or intended for use by the government as evidence in chief at the trial. Fed. R. Crim. P. 16(a)(1)(D).

B. Government not Required to Disclose: Fed. R. Crim. P. 16

Certain information in the possession of the government is not subject to disclosure except as provided in the Rule 16(a)(1)(A), (B), (C), and (D).

1. *Reports, Memoranda, Internal Documents.* The defendant does not have the right to discovery or inspection of reports, memoranda, or other internal government documents made by the attorney for the government or other government agents in connection with the investigation or prosecution of the case or statements made by government witnesses or prospective government witnesses except as provided in 18 U.S.C. §3500.

2. *Grand Jury Transcripts.* Grand jury transcripts except as provided in Fed. R. Crim. P. 6, and 16(a)(1)(A) may not be discovered and inspected by the defendant. Fed. R. Crim. P. 16(a)(3).

C. Defendant Required to Disclose: Fed. R. Crim. P. 16

Certain evidence in the possession of the defendant must be disclosed to the government.

1. *Documents and Tangible Objects.* If the defendant requests disclosure under Rule 16(a)(1)(C) or (D) and the government complies, the defendant upon request of the government must permit the government to inspect, copy or photograph books, papers, documents, photographs, or tangible objects within the possession custody and control of the government which the defendant intends to introduce as evidence in chief at the trial. Fed. R. Crim. P. 16(b)(1)(A).

2. *Reports of Examinations and Tests.* If the defendant requests disclosure under Fed. R. Crim. P. 16(a)(1)(C) or (D) and the government complies, the defendant on request of the government shall permit the government to inspect and copy or photograph any results or reports of physical or mental examinations and of scientific tests or experiments made in connection with a particular case in the control of the defendant which the defendant intends to introduce as evidence in chief at the trial or which were prepared by a witness whom the defendant intends to call at the trial when the results of the report relate to the testimony. Fed. R. Crim. P. 16(b)(1)(B).

D. Defendant not Required to Disclose: Fed. R. Crim. P. 16

Other information in the possession of the defendant is not subject to the disclosure.

1. *Reports, Memoranda, Internal Defense Documents.* Except for scientific reports or reports concerning the mental condition of the defendant, the government does not have the right to discovery or inspection of reports, memoranda or other internal defense documents made by the defendant or the defendant's attorneys or agents in connection with the investigation or defense of the case or of statements made by the defendant or by government or defense witnesses or by prospective government or defense witnesses made to the defendant or the defendants' attorneys. Fed. R. Crim. P. 16(b)(2).

E. Continuing Duty to Disclose: Fed. R. Crim. P. 16

The government and the defendant have the continuing duty to disclose additional evidence or material previously requested or ordered if discovered prior to or during a trial which is subject to discovery or inspection under Rule 16. The party must promptly notify the other party or the attorney or the court of the existence of the additional evidence or material. Fed. R. Crim. P. 16(c).

F. Regulation of Discovery: Fed. R. Crim. P. 16

1. *Protective and Modifying Orders.* Upon a sufficient showing the court at any time may order that discovery or inspection be denied, restricted, or deferred or make such other order as is appropriate. A protective order requires a motion by a party and then the court may permit the party to make such showing in the form of a written statement to be inspected by the judge alone. After this ex parte showing the court can order the entire text of the party's statement be sealed and preserved in the records of the court and made available to the appellate court in the event of an appeal. Fed. R. Crim. P. 16(d)(1).

2. *Failure to Comply with a Request.* If a party during the course of the proceedings is shown to have failed to comply with the discovery and inspection required by Fed. R. Crim. P. 16 the court may order such party to permit the discovery or inspection, may grant a continuance or prohibit the party from introducing the evidence not disclosed. The court may also enter any order it deems just under the circumstances. The court may further specify the time, place, and manner of making this discovery and inspection and prescribe such terms and conditions as are just. Fed. R. Crim. P. 16(d)(2).

G. Notice of Alibi: Fed. R. Crim. P. 12.1

1. *Notice by the Defendant.* If the government makes a written demand for notification of an alibi defense which states the time, date, and place at which the alleged offense was committed the defendant must serve within 10 days or at any different time as the court may direct a written notice of the defendant's intention to offer a defense of alibi. The notice by the defendant shall state

the specific place or places at which the defendant claims to have been at the time of the alleged offense and the names and addresses of the witnesses upon whom the defendant intends to rely to establish such an alibi. Fed. R. Crim. P. 12.1(a).

2. *Disclosure of Information and Witnesses.* After the defendant gives a notice of an alibi defense the government within 10 days but in no event less than 10 days before trial unless otherwise directed by the court, shall serve upon the defendant or the defendant's attorney a written notice stating the names and addresses of the witnesses upon whom the government intends to rely to establish the defendant's presence at the scene of the alleged offense and any other witnesses to be relied upon to rebut testimony of any of the defendant's alibi witnesses. Fed. R. Crim. P. 12(b).

3. *Continuing Duty to Disclose.* Prior to or during a trial, if a party learns of additional witnesses whose identity should have been included in the information required to be furnished under Fed. R. Crim. P. 12.1(a) or (b) the party must promptly notify the other party of the existence of this information and identify such additional witnesses. Fed. R. Crim. P. 12.1(c).

4. *Failure to Comply.* If any party fails to comply with the requirements of Fed. R. Crim. P. 12.1 the court may exclude the testimony of any undisclosed witness offered by such party as to the defendant's absence from or presence at the scene of the alleged offense. The defendant is not by this rule prohibited from testifying on the defendant's own behalf. Fed. R. Crim. P. 12.1(d).

5. *Exceptions.* The court can grant exceptions for good cause shown to any of the requirements of Rule 12.1(a)–(d). Fed. R. Crim. P. 12.1(e).

6. *Inadmissibility of Withdrawn Alibi.* The evidence of an intent to rely upon an alibi defense which is withdrawn at a later date or of statements made in connection with such intention is not admissible in any civil or criminal proceeding against the person who gave the notice of the intention. Fed. R. Crim. P. 12.1(f).

H. Notice of Defense Based upon Mental Condition: Fed. R. Crim. P. 12.2

1. *Defense of Insanity.* If a defendant intends to rely on the defense of insanity at the time of the alleged crime the defendant must timely notify the attorney for the government in writing of such intent. If the defendant fails to do so, insanity may not be raised as a defense. The court may for cause shown allow late filing of the notice or grant additional time to the parties to prepare for trial or make such order as may be appropriate. Fed. R. Crim. P. 12.2(a).

2. *Mental Disease or Defect Inconsistent with the Mental Element Required for the Offense Charged.* If the defendant intends to

introduce expert testimony relating to a mental disease or defect or other condition bearing upon the issue of whether the defendant had the mental state required for the offense charged the defendant must timely notify the attorney for the government in writing of such an intention. The court may for cause shown allow late filing of the notice or grant additional time for the parties to prepare for trial or make such other order as may be appropriate. Fed. R. Crim. P. 12.2(b).

3. *Psychiatric Examination.* In an appropriate case, upon motion of the attorney for the government, the court may order the defendant to submit to a psychiatric examination by a psychiatrist designated in the order of the court for this purpose. No statement made by the accused in the course of this examination shall be admitted in evidence against the accused on the issue of guilt in any criminal proceeding. Fed. R. Crim. P. 12.2(c).

4. *Failure to Comply.* Failure to give notice required by 12.2(b) or (c) may give rise to an order by the court to exclude the testimony of any expert witness offered by the defendant on the issue of the defendant's mental state. Fed. R. Crim. P. 12.2(d).

I. Depositions: Fed. R. Crim. P. 15

1. *Witness or Party.* A deposition of a witness or party may be taken in exceptional circumstances when required to preserve the testimony of that party or witness for use at trial. Fed. R. Crim. P. 15(a).

2. *Motion and Notice Required.* The party desiring to take a deposition must file a motion to do so with the court and serve notice on the other parties. Fed. R. Crim. P. 15(a).

3. *Discretion of Court.* The court has the discretion to determine if a deposition may be taken based on exceptional circumstances required to preserve testimony. Fed. R. Crim. P. 15(a).

4. *Books, Papers, Documents, etc.* Upon motion, the court may also require that any book, paper, document, record, recording, or other material, not privileged, be produced at the time of the taking of the deposition. Fed. R. Crim. P. 15(a).

5. *Notice of Taking.* Reasonable written notice of the time and place of taking of the deposition is required to be given by the party taking the deposition. The notice must state the name and address of each person to be examined. Fed. R. Crim. P. 15(b).

6. *Continuance.* The party upon whom the notice is served may by motion request the court to extend or shorten the time period for the taking of the deposition and the court has the discretion to determine if the time should be changed based on this motion. Fed. R. Crim. P. 15(b).

7. *Payment of Expenses.* The government has the obligation of paying the expenses of depositions taken at the request of the gov-

ernment and has the obligation of paying for depositions at the request of a defendant when the defendant is unable to pay for them. Fed. R. Crim. P. 15(b).

8. *Depositions Taken Pursuant to Civil Rules.* Depositions must be taken and filed in the manner provided in civil actions (See Fed. R. Civ. P. 30 and 32) except that no deposition shall be taken of a party defendant without consent and the scope and manner of examination and cross-examination shall be such as will be allowed in the trial itself. Fed. R. Crim. P. 15(d).

9. *Statements of Witness being Deposed.* The statements of the witness being deposed which are in the possession of the government shall be made available to the opposing side if the defendant would be entitled to that statement at trial under Fed. R. Crim. P. 16. See Section 3.4(B). Fed. R. Crim. P. 15(d).

10. *Use of Deposition.* A deposition may be used as substantive evidence if the witness is unavailable as defined by Fed. R. Evid. 804(a), or the witness gives testimony at the trial or hearing inconsistent with the deposition. It may also be used by any party for the purpose of contradicting or impeaching the testimony of the deponent. If only part of the deposition is offered in evidence by a party, an adverse party may require all of the relevant parts of the deposition to be offered. Any party may offer other part. of that deposition. Fed. R. Crim. P. 15(e).

11. *Objections to the Deposition Testimony.* Objections shall be stated at the time of taking the deposition. Fed. R. Crim. Proc. 15(f). See Chapter 9 Objections.

12. *Taking and Use of Deposition by Agreement.* A deposition can be taken orally or upon written questions by agreement of the parties. If the court consents, the deposition may be used in any way with which the parties agree. Fed. R. Crim. P. 15(g).

CASE LAW—LOCAL PRACTICE & PROCEDURE—IDEAS

Outline   Notes

3.5 Planning Civil Discovery

Information can be obtained by informal requests of the opposing attorney, mutual voluntary exchanges, and Fed. R. Civ. P. 29 stipulations. Effective discovery planning involves consideration of the following questions:

1. How should discovery requests be sequenced?
   a) What method should be employed first?
   b) Which side should proceed first?
2. What information can be discovered through the pleadings?
3. What effect will adding or deleting a party have upon the scope of discovery?
4. What information can be obtained through motions, affidavits, and statements in open court?
5. What data can be garnered through negotiation discussions?
6. Does the unusual case permit pre-complaint discovery pursuant to Fed. R. Civ. P. 27?
7. What information should be obtained through:
   a) Informal requests?
   b) Interrogatories?
   c) Requests for production of documents and things?
   d) Depositions?
   e) Physical examinations?
   f) Request for admissions?
   g) Rule 45 subpoenas?
8. Should a discovery conference be convened pursuant to Fed. R. Civ. P. 26(f)?

A. Supplementary Responses: FRCP 26(e)

Discovery requests which seek certain information must be supplemented. Responses must be supplemented if the information:

1. Includes the identity and location of persons having information.
2. Includes the identity of trial experts.
3. Renders prior responses incorrect or becomes a knowing concealment.
4. Completes a previous incomplete response.

CASE LAW—LOCAL PRACTICE & PROCEDURE—IDEAS

Outline   Notes

3.6 Depositions

A. Why Should a Deposition be Taken?

1. To obtain information.
2. To determine what the deponent knows.
3. To preserve testimony.
4. To obtain admissions.
5. To assess the demeanor of the deponent.

See Form 3-3 Deposition Worksheet.

B. Planning a Deposition: FRCP 28 and 30(a)

1. *When should the deposition be scheduled?* The closer in time the deposition is taken to the event or occurrence the fresher the memory of the deponent will be. It may be necessary to delay depositions until other information has been gathered or until the case has progressed to a certain point.
2. *Where should it be held?* Convenience will usually dictate the location of the deposition. There may be advantages or disadvantages to holding the deposition in the deposing attorney's office, in the deponent's office, in the opposing attorney's office, in a court reporter's office, or in a courthouse room.
3. *Whose deposition should be taken first?* Whoever's deposition is noticed first will be deposed first. The sequence of depositions may be important if the deponents have related information. Opposing party or adverse witness' depositions may be scheduled on the same day to avoid timing problems and to prevent the responses of one from influencing another.
4. *Who should be present?* Typically, the two attorneys, the deponent, and the court reporter will be present. A party has a right to be present. The addition of a party may influence the deposition; the inclusion of an expert may be helpful during the deposition of an opposing expert.
5. *Should a telephone deposition be arranged?* A stipulated deposition may be conducted over the telephone as a conference call. This method is less expensive than a face-to-face deposition, but the inability to observe the demeanor of the deponent may outweigh its economic advantage.

C. Taking the Deposition: FRCP 30(b)

A deposition notice for a party may be accompanied by a Rule 34 Request for Production or a Rule 45 subpoena duces tecum for a non-party.

D. Preserving the Record

Depositions will be recorded by stenographic means, or based on a court order or stipulation, by audio or video recording. A more accurate record will be maintained if:

1. All persons speak clearly.
2. An appropriate pace is maintained.
3. Difficult words are spelled.

4. Nonverbal gestures or descriptions are verbally described.
5. Unnecessary comments are avoided.

E. Preparing for the Deposition

Prior to the deposition an attorney should:
1. Organize the file information.
2. Decide what purpose or purposes this deposition will serve.
3. Assess what information the deponent might know.
4. Determine the best approach to obtain information.
5. Prepare an outline.
6. Prepare specific questions if necessary.

F. Proceeding with Deposition: FRCP 30(c)

Concerns which need to be addressed include:
1. Have preliminary procedures, including the oath, been completed?
2. Should any initial stipulations be specified?
3. Should any introductory statements be explained to the deponent?
4. What questions should be asked first?
5. How should the deposition proceed?
6. What documents or exhibits should be requested or identified?
7. How should objections be handled?
8. How can any unnecessary interference by other attorneys be prevented or controlled?
9. What concluding questions should be asked?
10. What stipulations or waivers should be noted on the record?

G. Questioning Strategies and Tactics

A deposition can be conducted in a more effective manner if examining attorneys:
1. Listen carefully.
2. Are curious.
3. Ask easy-to-understand questions.
4. Insist on responsive answers.
5. Probe for information.
6. Detail circumstances.
7. Ask about opinions, emotions, attitudes.
8. Ask about witnesses and materials.
9. Pursue admissions.
10. Continually assess the demeanor of the deponent.

H. Representing the Deponent: FRCP 30(e)

Attorneys who represent the deponent should:
1. Thoroughly prepare the deponent by explaining the case and file, reviewing information, and rehearsing anticipated deposition questions.
2. Make appropriate objections.

3. Instruct the deponent not to answer improper questions.
4. Protect the deponent, if necessary.
5. Control the deposing attorney, if needed.
6. Question the deponent at the end of the examination, if appropriate.
7. Consider concluding matters:
    a) Should the reading of the transcript be waived?
    b) Are there any changes that need to be made in the testimony?
    c) Should the signing of the transcript be waived?
    d) Should notice of its filing be waived?

I. Objections

Objections to form (vague, leading) must be asserted to be effective otherwise they will be waived. Other objections (relevancy, hearsay) will usually be automatically preserved by the rules and need not be made during the depositions. The judge will rule upon them if the deposition is used at trial.

J. Written-Question Depositions: FRCP 31

This discovery device provides information without the expense of oral depositions and without the problems of written interrogatories, but has limited use because of its lack of flexibility and the difficulties inherent in preparing written questions.

CASE LAW—LOCAL PRACTICE & PROCEDURE—IDEAS

Outline   Notes

3.7 Interrogatories   See Form 3-4 Interrogatories Worksheet.

A. Parties: FRCP 33(a)   Interrogatory questions may be submitted to any party to a civil action, but not to non-party witnesses.

B. Timing: FRCP 33(a)   Interrogatories may be submitted with the summons and complaint or may be served by any party at any time after an action has commenced.

C. Subject Matter   Interrogatories may seek any discoverable information, but have some practical limitations. Interrogatories may seek the identification of documents, but Rule 34 is the proper discovery device to obtain copies of documents. Interrogatories may inquire about a party's recollection, but depositions will be a more effective device to obtain such testimony.

Interrogatories can effectively obtain the following types of information:

1. Identities of persons who know some facts, who have witnessed an event, or who have hearsay information.
2. The existence, identity, and location of documents and things discoverable under Rule 34.
3. Specific information such as dates, amounts, distance, speed, measurements, location, dimensions, data, statistics, test results, and other types of objective information.
4. Relevant financial information.
5. Information about the business entity such as corporate status or partnership arrangements.
6. Liability insurance coverage.
7. Government licenses.
8. Similar events, incidents, or transactions involving third persons.
9. Identities of trial experts, employee experts, and specially retained experts.
10. Opinions and supporting data of trial and employee experts.
11. More definite explanations of allegations contained in pleadings.
12. Specific amounts of alleged damages.
13. Opinions and contentions that relate the law to the facts.

D. Form   The interrogatory document usually contains several parts:

1. *Prefatory explanations* concerning the bases for the requests and a reference to Rule 33.
2. *Instructions* which describe certain conditions concerning the nature and source of the information sought, allow an explanation if a party does not know an answer, and permit alternative responses if a document contains an answer.

3. *Definitions* which define specific terms or recurring words in the interrogatories and permit shortened questions.
4. *The questions* themselves.

E. Interrogatory Drafting

Interrogatories should be drafted as clear, understandable, concise, and direct questions. Some courts restrict the number of interrogatories drafted. Drafting refinements may be required to meet these restrictions.

Form interrogatories may or may not be useful. Care must be taken because form questions will not always be appropriate for the case.

F. Objections

Common objections to interrogatories include:
1. Irrelevant under Rule 26.
2. Vague and ambiguous.
3. Unduly burdensome.
4. Excessive number.

Upon the receipt of objections, the requesting party may schedule a court hearing to pursue the answers. The objecting party has the burden of establishing the legitimacy of the objections. Objections and answers must usually be submitted within 30 days after service of the request.

G. Answering Interrogatories

Questions must be interpreted and answered in good faith by the answering party. Answers to interrogatories must be in writing, under oath, truthful, and complete. Many jurisdictions require that the question be restated before each answer.

A party must respond with information, whether personal knowledge or hearsay and must conduct a reasonable investigation when the party has access to requested information. The attorney, client, and any other person with information should participate in drafting answers.

H. Business Records: FRCP 33(c)

Most jurisdictions permit a party to submit business records in lieu of answers if the records contain the information.

I. Effect of Interrogatories in Trial: FRCP 33(b)

Interrogatory responses may be introduced at trial as admissions or may be used for impeachment purposes. Usually, responses to interrogatories will match the evidence introduced by the answering party at trial. Answers to interrogatories do not limit a party to such proof. A party may introduce different information at trial, but may be impeached with the previous inconsistent answer.

CASE LAW—LOCAL PRACTICE & PROCEDURE—IDEAS

Outline   Notes

3.8 Production of Documents and Things

See Form 3-4 Production of Documents/Things Worksheet.

A. Documents and Things: FRCP 34(a)

Documents include writings, contracts, drawings, graphs, charts, photographs, records, data compilations, and computer information. Things include tangible items, land, and other property.

B. Custody of Documents and Things

The other party must have possession, or the custody and control of the documents or things.

C. Specific and General Requests: FRCP 34(b)

Requests need to be drafted with "reasonable particularity." That is, the request must make clearly apparent what is sought. Rule 34 requests should be drafted with definitions and descriptions that seek both general and specific categories of documents and things.

D. Time, Place and Manner

1. The request should include the proposed time, place and manner for:
   a) Inspection of documents, land or objects;
   b) Testing, sampling, or surveying that will be performed;
   c) Copying documents and photographing of land or objects; and
   d) Any other operation that will be performed.
2. Alternative requests include:
   a) The responding party can provide copies;
   b) The responding party can select the time and place for production; or
   c) The parties can agree later regarding the place, time and manner of production.

E. Responses by a Party: FRCP 34(b)

A party may respond by:
1. Providing full and complete disclosure.
2. Suggesting another time, place or manner for the production of documents and things.
3. Seeking a protective order.
4. Interposing objections.

F. Common Objections

Proper objections include:
1. No such documents presently exist.
2. The party does not have custody or control.
3. Irrelevant.
4. Trial preparation materials.
5. Mental impressions of lawyer.
6. Unduly burdensome request.
7. Testing procedures will destroy the evidence.

G. Testing Procedures

Testing should be conducted pursuant to a stipulation or court order to avoid later controversies. Agreements or orders for testing should include:

1. A testing procedure.
2. The right of all parties to examine the article before testing.
3. The right of all parties to be present during test.
4. The recording of the test.
5. The right of all parties to the test results and report.

H. Obtaining Documents and Things from Someone not a Party: FRCP 45

Documents and things may be obtained from a non-party by means of a Rule 45 subpoena which allows disclosures at depositions, motion hearings, and other places by court order. The subpoena describes the items sought and the time and place of disclosure.

CASE LAW—LOCAL PRACTICE & PROCEDURE—IDEAS

Outline   Notes

3.9 Requests for Admissions	See Form 3-6 Requests for Admissions Worksheet.
A. The Use of Requests for Admissions	Requests for admissions are used in civil actions to: 1. Establish a fact or legal proposition. 2. Obtain some information. 3. Limit issues for trial.
B. Who can be Served	Requests may be submitted to parties to the action.
C. Request Form: FRCP 36(a)	"Each matter of which an admission is requested shall be separately set forth": 1. That each of the following statements is true. . . . 2. That each of the following documents, exhibited with the request, is genuine. . . .
D. Drafting Techniques	Requests should be drafted using simple, concise, and precise words. The best requests for admissions seek a yes or no answer or a specific response that avoids misleading characterizations.
E. Scope of Admissions	Requests may include factual statements, opinions, and application of law to fact statements.
F. Responding to Requests: FRCP 36(a)	A party may: 1. Admit the request. 2. Deny, if appropriate. 3. Qualify a response. 4. Object. 5. Seek a protective order. 6. Seek an extension of time. 7. Fail to respond and have the requests become automatic admissions.
G. Asserting Denials	When the requested admission does not state the truth of the matter a specific denial may be interposed.
H. Qualifying Answers: FRCP 36(a)	Some responses may be qualified by admitting part and denying part, or by explaining "in detail the reasons why" a request cannot be admitted or denied.
I. Common Objections	An objection must state specific reasons, such as: 1. Irrelevant under Rule 26. 2. Privileged information.

3. Party does not have sufficient information after a reasonable inquiry.

J. Effect of an Admission: FRCP 36(e)   An admission is conclusive proof of the truth of the matter asserted.

K. Withdrawing or Changing an Admission   A party may only withdraw or change a response by court order for good cause shown.

CASE LAW—LOCAL PRACTICE & PROCEDURE—IDEAS

Outline   Notes

3.10 Physical Examinations

See Form 3-7 Physical Examination Worksheet.

A. FRCP 35 Examinations

These include physical, mental and blood examinations of an adverse party.

B. Types of Cases

Any civil case in which the physical, mental or blood condition of a party is in "controversy" is appropriate for a Rule 35 proceeding. Personal injury actions often involve such examinations.

C. Arranging Examinations

A court will order an examination based on a motion or stipulation that explains the good cause for the examination. The court order will include the time, place, manner, conditions, and scope of the examination.

D. "Good Cause"

This term means that the requesting party needs the information which is relevant under Rule 26.

E. Conditions of an Examination

The examination usually occurs at a time and place convenient for the examining doctor and the party. The party's attorney and a "friendly" doctor may also be present if the situation warrants. The scope of the examination should be limited to the issues in controversy.

F. Selection of the Doctor

The court appoints the doctor and usually adopts the recommendation of the requesting party. This doctor not only will conduct the examination and prepare a report but may also be an expert trial witness.

G. Drafting the Request

A notice of motion and motion must be served on the party or person to be examined and all other parties. Rule 35(a) requires the court order to specify the time and location of the examination, the manner in which the examination will be conducted, any conditions restricting the exam, the scope of the exam, and the persons who will be present.

H. Alternative Responses to a Rule 35 Motion

A responding party may respond with:
1. Cooperative compliance.
2. A stipulated agreement detailing the time, place, manner, conditions, and scope.

3. Objections based upon violations of Rule 35.
4. A motion seeking a protective order.

I. After the Examination The doctor usually completes a report which is forwarded to all parties.

CASE LAW—LOCAL PRACTICE & PROCEDURE—IDEAS

Outline   Notes

3.11 Enforcing Discovery Requests

A. *What Should First be Done if a Party Fails to Respond to a Discovery Request?*

A request by telephone or letter should be made to remind the party about the delay and to demand discovery.

B. *What if the Party Continues to Fail to Fully Respond?*

Rule 37 provides for enforcement of discovery rights. An order may be obtained compelling discovery.

C. *What if the Party Fails to Comply?*

Sanctions may be imposed by the court:
1. Expenses including costs and lawyer's fees may be imposed.
2. Facts may be deemed admitted.
3. Pleadings may be stricken.
4. Proceedings may be stayed.
5. Evidence may be barred.
6. The party may be held in contempt.
7. The action may be dismissed.

D. *Are Discovery Orders Appealable?*

Rarely. They are subject to appellate review on a final judgment, but rarely as an interlocutory appeal.

CASE LAW—LOCAL PRACTICE & PROCEDURE—IDEAS

Outline   Notes

3.12 Avoiding Mistrials and Reversals

A. Do Not Create or Preserve False Evidence

Creating or preserving false evidence is absolutely forbidden. See DR 7–102(A); Model Rule 3.4(b). Giving false answers to interrogatories or allowing a witness to commit perjury during a deposition violates this prohibition. See, e.g., *Commission on Professional Ethics v. Crary*, 245 N.W.2d 298 (Iowa 1976); *North Carolina State Bar v. DuMont*, 286 S.E.2d 89 (N.C. 1982).

B. Withholding Evidence

An attorney must comply with requests for discovery. DR 7–102(A)(3) states, "In his representation of a client, a lawyer shall not . . . [c]onceal or knowingly fail to disclose that which he is required by law to reveal." See also Model Rule 3.4(D).

The duty to disclose relevant evidence sometimes conflicts with the attorney's duty with respect to the attorney-client privilege. The attorney-client privilege may occasionally justify withholding evidence requested during discovery. See *In re Grand Jury Proceedings*, 473 F.2d 840 (8th Cir. 1973) (summaries of interviews protected by work product doctrine); *State v. Olwell*, 394 P.2d 681 (Wash. 1964) (withholding of suspected murder weapon).

Nevertheless, the general rules of civil procedure will usually apply. See generally Fed. R. Civ. P. 26–37. Consequently, the attorney should develop a conscientious attitude towards complying with requests for discovery.

C. Comply With Court Orders

Although an attorney's failure to comply with opposing counsel's request for discovery will not always entail sanctions against the attorney, the likelihood of sanctions increases when an attorney disobeys a court's order for discovery.

The trial court is given wide latitude in imposing sanctions for failure to comply with discovery orders. The court may:
1. Order that certain facts or matters are established.
2. Order that certain claims or evidence not be admitted at trial.
3. Strike all or parts of the pleadings.
4. Stay further proceedings until the discovery order is complied with.
5. Dismiss all or part of the action.
6. Enter a default judgment.
7. Find the attorney in contempt.
8. Award reasonable expenses, including attorney's fees.

The most severe sanction is, of course, dismissing the action with prejudice. Dismissal will only be used in the most egregious circumstances. See *National Hockey League v. Metro Hockey Club, Inc.*, 427 U.S. 640, 96 S.Ct. 2778 (1976) (crucial interrogatories unanswered after seventeen months); *Factory Air Conditioning Corp. v. Westside Toyota*, 579 F.2d 334 (5th Cir. 1978) (interrogatories unanswered after six months). The purpose of dismissal in these types of cases is not only to penalize the offending party, but to act as a deterent to others.

On the other hand, the simple negligence of an attorney will usually not be sufficient grounds for dismissing a client's action. *Marshall v. Segona*, 621 F.2d 763 (5th Cir. 1980). In fact, dismissal is reserved for those situations where other sanctions cannot achieve the same deterent effect. Likewise a good faith misunderstanding of a court's order will not be grounds for dismissal. See *United Artists Corp. v. Freeman*, 605 F.2d 854 (5th Cir. 1979). The best practice will be to avoid these issues by complying with court orders.

D. Respond Promptly to Requests for Admission

Although it is unlikely that the failure to answer a request for admission will ever result in a mistrial or reversal, this discussion is included because of the impact a failure to answer these requests will have on the case. Rule 36(a) of the Federal Rules of Civil Procedure states that requests for admission are "admitted unless, within 30 days after service of the request, or within shorter or longer time as the court may allow," the request is answered or objected to. The possibility exists that the case could be lost because a crucial issue is admitted. See *Brook Village N. Assoc. v. General Elec. Co.*, 686 F.2d 66 (1st Cir. 1982); *Brown v. Arlen Mgmt. Corp.*, 663 F.2d 575 (5th Cir. 1981).

The court may, however, grant a motion seeking to nullify the effect of an unanswered request for admission. See Fed. R. Civ. P. 36(b); but see *Brook Village*, supra, (trial court may not reverse default admission after trial because evidence contradicted admission). This will depend on how the court views the attorney's failure to respond to the request and the effect of granting or not granting the motion on the parties. See *Gutting v. Folstaff Brewing Corp.*, 710 F.2d 1309 (8th Cir. 1983) (costs of depositions not considered prejudicial effect). The attorney should avoid these potential problems by responding to requests for admission within the 30 day time limit.

CASE LAW—LOCAL PRACTICE & PROCEDURE—IDEAS

Outline   Notes

3.13 Bibliography   TEXTS

R. Haydock and D. Herr, *Discovery Practice* (Little, Brown & Co.,
Boston, MA, 1982).

R. Haydock and D. Herr, *Discovery: Theory, Practice, Problems* (Little,
Brown & Co., Boston, MA, 1983).

R. Haydock and J. Sonsteng, *Deposition manual for Demonstration
Videotapes* (Nat'l Ist. for Trial Advocacy, St. Paul, MN 1982).

K. Hegland, *Trial and Practice Skills in a Nutshell* 251–74 (West Pub.
Co., St. Paul, MN, 1978).

R. Keeton, *Trial Tactics and Methods* 390–440 (West Pub. Co., St.
Paul, MN, 1973).

J. Kelner & F. McGovern, *Successful Litigation Techniques* Ch. 5
(Matthew Bender, New York, 1981).

A. Morrill, *Trial Diplomacy* 179–211 (Court Practice Inst., Chicago,
IL, 1972).

FACTUAL INVESTIGATION WORKSHEET   **Form 3-1**

Case _____   File _____

1. Witness Interviews

Name   Fact Summary
Date
Interviewer
Impression of Witness

Statement Provided

Name   Fact Summary
Date
Interviewer
Impression of Witness

Statement Provided

Name   Fact Summary
Date
Interviewer
Impression of Witness

Statement Provided

Name   Fact Summary
Date
Interviewer
Impression of Witness

Statement Provided

FACTUAL INVESTIGATION
WORKSHEET   Form 3-1 (continued)

Case _____   File _____

2. Sources to Locate Witnesses and Information

Telephone Directory   Employees
Department of Transportation   Friends
City Directory   Relatives
Other

3. Documents

Statements   Bills, receipts
Writings   Photographs
Contracts   Diagrams
Leases   Coroner's Report
Records   Transcript of Traffic
Police Reports   Court Hearings
Highway Traffic/Motor   Business Records
   Vehicle Records   Government
Weather/Newspaper   Documents
   /TV Reports   Medical Records
Court Records   Hospital Records
Advertising Brochures/   Employee Records
   Warranties   Movies
Videotapes

4. Physical Evidence

5. Scene

6. Other Investigation

INVESTIGATION WORKSHEET

Form 3-2

Case _____   File _____

1. What facts corroborate or supplement the client's version of the case?

2. What facts weaken or contradict the client's version of the case?

3. What facts corroborate or supplement the opposing party's version of the case?

4. What facts weaken or contradict the opposing party's version of the case?

INVESTIGATION WORKSHEET   Form 3-2 (continued)

Case _____   File _____

What can be proved?	Why should it be proved?	Who will prove it?	How will it be proved?	Where can exhibits be obtained?

DEPOSITION WORKSHEET   **Form 3-3**

Case _____   File _____

Deposition Planning

Prospective Deponent   Purpose/Facts

Location

Date/Time

Prospective Deponent   Purpose/Facts

Location

Date/Time

Prospective Deponent   Purpose/Facts

Location

Date/Time

Prospective Deponent   Purpose/Facts

Location

Date/Time

Depositions Completed

Deponent Transcript	Reviewed	Signed	Filed	Indexed

INTERROGATORIES WORKSHEET

Form 3-4

Case _____   File _____

Party	Date Served	Subject Matter	Answers Due	Answers Received	Answers Adequate

PRODUCTION OF DOCUMENTS/
THINGS WORKSHEET

Form 3-5

Case _____   File _____

Party	Date Served	Items Sought	Response Due	Response Made	Response Adequate

REQUESTS FOR ADMISSIONS WORKSHEET   Form 3-6

Case _____   File _____

Party	Date Served	Requests	Response Due	Response Made	Response Adequate

PHYSICAL EXAMINATIONS WORKSHEET   **Form 3-7**

Case _____   File _____

Motion Served	Motion Hearing	Court Order/ Stipulation	Examinee	Examiner	Conditions	Report

Chapter 4
THE JURY SELECTION PROCESS

Every person is a volume, if you know how to read. . . .
—William Ellery Channing

Minds are like parachutes. They only function when they are open.
—Thomas Robert Dewar

4.1 Description   Jury selection is the process of removing the least acceptable persons from a pre-selected panel of jurors. With counsel of equal ability, the resulting panel will be as balanced as possible. This process usually involves questioning of prospective jurors by the attorneys and/or the court. Questions asked during jury selection attempt to obtain information about the prospective juror's perceptions, opinions, experiences, and personalities. Each attorney then attempts to strike unfavorable jurors using challenges for cause and preemptory challenges.

4.2 Purposes   There are several main purposes of jury selection:
A. To obtain information about the jurors;
B. To determine the attitudes and feelings of the jurors;
C. To educate the jurors concerning the case;
D. To obtain a commitment from the jurors;
E. To have a juror disqualify himself or herself;
F. To select a favorable jury; and
G. To establish rapport with the jurors.

A. Obtaining Information About the Jurors   The attorney needs to acquire factual information about the jurors to support a challenge for cause and to form a basis for exercising preemptory challenges.

B. Determining Attitudes   Knowledge of attitudes and feelings in addition to factual knowledge is also necessary to knowingly and intelligently select a jury.

C. Educating the Jury   The attorney may discreetly use jury selection to educate and inform the jurors about aspects of the case. The attorney should not, however, attempt to argue the case during jury selection.

155

D. Obtaining Commitment	It may be effective to obtain a promise from the jurors that they will do or not do something.
E. Disqualifying a Juror	A juror may agree that because of apparent or implied bias, prejudice, or interest that they should not be a juror in a case.
F. Selecting a Fair and Favorable Jury	A jury needs to be selected that will be fair and hopefully favorable to the client's cause.
G. Establishing Rapport	Voir dire questions need to be designed to establish a favorable rapport between the jurors and the attorney and the client.

CASE LAW—LOCAL PRACTICE & PROCEDURE—IDEAS

Outline   Notes

4.3 Preparation and Organization

A. Advance Investigation

The lawyer should collect as much information as possible about the prospective jurors. If a list of jurors is available before trial, the attorney should obtain a copy of the list and review it. Addresses will provide generalized information concerning neighborhood, house size, socio-economic position with little investigation. If time, money, and resources are available, the potential jurors should be investigated. All available information will serve as a basis for presenting challenges for cause and for exercising peremptory challenges.

B. Selecting a Theory

Some lawyers prepare a jury profile in advance and select those jurors who best fit within that profile. Other lawyers select jurors based on intuitive feelings developed during the course of voir dire. Theories on how to select a jury are probably as diverse as the number of lawyers who actually pick a jury.

A lawyer may want to consider the following factors whatever the theory used: age, social background, marital status, family status (children), family history (parents, siblings), education, occupation (self, spouse, family), employment history, residence history, personal history, hobbies, activities and experiences relevant to the case. Some theories for jury selection include similarity to parties, ethnic characteristics, religion, work, social class, body language, attitudes, and overall impression.

In the last analysis, the success of the jury selection process depends on the lawyer's ability to relate to the people who are being questioned as prospective jurors, to use the limited information available, and to make accurate judgments about people. Thus, the jury selection process should be viewed as an art rather than a science, even in cases where social scientific methodology is employed. The more information the lawyer can obtain about each juror, the more trustworthy the art becomes.

C. Selection Considerations

In selecting jurors an attorney should:

1. Consider the type of person the attorney and the client normally appeal to and what type may be aggravated by either the attorney or client.
2. Think about what the impact witnesses will have on particular jurors.
3. Consider who will be most receptive to the case, and who will be receptive to the other attorney's case and client.
4. Who will follow the "letter" of the law and who will "bend" the rules.
5. Determine what level of intelligence is required by the case.
6. Try to determine who the foreperson will be.

7. Consider the ethnic, social, and cultural background of each juror.
8. Consider the impact a juror's gender may have on the case.
9. Look at each juror's body language.
10. Note any associations or "cliques" among jurors.
11. Remember that strong-willed or opinionated jurors may deadlock a jury.
12. Note jurors who arrive late, talk during voir dire, or display other questionable conduct which may demonstrate a lack of interest or seriousness.
13. Consider how cohesive the jurors will be together.
14. Determine whether, as a plaintiff, a more harmonious group of jurors will be desirable, or whether, as a defendant, jurors who are more individualistic and do not follow a crowd are more desireable.

See Form 4-1 Jury Selection Worksheet.

CASE LAW—LOCAL PRACTICE & PROCEDURE—IDEAS

Outline   Notes

4.4 Selection Procedures

A. Generally

No other aspect of trial procedure varies as widely as the voir dire process. At one extreme, the trial judge allows the lawyers to conduct the entire voir dire process. At the other extreme, the trial judge conducts the entire voir dire examination and the lawyers only submit written questions to the court which the judge may ask. Probably the most common procedure used is somewhere in between. Federal court trial judges assume more control over the voir dire process and because of money and time considerations the trend seems to be in that direction.

B. Specific Procedures

It is essential for the trial attorney to know the specific procedures employed in the jury selection process. Answers to the following questions will vary from jurisdiction to jurisdiction and may be obtained by experience, by research, or from information provided by colleagues, the clerk, the bailiff, the court reporter, the law clerk, or the judge:

1. What are the requirements for jury service? Where do the jurors go? How they are processed? What are they told and what explanations, pamphlets, slides, or movies are provided them?
2. How many prospective jurors will sit on the initial panel? How are they selected?
3. What information is available about the panel members? What will be provided the attorneys?
4. Who begins the voir dire questioning: The plaintiff/prosecutor or defense? How much time will usually be available? Will questioning of individual prospective jurors be allowed or must the questions be addressed to the entire panel?
5. Is the judge present during voir dire? Is voir dire recorded by a reporter?
6. How are challenges made? Does the jury remain in the room during the striking process? What grounds must be established for cause?
7. Are the peremptory challenges made after all the questioning is done or one juror at a time? Who goes first? Is a sheet of paper passed between the adversaries that has the jurors' names on it to be crossed off? If a paper is passed, does each lawyer take one strike and pass the paper or is more than one strike taken at a time?
8. How are jurors sworn? Are they sworn both before and after voir dire? Must the lawyers stand during the swearing in?
9. Under what circumstances are the replacement jurors called? Where do they sit?
10. What preliminary explanations will the judge make to the jury?

11. Will the jurors be allowed to take notes?

C. Preliminary Instructions
After the jury has been sworn by the clerk and before opening statements the trial judge may instruct the jurors to:
1. Refrain from discussing the case among themselves or with other persons;
2. Avoid approaching or conversing with counsel, witnesses, or other persons;
3. Direct any questions or problems to the bailiff; and
4. Follow the directions of the bailiff, who is in charge of the jurors, regarding the physical facilities and supplies.

The judge may also provide jurors with instructions regarding the following:
1. An explanation of important general principles of law applicable to the case, such as the burden of proof or definitions of legal terms;
2. An explanation of the specific laws applicable to the case;
3. The functions of the judge and that the judge will be the source of the law;
4. The responsibilities of the attorneys and that statements and arguments by them should not be considered evidence;
5. A summary of the issues of the case or a reading of the charge or complaint;
6. The identity of the parties and their counsel;
7. Whether note taking is permitted;
8. Any other instructions the attorneys request which the court deems appropriate; and
9. Instructions favored by a particular judge.

CASE LAW—LOCAL PRACTICE & PROCEDURE—IDEAS

Outline   Notes

4.5 Selection Process

A. Generally

The selection process begins as soon as the prospective jurors enter the courtroom. An attorney should observe the jurors as they take their seats and notice their appearance, conduct, and any apparent pecularities. This first impression and personal intuitive responses may be helpful in later making a final selection.

B. Notes

Many attorneys take notes concerning the jurors during voir dire. These notes may be written on a chart listing the jurors names. This chart may be constructed by an attorney as the clerk reads the names of the prospective jurors or may be provided by the clerk to the attorneys. The chart should be designed so there is sufficient room for notes to be taken during voir dire. See Form 4-2 Jury Selection Chart. The notes may include observations by the attorney, responses by the jurors, and other factors which rate the prospective juror as favorable or unfavorable. This information will aid the attorney in determining who to challenge and who to select.

Note taking can create some problems during voir dire. The recording of the information may unnecessarily interfere with and delay the attorney asking questions; many jurors will be suspicious, bothered, or offended by such note taking; individual written notes may not be accurate in the selection process as a total assessment of each juror; and extensive note taking may keep the attorney from watching and listening to the jurors. For these reasons many lawyers do not take notes or do so in a shorthand way that is neither distracting nor offensive.

C. Addressing the Jurors

Jurors should be addressed by their last names. Woman jurors may prefer to be addressed as Mrs., Ms., or Miss. It may be necessary to ask which way they prefer to be addressed. Some jurors will be more sensitive to this issue than others, and it is important to correctly address each juror. The attorney could ask their preferrence, or the attorney could request that the clerk or the judge ask their preference.

D. Areas of Questioning

There are several areas of questions that should be considered with every juror. These areas include:

Obtaining Information:
1. Address
2. Educational level
3. Employment status
4. Marital status
5. Family status
6. Relationship with parties, attorneys, and witnesses

7. Whether jurors have heard about the case or have any information about the case
8. Previous jury experience
9. Experience with court system
10. Experience or education in fields relating to case
11. Whether juror would suffer any personal hardship as juror

Probing Opinions and Attitudes:
1. About liability issues
2. About damage issues
3. About facts
4. About legal principles
5. About client
6. About problems with case
7. About weaknesses in the case
8. About other issues

There will be some areas that it may be tactically better to avoid during voir dire. Age, religion, and private concerns are examples. The age of a juror that can be determined by appearance is usually sufficient, and there is no need to ask a sensitive question that will bother some and offend many jurors. Questions concerning religious beliefs or personal matters when not germaine to the case often are embarrassing and uncomfortable. The risk of offending some or all of the jury panel is so high that care and delicacy must be exercised before questioning in these areas.

E. Selection of Question Areas

It is very difficult to select questions that will not at some point embarrass or cause one or more jurors to become uncomfortable. The attorney must be sensitive to the jurors position and probable reaction particularly to personal questions. In some situation it may be advisable to avoid inquiring into certain areas to avoid offending the jurors. In many other situations, it will be necessary for the attorney to pursue some questions because that information is vital to the selection process and because the best interests of the client require such probing. In these circumstances the attorney should be as careful as possible in phrasing questions that will reduce the chance of any adverse reaction on the part of the jurors.

F. Types and Forms of Questions

There are several types of questions that may be asked during voir dire. These types include:

1. Specific questions directed to the entire panel which require a yes or no answer and may require follow-up questions.
2. General questions to the panel which require an explanatory response.

3. Specific questions directed to an individual juror that require a yes or no or short explanation response.
4. General questions to an individual juror which requires a narrative explanatory response.

The form of a question will depend upon its purpose. If the question seeks specific information, the question should be phrased to generate a specific response. The following questions demonstrate examples of such questions:

> Where do you live?
> Do you know the plaintiff, Denise Baker?
> Have you sat as a juror in a previous case? What kind of case was it?

If the question seeks opinions and attitudes of the jurors the question may be phrased either as an open ended or a leading question. Examples of such questions include:

> Does the fact that this case involves the tragic death of a child influence you one way or the other in your consideration of the facts?

> This case involves a claim of sex discrimination. How do you feel in general about a woman who claims that a man discriminated against her and hired someone else and not her?

> What feelings do you have if your son or daughter were to date someone of a different race?

> The fact that this case involves a large corporation will not influence you one way or the other in reaching a verdict based on the facts, will it?

If the question is designed to provide information to the jurors, the preface to the question may be more important than the question or response. Some examples include:

> The plaintiff in this case is a widow, did any of you know her deceased husband, Mr. Baker? An expert design engineer will testify in this case. Her name is Darlene Cooper. Have any of you seen her on television or read any of her books?

If the question is designed to obtain a commitment or promise from the jurors then the question should seek a yes or no response. Some examples include:

Will you be able to put aside any feelings of sympathy you may have for the plaintiff and return a verdict based solely on the evidence presented?

The defendant in this trial is unemployed and has to receive income from welfare payments to provide for her family. You will not allow the fact of her exercising her right to receive welfare to affect your judgment in this case, will you?

During this trial I, as the lawyer, have the duty to protect my client's interests. This may require me to object to the introduction of certain evidence by the plaintiff. Do you promise that you will not hold against my client any disagreement you might have with me when I object and attempt to exclude certain evidence from your consideration?

If the questions are intended to result in an individual juror agreeing not to want to sit as a juror, the questions should be leading and suggestive of the answer. An example is:

Mr. Morrow, you said your daughter is a doctor. You understand that this case involves medical malpractice by a doctor? Evidence in this case may make you uncomfortable and may make it somewhat difficult for you to decide because you may think of your daughter? Do you agree that the parties in this case may wonder to what degree you may be affected by your relationship with your daughter? Do you agree that you would be more comfortable sitting in another case that did not involve issues that relate so closely to your family interests?

Since the questioning process serves many purposes, the type and form of questions will be mixed and will vary according to the case plan and the particular goals of the examiner.

G. Conduct of Voir Dire

An attorney needs to consider many factors in determining how to conduct jury questioning. These factors include:

1. *First Impressions.* An attorney who makes a good impression during voir dire will benefit from the lasting effect of this impression with the jury.
2. *Sincere, Honest Advocate.* An attorney needs to be viewed by the jurors as a sincere and honest advocate. This attitude needs to be initially projected during voir dire. It is vital for the attorney to be perceived by the jurors as a lawyer with integrity. This perspective will significantly bolster the credibility and persuasiveness of the attorney throughout the trial.

3. *Rapport.* The attorney should attempt to reduce any anxiety, fear, nervousness, or tension the jurors may naturally feel and to begin establishing rapport with them. A respectful attitude, a caring approach, eye contact, attentive listening, and a genuine interest will help establish the proper rapport. The more comfortable and at ease the jurors become with the attorney the more attention and concentration they can devote to the case. The greater the affinity jurors feel toward a lawyer the more effective an advocate that attorney will become.

4. *Scope.* The scope of questioning will depend upon what questions the judge has asked the jurors and what information the attorney feels is necessary to make as valid a decision as possible about a juror. The attorney will need to inquire into those areas the judge did not cover. If an attorney wishes to ask some questions in legally sensitive areas (about insurance) or personal information (hardships) it may be advisable to request that the judge ask such questions to avoid the attorney from appearing to create a problem.

5. *Questions.* The type of questions that should be asked depends upon the preferences of the attorney, the character of the jurors, the nature of the case, and the time available for voir dire. General questions directed to the panel as a whole will usually be appropriate if yes or no answers or short explanations are expected. Specific questions directed to individual jurors may be asked as follow up questions or as probes into new areas. Questions should be asked in a manner which involve all jurors. A mix of general and specific questions will usually maintain the attention of all the jurors. It is important for all the jurors to be treated similarly. If one juror is asked several specific questions but another juror is asked only a few questions, that second juror may resent being treated differently.

   The jurors will also need to know how they are expected to respond to questions. The attorney, especially in asking questions to the entire panel, should make clear whether the jurors should respond verbally or by raising their hand.

6. *Planned Questions.* The attorney must initially appear to the jurors as a well prepared professional. The use of planned questions prepared before voir dire will help create that appearance. Questions may be written out or the topic of inquiry can be listed as an aid during the actual questioning. Unplanned, spontaneous questions may appear to be aimless, rambling, and poorly phrased. A well structured and thoughtful line of questions will further assist the attorney in being able to watch, listen, and appropriately explore unexpected answers. Preparation will assist in establishing the attorney as a credible, persuasive advocate.

7. *Obtaining Commitments.* An attorney during voir dire may attempt to obtain a promise from the jurors not to hold some fact or weakness against a client. There is some debate about the efficacy of such a commitment. It appears that most jurors will hold themselves and the other jurors to such promises if made. Studies of videotaped jury deliberations confirm the notion that some jurors will speak up and remind other jurors about a commitment if the subject matter of the promise arises as a factor in the verdict.

8. *Avoiding Argument.* A juror may cause problems during voir dire. The juror may disagree with the content or tone of a question or may misunderstand an inquiry. The attorney must remain calm and react in a controlled, professional way. It may be advisable for the attorney to accept the blame for asking an awkward or unclear question and rephrase it rather than imply that the juror is at fault. An admission by a lawyer that a question was inappropriate or that the lawyer was wrong may assist in establishing a sense of humility and rapport between that attorney and the jury.

H. Rehabilitation

After a lawyer completes the voir dire of a panel or an individual juror and obtains some information that may support a motion to challenge a juror for cause, many jurisdictions permit the opposing attorney to ask more questions of a prospective juror to develop new information to rebut any facts or inferences supporting a challenge. In some jurisdictions the judge may intervene and ask some rehabilitative questions. Typically such rehabilitation concludes with a general question such as "You will be able to set aside your attitude and feelings about the matter and be a fair and impartial juror, won't you?" The purpose of rehabilitation is to prevent a challenge for cause and to force the opponent to use one of a limited number of peremptory challenges.

CASE LAW—LOCAL PRACTICE & PROCEDURE—IDEAS

Outline   Notes

4.6 The Final Selection Process

A. Challenge for Cause

See Form 4-3 Final Jury Data.

A challenge for cause is usually governed by local statutes. Statutes may disqualify certain types of persons such as judges, lawyers, relatives, and other individuals who may not be impartial. The judge or clerk in a case will usually screen the jurors and automatically disqualify individuals who fall within certain categories of persons.

The challenge for cause is made by an attorney when a prospective juror is prejudiced against a party or the case, has been involved in similar litigation, or has some other interest which makes the juror unlikely to be impartial. The challenging attorney must show that there is an obvious sympathy, bias or prejudice that would make it impossible for a particular juror to be fair. There are no limits on the number of challenges for cause, but they will seldom be granted by the court. Consideration of time and expense usually influence the court to be conservative in the excusing of jurors for cause.

An attorney may be able to have a juror disqualify himself or herself from sitting as a juror because of discomfort or interest. It is unlikely that a juror will voluntarily admit that he or she will be unfair as a general proposition. It is more likely that a juror may agree not to want to sit as a juror if the attorney can suggest specific reasons why the juror may be uncomfortable, may have difficulty setting aside some experience, and may prefer to sit on another case. This series of questions has the juror first recognize the need to have all jurors appear to be fair in a case and then realize that the juror may be a perceived source of unfairness.

B. Peremptory Challenges

The number and procedure involved in using peremptory challenges is also controlled by local statutes. Peremptory challenges are discretionary challenges that may be used as the attorney pleases. The attorney does not need to publicly explain the reasons for striking a juror. Of course, the attorney should have a tactically appropriate reason but it need not be stated on the record.

Peremptory challenges are limited in number. It is necessary for an attorney to know the number of challenges in the jurisdiction for both civil and criminal cases. Typically in a civil case with a six person jury, each party will have 2 or 3 preemptory challenges with a panel of 10 or 12 prospective jurors. In a criminal case with a 12 person jury, the prosecution and defense may have between 3 and 6 challenges with a panel of 20 or 24 prospective jurors. The defense usually has more challenges than the number allowed the prosecution.

C. Challenge to the Array

A challenge to the array is a claim that the process used to select potential jurors is unlawful or unfair. This challenge is rarely used today because prospective jurors are usually selected randomly using modern statistical methods and computers.

D. Using Challenges

An attorney does not need to challenge any juror or use any peremptory challenges. There should be a reason for every challenge. The attorney should keep an eye on the replacement juror, particularly after getting down to the last couple of peremptory challenges. The replacement juror may be worse than the excused juror. If local procedure permits, jurors should not be challenged immediately. It is much easier to make judgments about which jurors should be removed if the preemptory challenges do not have to be exercised until after all the questioning is complete. Once the whole panel has been questioned a ranking of jurors can be accomplished and the other side may be equally concerned about a problem juror and use a challenge to dismiss that juror.

E. Use of Client

Some attorneys use their clients' feelings about a juror to assist in making a decision about whom to strike from a panel. Other attorneys never consult with a client and prefer to use their own judgment. In deciding whether to use the client as a resource, an attorney should consider the relationship with the client, the attorney's independence in the case, the perception of the jurors concerning the relationship, the ability of the client, and the attorney's preference.

F. Alternate Jurors

Most trials that will be lengthy or complex will include alternate jurors in addition to the regular jurors. An alternate juror will replace a regular juror if that regular juror becomes ill or unable to attend the trial. The selection process for alternates occurs at the same time and is identical to the procedure used for the other jurors. Typically one alternate juror will be selected for a 6 person jury and two to three for a 12 person jury.

CASE LAW—LOCAL PRACTICE & PROCEDURE—IDEAS

Outline   Notes

4.7 Avoiding Mistrials and Reversals

A. Do Not Use Voir Dire as an Opportunity to Interject Inadmissible Evidence

A trial lawyer is given wide latitude, subject to the discretion of the court, in questioning prospective jurors. *Lamaak v. Brown*, 259 Iowa 1324, 147 N.W.2d 915 (1967); *Ruby v. Chicago, M. & St. P. Ry.*, 129 N.W. 817 (Ia. 1911). This is necessary in order to allow the intelligent exercise of peremptory challenges and to expose sufficient grounds for challenges for cause.

The greatest area of difficulty in voir dire, from an ethical standpoint, occurs because lawyers see it as an opportunity to immediately lay their case before the jury. Some would argue that a lawyer has a duty to do so. Consequently, there is a line drawn between when it is ethical, for example, to disregard the evidentiary prohibition against the mention of insurance in a personal injury suit. A prospective juror may be asked if he has any interest in or relationship to insurance companies if the question is asked only for that purpose. Such questions must be asked in the good faith belief that some jurors may, in fact, have such a relationship to or interest in specific insurance companies. *Imparato v. Rooney*, (95 Ill. App. 3d 11, 419 N.E.2d 620 (1981). But if the question is asked in such a way as to inform the jurors that the defendant is insured, the question is unethical and is grounds for a new trial. It is equally unethical to use voir dire to inform jurors that the defendant is *not* insured. *Rom v. Calhoun*, 227 Minn. 143, 34 N.W.2d 359 (1948). However, in one jurisdiction, letting it slip that a defendant is *not* insured may not warrant a new trial since it is to be assumed by the jury that insurance does not exist. *Laguna v. Prautz*, 300 N.W.2d 98 (Ia. 1981). To avoid such situations it may be best to request that the judge ask sensitive questions.

B. Keep the Voir Dire Relevant to the Issues at Trial

Any use of voir dire to prejudice the jury is unethical. Thus, formulating questions that inform the jury that a defendant is wealthy or an atheist, if not relevant, are not allowed. The basic rule is that evidence may be referred to in voir dire as long as it bears upon an issue at trial and will be brought out at trial.

C. Do Not Curry the Favor of Jurors

Communication with jurors before trial is forbidden except in the course of official proceedings (DR 7–108(A)). Once the jury is impaneled, the same prohibition governs. Also, "currying favor" of any juror, such as expressing concern for their comfort, should be scrupulously avoided. See Rule 19(i), Code of Trial Conduct of the American College of Trial Lawyers. While it may be obvious that an attorney should not accept an offer of drinks from a juror or to arrange the purchase of life insurance from one, both have been done. The acceptance of drinks by counsel was found to be clearly misconduct; however, it was not grounds for reversal. *Omaha Bank for Coops. v. Siouxland Cattle Coop.*, 305 N.W.2d 458 (Ia. 1981). The attorney who set up the life insurance deal with a juror was for this, among other reasons, disbarred. *In re Heiden*, 217 Or. 134, 341 P.2d 1107 (1959).

Finally, it is the duty of counsel to bring any juror misconduct of which they are aware to the immediate attention of the court. This information cannot be secreted and then used as ammunition for a new trial after one has lost the case. *See State v. Durfee*, 322 N.W.2d 778 (Minn. 1982).

CASE LAW—LOCAL PRACTICE & PROCEDURE—IDEAS

Outline   Notes

4.8 Bibliography   TEXTS

G. Bellow & B. Moulton, *The Lawyering Process* 663–76 (1978).

P. Bergman, *Trial Advocacy in a Nutshell* 363–72 (1979).

C. Boardman, *Jurywork: Systematic Techniques* (Nat'l Jury Project, N.Y. 2d ed. 1983).

S. Goldberg, *The First Trial in a Nutshell* 44–47, 166–79, 182–90 (1982).

K. Hegland, *Trial and Practice Skills in a Nutshell* 86–100 (1978).

J. Jeans, *Trial Advocacy* Ch. 7 (1975).

R. Keeton, *Trial Tactics and Methods* 245–94 (1973).

J. Kelner & F. McGovern, *Successful Litigation Techniques* Ch. 10 (1981).

T. Mauet, *Fundamentals of Trial Techniques* 23–47 (1980).

J. McElhaney, *Effective Litigation* 109–11 (1974).

A. Morrill, *Trial Diplomacy* 1–21 (1972).

J. Sonsteng and R. Haydock, *Voir Dire Manual for Demonstration Videotapes* (Nat'l Inst. for Trial Advocacy, St. Paul, MN 1982).

JURY SELECTION WORKSHEET   **Form 4-1**

Case _____   File _____

What kind or type of person could probably best identify with the parties, attorneys, witnesses, and issues in the case?

What kind or type of person would probably be least likely to identify with the parties, attorneys, witnesses and issues in the case?

JURY SELECTION CHART

Form 4-2

Name of Case: Date of Trial:

Juror Information	1	2	3
Name			
Address			
Approximate age/ demeanor/dress			
Know case			
Know witness			
Occupation			
Employer			
Education			
Marital status			
Spouse's occupation			
Spouse's employer			
Children			
Past claims/ lawsuits			
Similar case experience			
Past/present jury duty:			
Civil			
Criminal			

JURY SELECTION CHART   Form 4-2 (continued)

Juror Information	1	2	3
Opinion about issues			
Attitude toward facts			
Attitude toward law			
Attitude toward problems			
Do I and client like this juror?			
Does juror like me and client?			
Hardship reasons			
Overall rating 0–10			
Other factors/ reasons			
Other			
Other			

JURY SELECTION CHART   Form 4-2 (continued)

Name of Case: Date of Trial:

Juror Information	4	5	6
Name			
Address			
Approximate age/ demeanor/dress			
Know case			
Know witness			
Occupation			
Employer			
Education			
Marital status			
Spouse's occupation			
Spouse's employer			
Children			
Past claims/ lawsuits			
Similar case experience			
Past/present jury duty:			
Civil			
Criminal			

JURY SELECTION CHART

Form 4-2 (continued)

Juror Information	4	5	6
Opinion about issues			
Attitude toward facts			
Attitude toward law			
Attitude toward problems			
Do I and client like this juror?			
Does juror like me and client?			
Hardship reasons			
Overall rating 0–10			
Other factors/ reasons			
Other			
Other			

JURY SELECTION CHART   **Form 4-2 (continued)**

Name of Case: Date of Trial:

Juror Information	7	8	9
Name			
Address			
Approximate age/ demeanor/dress			
Know case			
Know witnesses			
Occupation			
Employer			
Education			
Marital status			
Spouse's occupation			
Spouse's employer			
Children			
Past claims/ lawsuits			
Similar case experience			
Past/present jury duty:			
Civil			
Criminal			

JURY SELECTION CHART Form 4-2 (continued)

Juror Information	7	8	9
Opinion about issues			
Attitude toward facts			
Attitude toward law			
Attitude toward problems			
Do I and client like this juror?			
Does juror like me and client?			
Hardship reasons			
Overall rating 0–10			
Other factors/ reasons			
Other			
Other			

JURY SELECTION CHART   Form 4-2

Name of Case: Date of Trial:

Juror Information	10	11	12
Name			
Address			
Approximate age/ demeanor/dress			
Know case			
Know witnesses			
Occupation			
Employer			
Education			
Marital status			
Spouse's occupation			
Spouse's employer			
Children			
Past claims/ lawsuits			
Similar case experience			
Past/present jury duty:			
Civil			
Criminal			

JURY SELECTION CHART   Form 4-2 (continued)

Juror Information	10	11	12
Opinion about issues			
Attitude toward facts			
Attitude toward law			
Attitude toward problems			
Do I and client like this juror?			
Does juror like me and client?			
Hardship reasons			
Overall rating 0–10			
Other factors/ reasons			
Other			
Other			

FINAL JURY DATA

Form 4-3

Case _____   File _____

Challenges for cause

    Plaintiff/Prosecutor

    Defendant

Peremptory Challenges

    Plaintiff/Prosecutor

    Defendant

Juror Position Chart

Alternate Juror(s)

    1.   2.

Chapter 5
OPENING STATEMENT

A mind conscious of integrity scorns to say more than it means to perform.

—Robert Burns

Speeches cannot be made long enough for the speakers, nor short enough for the hearers.

—James Perry

5.1 Purposes

The opening statement is the first oral presentation by an attorney at trial directly addressing the facts and issues to be presented during the trial. The opening statement usually occurs immediately after voir dire and is confined to a statement of the facts. The opening statement does not include or permit argument or the drawing of inferences by the attorney.

There are two main purposes of the opening statement. The first is to acquaint the jury with the case and the party's positions. The second is to persuade the jury of the merits of the case. A description of the case includes a description of the parties, the scene, and the events.

The second purpose of the opening statement is really the purpose of the entire trial. An attorney who can persuade the jury of the merits of the case during the opening statement will significantly improve the chances of obtaining a favorable verdict. The value of a first impression is immeasurable in the courtroom. The attorney will appear more credible throughout the trial if the opening statement is effective.

The opening statement may also be used to achieve several other purposes. For example, it can be used to emphasize the theme of the case or to fill any voids or gaps in the case. The opening statement can also be employed to prepare the jury for a particular witness or to reduce the element of surprise from the other side's case.

5.2 What Can be Presented

A. Facts

Facts, even those in dispute, may be described and explained, so long as they can be proved during trial. The attorney might even discuss important facts which will be developed by opposing counsel. The facts to be presented should minimally include the major facts of the case. The term "facts" throughout this chapter will include all facts and any lay or expert opinions admissable in a case.

B. Argument

Opening statement does not permit an attorney to present arguments, draw inferences, propose conclusions, or otherwise comment on the evidence. Closing argument will afford the attorney the opportunity to present such arguments and conclusions. However, an attorney may be able to present the issues or theories of a case by prefacing such remarks with the statement "the evidence will show".

C. The Law

The judge is the person who explains the law to the jury. It is permissable for an attorney to make short, accurate references to the law during opening if necessary for the jury to understand the case. It may be necessary for the attorney to describe the legal elements of the case and the burden of proof and show how the facts will prove the elements and meet the burden of proof.

D. A Fact Test

One method to determine whether an attorney can include a statement during opening is to determine whether a witness, a document or some other form of evidence will provide such information. If the answer is yes, the statement may be referred to during opening; if no, then it is inappropriate and objectionable. Some judges and opposing lawyers will allow more latitude in an opening statement. Knowledge of this information will permit an attorney to present an opening statement with a broader scope.

CASE LAW—LOCAL PRACTICE & PROCEDURE—IDEAS

Outline   Notes

5.3 Preparation & Organization	See Form 5-1 Opening Statement Planning Worksheet.

A. *Knowing the Case*   The attorney needs to become familiar with every fact, inference, and aspect of the case. This knowledge will be necessary to analyze and select the theories of the case, establish the overall themes, plan the trial presentation, and determine which facts need to be proved in the case and presented in the opening statement.

B. *Developing Issues and Themes*   The issues and central theme of a case should be decided, thought out, and organized before the trial begins.

1. *The Issues.* The issues are the key or pivotal questions of fact raised by the contentions of the parties. After deciding what issues exist, the attorney should select the issues to be stressed to the jury. The early presentation of these issues may provide a framework for the trial that focuses attention on these issues and away from the opponent's case.

2. *The Themes and Theories of the Case.* The themes of a case are the major concepts central to the case. The theories of a case consist of the legal and factual theories that support the themes. See Section 1.3(E) and (F). The opening statement is the time to present the themes and theories in a comprehensive and complete way. The jury may have some idea about the case based upon the judge's preliminary instructions, statements, and questions during jury selection. In opening statement, the attorney explains to the jury how the various parts of the trial will fit together.

   The attorney should select words which reflect and reinforce the themes of the case. These theme words should be used during the opening statement as the attorney describes the story of the events. Theme words should be repetitively used throughout the trial to reinforce the theories and issues of the case.

C. *Opening Statement Based on Closing Argument*   The final argument is the part of the trial towards which everything else must point. If a fact, issue or position is not a part of the final argument it should not be a part of the opening statement or the rest of the case. The opening statement must be consistent with the factual and legal themes, the evidence, and the positions presented in the final argument. The opening statement should be based on what will be said in final argument.

D. *Anticipating Opposition's Positions*   An attorney needs to review the case from the perspective of the opposition and take such matters into account when preparing an opening statement. It is necessary to anticipate the other side's position in an attempt to defuse the opposition. The more an attorney knows about the theories, arguments, and positions of the opponent the more complete the opening preparation will be.

E. Pretrial Rulings　　　When selecting the facts which will be presented during opening statement, the attorney must ascertain whether an in limine ruling regarding certain categories of evidence is necessary before presenting or preparing the opening statement. The opening statement may not refer to evidence that will not be admissible during trial. Some questionable evidence which may not be admissable will create a problem for an attorney. Tactically an attorney may not want to refer to evidence which the opposing lawyer may object to during the opening and which the jurors will never receive during the trial. Pretrial evidentiary rulings will permit the attorney to plan the opening statement knowing exactly what information will be available during the trial.

F. Selecting Visual Aids　　　The attorney must decide whether to use any visual aids or trial exhibits during the opening statement. Consideration should be given to the impact a visual aid may have on the jury and whether the attorney is capable of being comfortable and effective using this tool. Visual aids may be a prepared outline of the opening statement on foam core board, poster board or overhead transparency, a chart or diagram, or the use of a blackboard during opening statement. Trial exhibits, which include real and demonstrative evidence, may sometimes be used during the opening statement. If visual aids or exhibits will be used during the opening statement, the attorney should inform the court and opposing counsel prior to trial in order to obtain permission for their use and to resolve any objections.

G. When to Present or Reserve the Opening Statement　　　The plaintiff/prosecution has the burden of proof in a case and gives the first opening statement. The plaintiff's opening statement occurs immediately after voir dire. After the plaintiff presents an opening statement, the defense has an opportunity to do the same. The defense will also have the option of reserving the opening statement until after the plaintiff has presented the case.

The best practice for the defense is usually to give the opening statement as soon as possible to counter an effective opening statement. The defense will normally want to tell the defense side of the story as soon as possible so that the jurors will keep open minds about the case until the defense can present its case. When the jurors understand the defense case they will be able to place the plaintiff's case in perspective. The criminal defense attorney may sometimes reserve the opening statement to prevent the prosecutor from learning what theories or defenses will be presented during the trial. However, this option may not always be available depending upon the local practice.

While opening statement may be waived, it should never be waived in a jury trial because it is an excellent vehicle for persuasion and an essential part of the overall trial presentation.

H. Written Outline and Detailed Script

The material for an opening statement needs to be organized into an outline format. The outline should include the introduction, the body, and the conclusion. The use of an outline helps organize the facts and theory of the case into an easily usable and readily accessible format. As the attorney prepares other aspects of the trial, this outline may be modified or altered and needs to remain flexible.

Some attorneys will find it advantageous to write or dictate a complete opening statement. This draft may then be reviewed and improved. With this format, the attorney will know that the final script of the opening statement will contain everything that needs to be presented. The drawback of using a script during an opening statement is the temptation to read the opening statement to the jury. Reading a script of the opening statement will appear dry and impersonal to the jury. A better approach for the attorney who wishes to use a script is to prepare a key word outline of the script. After becoming completely familiar with the script, the attorney should be able to present the opening statement using only the key word outline. When notes or outlines are used they should be used in a candid, forthright fashion.

I. Practice

After the attorney has prepared the outline or script, practice and rehearsal are necessary to be adequately prepared for the presentation at trial. The attorney who practices the opening statement several times prior to trial will find the time well spent. The attorney may want to think through the opening statement silently and then practice verbally concentrating on its content. As the content of the opening statement is mastered, the attorney can work on stylistic improvements. After this preparation the attorney should continue practicing and rehearsing the opening statement to an audience of colleagues or others, in front of a mirror, or on videotape for later review and critique. The attorney should practice presenting the opening statement until it can be done without referring to notes. Practice and rehearsal time can be stolen from non-law, non-productive activities which permit two tasks to be accomplished at once, i.e. drive time, lawn mowing, garden weeding, dishwashing, clothes folding, house cleaning, day dreaming.

J. Local Requirements

The attorney needs to determine before the trial whether the trial judge has any special requirements or limitations regarding the opening statement. This procedure will avoid having the opening statement interrupted by the trial judge and reduce the chances of opposing counsel making objections. Local practice and procedures, such as the prohibition of the use of trial exhibits during opening statements, may restrict how an opening statement can be presented.

CASE LAW—LOCAL PRACTICE & PROCEDURE—IDEAS

Outline   Notes

5.4 Structure of an Opening Statement

Opening statements must be presented in a structured fashion. Any reasonable structure is appropriate as long as it is simple and understandable. The structure must be designed so that the entire case can be framed within it and so that the jury can relate the facts and themes to the structure clearly and easily.

Most opening statements will be effectively presented as a chronological story. Other structures will be appropriate depending upon the circumstances. An attorney can present the facts in the order in which the witnesses will testify and present the information. An attorney can employ a flashback technique by first explaining the end of the story and then flashing back to earlier events. This approach would permit an attorney to first describe the damages in a civil case and then the events surrounding liability. An attorney can also present the facts in a topical sequence explaining the trial information in subject matter clusters. Still other structures may be appropriate for specific fact situations.

A. Introduction

An opening should begin with an introduction that initially draws the jurors and their attention and interest to the presentation and the case. The jury's attention level will usually be high at the beginning of the opening statement and full advantage should be taken of this opportunity. A statement that begins with the start of the factual story presented in an interesting and dramatic way may be the most effective means to maintain the jury's interest.

The beginning of an opening will depend in part upon what has occurred during the jury selection process and what introductory remarks and instructions the judge may have given. The beginning remarks of an opening statement may need to be tailored around what has occurred in the case. An attorney who wishes to begin an opening statement in a certain way may request that the judge make certain preliminary remarks concerning the identity of the client, or attorneys, or the purpose of an opening statement.

B. Explanation of Purposes

Many attorneys will begin an opening with an explanation of who they are, who they represent, and the purposes for an opening statement. Typically prefatory explanations include:

This opening statement allows me an opportunity to explain to you the evidence that will be presented through the testimony of witnesses and through documents. The evidence will be presented in bits and pieces and not in the order in which the events occurred. This opening statement will identify the witnesses and will provide you with a summary of what they will say. This overview of the facts and events of this case will act as a roadmap that will lead you to an understanding of the case.

The advantage of these or similar preliminary remarks is that the jurors may better understand the purpose for an opening statement. The disadvantage of such remarks is that they may not be the most persuasive and effective way to begin the presentation of the story to the jury. An audience generally remembers best what it hears first and last. The attorney should consider what the jury must remember and since this preliminary introductory information is most likely not a part of the key theme or theory of the case, it may be better placed in the body of the presentation or left out entirely.

C. The Story   The attorney should assume that the fact finder knows nothing about the case or the matters concerned and should design a presentation to explain each fact and element of the case in understandable terms. The lawyer's knowledge of the case will be extensive and may cause obvious facts to be overlooked or avoided. The attorney must keep in mind that the fact finder will be hearing the full case for the first time.

The most effective opening statement presentation will usually be the attorney telling the story of the facts to the jury. This factual story will constitute much of the content of the opening statement. It should parallel the substance of the trial evidence and the description that will be given in the closing argument. The opening statement should include a description of what did not happen as well as what did happen in certain cases. It may be necessary for an attorney, particularly a defense counsel, to explain to the jury what the evidence will not show as well as what the evidence will show.

The story should be told with simple language, in as dramatic a fashion as appropriate, and with a persuasive style. The things that make a story very interesting and very believable that appear in the great works of literature, art, and theater are the same things that may make an opening statement more effective.

D. The Scene and the   The opening statement must include a description of the scene
Characters   of the event and the characters who will testify as witnesses in the case. Where these descriptions appear in the presentation depend upon the development and structure that has the most persuasive impact.

Some attorneys will attempt to present the characters by personalizing their witnesses and by attempting to depersonalize the opposing party's witnesses. Depersonalization may be created by impersonal references made about those characters including identification by their last name or as the plaintiff or defendant instead of by name if the person is a party.

E. Conclusion   An opening statement should conclude with a strong ending. This effect may be achieved with a concise summary of the vital facts, with a compelling statement justifying a verdict, or with a dramatic summary of the major theme of the case. The jurors will more likely remember what is said at the end of the opening statement rather than what is said during the middle and this factor should be taken advantage of during concluding remarks. The final words should be well thought out so that no matter how lost the attorney gets there will be an ending that is, both in words and delivery, a conclusion. The style and delivery should be consistent with the entire presentation. A strong presentation can be ruined by an apologetic or weak conclusion.

F. Length

The opening statement should be long enough to cover the essential aspects of the case, yet short enough to maintain the jurors' attention. It is difficult to suggest an optimum length for an opening statement because much depends upon the circumstances and complexity of a case and the speaking pace of an attorney. Some opening statements may only last five minutes; others will extend for more than an hour or two. Many opening statements last between ten to twenty minutes. The longer an opening statement is the longer the attorney must be concerned with preserving the interest of the jurors.

G. An Opening Statement Test

Questions that may assist in determining whether an opening statement has been properly constructed include the following inquiries:
1. Does the opening statement tell the jury what happened?
2. Does the opening statement tell the jury why to find for the client?
3. Does the opening statement make the jury want to find for the client?
4. Does the opening statement tell the jury how to find for the client?
5. Does the opening statement have a structure that is clear and simple?
6. Is the opposing statement consistent with what will be proved and with what will be argued in final argument?

See Form 5-2 Opening Statement Worksheet.

CASE LAW—LOCAL PRACTICE & PROCEDURE—IDEAS

Outline   Notes

5.5 Content of Opening Statement

The following matters represent considerations which apply to opening statements. The exact content of an opening will, of course, depend upon the facts and circumstances of a case.

A. Detailed Information

The facts presented during an opening statement should be as detailed as necessary. The advantage of providing a very detailed story is that it will usually be perceived by the jury or judge as more credible and more persuasive. The disadvantage in presenting detailed specific facts is that it increases the risk that the evidence will not be presented with the specificity that the opening statement suggests. Detail that provides necessary information for a full understanding or that explains sources of corroboration or credibility will usually bolster the essential aspects of the case.

B. The Use of Exhibits

Real evidence, demonstrative evidence, visual aids, deposition transcripts, witness' statements, pleadings, and other exhibits that have been carefully selected may be used during an opening statement to make the presentation more understandable and more effective. The design, placement and use in the presentation are as important as the exhibits themselves. The impact words and colors on a visual aid, the importance of an exhibit in the trial, the location in the room for clear viewing and easy access, the placement in the structure of the presentation, and the style of the lawyer in the use of and reference to an exhibit are important considerations in determining whether an exhibit will aid in or interfere with the opening statement presentation.

C. References to the Law

Opening statement is not the place for frequent or substantial references to the law. Lengthy explanations of the law are reserved to the judge and to the attorneys during closing argument. Some reference to the law will usually be appropriate. The attorney must know the local rule and procedure in regard to how much law can be discussed in opening statement in order to determine how to weave the law and facts together so that the jury has a clear structure upon which to relate the facts to the elements and to the burden of proof. While the attorney may briefly tell the jury what the appropriate law is for the case, the jurors may already know this so there may be no need for the attorney to explain this matter again.

D. Case Weaknesses

An attorney must consider whether to describe weaknesses in a case. The better practice is to present those weaknesses in a candid and forthright manner. The weak points of the case may have been mentioned during voir dire and may require less attention in the opening statement. Weaknesses in a case which have not been explained to the jurors and which most likely will be mentioned during the opposition's opening statement or later in the case should be addressed during opening statement. An open and candid disclosure of such information will usually increase the sincerity and credibility of the attorney and will often reduce the impact of the opposition's tactics.

E. Qualifying Remarks

During opening statement an attorney may use as a preface the phrase: "The evidence will show." Some judges may require an attorney to employ this or a similar phrase periodically during an opening to prevent the presentation from sounding like argument. Many attorneys will prefer not to use this phrase because they believe it reduces the impact of the story. It may be more effective in telling a story not to remind the audience that what is being said has yet to be proved. A qualifying introduction such as "the evidence will show" used as a preface to the presentation of a theme or argument may be an effective tactic to prevent an objection. However, if this tactic is overused and it becomes apparent that it is being used to argue or to introduce otherwise inappropriate information into the opening statement, objections will be sustained and the attorney will lose credibility with the judge and jury.

Some attorneys advise the jurors that what an attorney says during opening does not constitute facts and that it is the function of the jurors to determine the facts after hearing the evidence during the trial. Comments like this may also reduce the intended impact of an opening statement presentation. Defense counsel may tactically want to make such comments in an attempt to reduce the effectiveness of the plaintiff's opening statement and to remind the jurors that they must determine the evidence as it is introduced during the trial.

F. Request for Verdict

An opening statement should contain an explanation of the verdict that the facts will support. This explanation should be clear and distinct so the jury understands what conclusion they must reach to find for a party. Some attorneys will say that the facts require that the jury return a verdict because the client is entitled to or has a right to such a verdict. It may be more effective for the attorney to explain to the jurors that they will have an opportunity, and even a duty, to return a verdict based upon the facts of the case.

An attorney for a plaintiff who seeks damages may or may not want to advise the jury regarding the specific amount of damages that should be awarded. The attorney needs to make a tactical judgment depending upon the circumstances of each case whether it is better for the jury to first hear specific amounts of damages during the trial with a summary amount requested during closing argument or better to suggest some amount of damages to the jury in opening statement so that they have some understanding and predisposition towards that amount during the trial.

G. *Understatement*

Understatement can be a useful credibility-building device for an opening statement presentation. Understating a case will set the expectation of the jury at a level which will be exceeded at the trial. The presentation of the evidence at the trial will then surpass the jury's expectations, enhancing the credibility of the case and the attorney. The use of understatement does have disadvantages. It may reduce the attorney's ability to explain the facts in a persuasive way, and jurors may perceive an understated case to be weaker than the attorney intended.

H. *Overstatement*

The attorney should avoid the use of overstatement during an opening statement. The jury may be initially impressed, but this initial impression will not last long once the jury realizes the evidence presented during trial does not match what the attorney stated during the opening statement. Further, opposing counsel may comment during closing argument about the absence of the exaggerated evidence from the trial.

I. *Promises*

An opening can be presented effectively if an attorney "promises" the jury that certain evidence will prove a certain fact—as long as the attorney can fulfill that promise. Often a promise cannot be kept causing the jury to disbelieve the facts of the case as well. A promise is a tactical approach that must be employed carefully.

If a lawyer does make promises during an opening or otherwise asserts that certain evidence will be forthcoming, the opposing lawyer should note all these statements and mention during closing argument all promises not kept.

J. *Improper Comments*

An attorney may not comment about the evidence or the credibility of the witnesses or assert personal opinions. It is also inappropriate for an attorney to denounce or attack the opposing party or attorney.

CASE LAW—LOCAL PRACTICE & PROCEDURE—IDEAS

Outline   Notes

5.6 Presentation and Delivery

The manner in which the attorney delivers the opening statement will affect the jurors' understanding of the facts of the case, will significantly influence their initial impression of the attorney and the strengths and weaknesses of the clients' case, and will shape their perspective of the entire trial. The more effective and persuasive the attorney can be in presenting an opening statement the greater the chance that a favorable verdict will be reached by the jury. The following factors are matters that will affect the quality of the opening presentation delivered by an attorney. The following factors relating to presentation and delivery parallel most of the considerations that are discussed in Section 10.4 regarding final argument.

A. Confidence

The attorney during an opening statement should appear to be confident, in control, and have command of the case. Jurors will usually be impressed by attorneys who are forceful yet tactful, candid yet not condescending, and positive yet realistic.

B. Sincerity

The appearance of sincerity and a belief in the merits of the client's cause are necessary in order to be effective. A failure to appear sincere will invariably cause the jury to think that if the attorney does not believe in or care about the case, the jury does not need to care.

C. Interest

A story told in an interesting manner will hold the jury's attention and sound more persuasive than a story told in an uninteresting or boring fashion. Interest may be established and maintained in any number of ways. The attorney must first appear to be interested in the case. A story told in a compelling, energetic, and enthusiastic manner will be a more effective approach than a dull, listless, monotone approach.

D. Integrity

An attorney must appear fair in the eyes of the jury. The jury will not trust an attorney who appears sneaky or underhanded. The attorney has the initial opportunity during opening statement to establish integrity and to present a trusting and fair appearance. In order to maintain this integrity the attorney must not oversell or overstate the case. The facts, witnesses and emotion of the case must live up to the opening statement presentation.

E. Attitude

The attorney must approach and treat the jurors with respect. The jurors should be treated as equals and not demeaned. Any different treatment will only insult and alienate the jury.

F. Stance

It will usually be more effective for an attorney to stand in front of the jury box and not behind a lectern or table. This stance will usually hold the juror's attention more than if the attorney hides behind a lectern. This is not to say that an effective opening cannot be presented using a lectern, but a lectern may unnecessarily interfere with an attorney establishing an effective presence with the jury.

The attorney must maintain an appropriate distance from the jurors. This distance should neither be too far away so that personal contact is lost nor too close so that the jurors feel uncomfortable. The exact distance will depend upon the number of jurors, the size, energy, and presence of the attorney, the size, shape, and acoustics of the courtroom, and the content of the statement being made. A distance of between five and eight feet can be used as an appropriate guide, but the distance should be flexible and vary in different circumstances. An attorney can approach closer or stand further away to make a point more effectively.

G. Posture   An attorney's body language must match what is being said. Jurors may be adversely affected by any inconsistencies. Good posture is essential for an advocate. Good posture does not require that the attorney stand stock still and straight as a rod during opening. A comfortable non-slouching posture should be appropriate.

Some movement and gestures are useful particularly if the opening is long. Movement, stance, pacing, and timing should be orchestrated so as not to be distracting. An attorney may use movement as a transition or to make a point more effectively and should avoid movement that appears purposeless.

H. Dress   The attorney's appearance is an important consideration throughout the trial. A speaker's appearance will often affect the listener's perceptions about that person. An attorney who is tastefully dressed and well groomed will usually appear more professional and credible to the jury.

I. Gestures   Effective speakers usually employ gestures to make a presentation more interesting. An attorney needs to incorporate appropriate gestures into a presentation. The lack of any gestures, the use of awkward hand movements, or wild gesticulations need to be avoided. Gestures should be natural, firm, and purposeful.

J. Eye Contact   Establishing eye contact with jurors will help the attorney in creating a sincere and courteous relationship with the jury. Looking jurors in the eye while talking will substantially increase the impact of what is being said. However, staring at a juror will undoubtedly make the juror uncomfortable and adversely affect the attorney's rapport with that juror. It is vital for the attorney to periodically make eye contact with each individual juror.

K. Vocal Control and Pace   The tone, volume, modulation, and pace of an attorney's delivery will affect the listening capabilities of the jurors. A dull, monotone presentation will be just as ineffective as ranting and raving. A balanced and well-modulated approach will usually be most effective.

Sometimes the best thing an attorney can say is nothing. Silence can be an effective way to highlight a point, to gain attention, or to create a transition. An attorney needs to learn to tolerate appropriate silence in the courtroom and to use it constructively.

L. Word Choice   1. *Simple Language.* Clarity of expression is important. The words the attorney chooses to use during opening statement will affect the understanding of the jury. Simple and clear language is preferable to complex legalese. Large words used just to show off vocabulary skills will turn off the jury. Overly simplistic words may give the jury the impression of being talked down to. The attorney must balance the need for simple language against the danger of appearing condescending.

2. *Factual Words.* Factual words and not conclusory words should be used. These words will more accurately reflect the content of the evidence and reduce the opportunity for opposing counsel to object.

3. *Impact Phrases.* Descriptive words will be useful in emphasizing the important facts of the case, will create a more vivid image of the events for the jury, and will more easily be remembered by the jurors. Impact language includes those words that more graphically describe a situation. "Smashed" instead of "hit," "huge" instead of "large," "shrieked" instead of "yelled," are examples of descriptive impact words. These type of words should be selected as long as they accurately reflect the facts of what happened. Care must be taken not to misuse such language. They should be descriptive fact words and not non-testimonial conclusions. Their use should not exaggerate the evidence that will be introduced. Impact words may be obtained from a Thesaurus, a dictionary, and from works of literature and drama.

M. Transitions   The opening statement will be more effective if the attorney employs transitions in the presentation. Prefatory remarks, silence, a louder voice, a softer voice, movement, gestures, chronology, and logic are all devices which can signal a transition.

N. Drama   To the extent possible and appropriate, the opening of a case should be presented in a serious, dramatic manner. The attorney should deliver an opening taking full advantage of the theatre of the courtroom.

Some opening statements may permit an attorney to create suspense as well. If the attorney understates some facts, the natural curiosity of the jury may be such that they will pay very close attention when the complete facts are introduced at trial. For example, during opening the attorney can tell the jury about the substance of a conversation but leave the exact words for the witness to state during trial.

O. A Positive, Assertive Position

An attorney should avoid an opening statement that only responds to or anticipates an opponent's facts and theories. Doing so may cause the jury to perceive the attorney as a person without original positions. In trial work, the best defense is a good offense; an opening statement should assert positive positions.

P. Developing Own Style

An attorney must deliver the opening in a style that reflects that attorney's abilities. An attorney should avoid copying and mimicking another lawyer's style but should be open to adapting and reworking what someone else has done if it appears effective.

Q. Observing the Jurors' Reaction

The attorney should observe the jurors' reactions during the opening statement and mold the presentation to the reactions of the jurors. The initial impressions displayed by a jury during the opening statement will also be useful in determining how the evidence is later presented and what might be an effective closing argument. Some jurors will be more likely to express a reaction regarding the facts of the case during the opening statement and less likely to display reactions as the trial progresses.

It is, however, difficult to accurately determine what a person is thinking just by watching them during a presentation. Care must be taken not to overreact, not to completely change an approach because of a perceived reaction and not to focus on one or two jurors because they seem to be responding positively.

An attorney may need to revise a presentation depending upon the location of the trial and the types of individual jurors. An aggressive, hard driving style may be effective in some large, urban areas but may be inappropriate for jurors in a rural area.

R. Notes and Outlines

An attorney in properly preparing for a case will learn the facts well enough that an opening statement may be presented without notes in most cases. Presenting a memorized opening or reading an opening statement will sound flat and contrived. Occasional references to notes may be appropriate, as long as such references do not unreasonably interfere with or detract from the presentation. Often notes are used only as a crutch which an attorney does not need.

When notes are necessary the attorney should not pretend not to use them or try to sneak a peek. An obvious use of notes done honestly and openly can be effective. It can even be used as a tool to develop rapport with the jurors, most of whom would be very uncomfortable in a public speaking situation.

Prepared outlines can be effectively used in an opening if conducted with the use of visual aids. An overhead transparency, a pre-prepared diagram, or a blackboard may contain an outline of the opening which will highlight important matters for the jurors and assist the attorney in explaining the facts. Any visual aid should be simple, impacting, and uncluttered.

CASE LAW—LOCAL PRACTICE & PROCEDURE—IDEAS

Outline   Notes

5.7 Objections and Motions

A. Objections

Section 9.6 lists available objections that may be asserted during opening statement. Tactically an attorney may not want to object but rather to write down what was said and to use it against the opposing attorney in closing argument. Most attorneys will not object during opening statement unless the opponent is saying or doing something that is clearly improper and damaging to the case. It may be necessary in these situations to object and request a curative instruction to preserve an issue for appeal. Many attorneys extend a courtesy to each other so that the opening statements are uninterrupted and zealous; effective but not bizarre behavior is accepted without objection.

B. Motions on the Opening Statement

An action may be dismissed or a directed verdict may be ordered on admissions made by counsel during opening statement. See *Best v. District of Columbia,* 291 U.S. 411 (1934); *St. Paul Motor Vehicle Co. v. Johnston,* 127 Minn. 443, 149 N.W. 667 (1914). Very few judges will grant this type of motion today, but making the motion may startle the opposing attorney and show determination.

Other possible motions include:

1. A motion to have the court set constraints on opponent's opening regarding time, scope, detail, and demeanor.
2. A motion by plaintiff to present additional facts in rebuttal to defendant's opening after defendant is finished.
3. A motion by defendant for a compulsory nonsuit.

CASE LAW—LOCAL PRACTICE & PROCEDURE—IDEAS

Outline   Notes

5.8 Avoiding Mistrials and Reversals

A. Guard Against Overly Prejudicial Statements

While an opening statement should be persuasive, it should not be excessive, such as characterizing a defendant as Aesop's fabled "fox in the chicken coop" or other exaggerated allegories. *U.S. v. Singer*, 482 F.2d 394 (6th Cir. 1973). Overly prejudicial remarks, which cannot be cured by a judge's admonitions to the jury to disregard them, will serve as a basis for a mistrial.

B. Limit Opening Statement to What Can be Offered or Proven at Trial

The opening statement must remain within the bounds of what a lawyer hopes to introduce at trial. Consequently, an opening statement which misstates evidence or characterizes it in a way that cannot be proved is impermissible. It may be unethical to conceal or withhold a position on which one intends to rely. Rule 22(b), Code of Trial Conduct of the American College of Trial Lawyers. It is unethical to proffer evidence that cannot be supported or which is, in fact, false. DR 7–102; *People v. Wallin*, 621 P.2d 330 (Colo. 1981).

C. Avoid Irrelevancies

Facts which may be true but are irrelevant should be avoided. For example, it is improper to refer to a party's family situation unless germane to an issue at trial. See *Tennis v. General Motors Corp.*, 625 S.W.2d 218 (Mo. 1981). See also DR 7–106.

D. Do Not Object to Opposing Counsel's Argument Merely to Harass

Repeated objections to an opposing attorney's opening statement are unethical if done only for harassment. DR 7–106(C)(6) prohibits conduct that is undignified or discourteous and degrading to a tribunal. A tribunal has been held to include all members of the entire forum, which includes opposing counsel. *State v. Turner*, 217 Kan. 574, 538 P.2d 966 (1975). EC 7–37 admonishes against haranguing and offensive tactics.

E. Do Not Argue from a Personal Viewpoint

Personal remarks or personal viewpoints have no place in the opening statement, although slipping into an occasional "I believe" will not seriously prejudice a case. The lawyer's remarks are not evidence and the judge may warn the jury to ignore them. The concern here, again, is whether the remarks will so seriously prejudice a jury as to create the need for a new trial or reversal. *Sanders v. Wheaton*, 273 Ark. 416, 619 S.W.2d 674 (1981); *Funk v. Venture Stores*, 94 Ill. App. 3d 115, 418 N.E.2d 498 (1981). DR 7–106(C)(3)–(4). A lengthy harangue on the size and expense of the opposing counsel's law firm, and how one's own poor client could not afford such services, will more than likely require a new trial. *Anderson v. Hawthorne Fuel Co.*, 201 Minn. 580, 277 N.W. 259 (1938).

CASE LAW—LOCAL PRACTICE & PROCEDURE—IDEAS

Outline   Notes

5.9 Bibliography

TEXTS

G. Bellow & B. Moulton, *The Lawyering Process* 826–965 (Foundation Press, Mineola, NY, 1978).

P. Bergman, *Trial Advocacy in a Nutshell* 248–58 (West Pub. Co., St. Paul, MN, 1979).

S. Goldberg, *The First Trial in a Nutshell* 98–102, 191–209 (West Pub. Co., St. Paul, MN, 1982).

K. Hegland, *Trial and Practice Skills in a Nutshell* 101–13 (West Pub. Co., St. Paul, MN, 1978).

J. Jeans, *Trial Advocacy* Ch. 8 (West Pub. Co., St. Paul, MN, 1975).

R. Keeton, *Trial Tactics and Methods* 270–80 (Little, Brown & Co., Boston, MA, 1973).

J. Kelner & F. McGovern, *Successful Litigation Techniques* Ch. 11 (Matthew Bender, New York, 1981).

T. Mauet, *Fundamentals of Trial Techniques* 49–83 (Little, Brown & Co., Boston, MA, 1980).

J. McElhaney, *Effective Litigation* 109–22 (West Pub. Co., St. Paul, MN, 1974).

A. Morrill, *Trial Diplomacy* 22–31 (Court Practice Inst., Chicago, IL, 1972).

OPENING STATEMENT PLANNING WORKSHEET Form 5-1

Case _____   File _____

1. The issues in this case are

2. The themes of this case are

3. Key facts of the case are

4. Pretrial rulings to be obtained include

5. Visual aids and exhibits to be used during Opening include

OPENING STATEMENT WORKSHEET Form 5-2

Case _____   File _____

Introduction

Story

Theme Phrases

Impact Words

Visual Aids/Exhibits

Case Weaknesses

Request for Verdict

Conclusion

Chapter 6
DIRECT EXAMINATION

Any fact is better established by two or three good testimonies than by a thousand arguments.

—Nathaniel Emmons

A word or nod from the good has more weight than the eloquent speeches of others.

—Plutarch

6.1 Purposes   An attorney by asking questions on direct examination attempts to communicate relevant information to the fact finder through the witness. A witness by answering questions on direct examination attempts to describe or explain all or part of an incident in a persuasive, credible manner. Direct examination constitutes the most common device to present evidence in a case.

The task of the trial lawyer will be to recreate through the testimony of the witness an historical event in the theater of the courtroom. The focus of attention will generally not be on the lawyer but on the witness. The most marvelously presented direct examination will seldom be appreciated and the credit will go to the witness, the luck of the case, the simplicity of the facts, the support of the law, and the rulings of the judge.

A lawyer may seek to meet three goals with direct examination:
1. To present evidence that is legally sufficient to support a prima facie case that will overcome a motion for a directed verdict or a motion to dismiss.
2. To convince the fact finder of the integrity of the evidence and the truth of the case, thereby persuading the fact finder to find for the client in the terms established by the attorney.
3. To counter or contradict evidence submitted by the opposition.

6.2 Preparation & Organization

A. Considerations in Preparation

1. *Rules of Procedure.* State or federal rules of procedure may limit the way in which the story will be told. Local court rules may also be a limitation, and individual judges may have their own rules which may affect the presentation. Opposing counsel may

210

have an interpretation of the rules of procedure that may either permit the lawyer certain flexibility or limit the lawyer's presentation through objections.

2. *Rules of Evidence.* State, federal, local, or individual courts may relax or expand the rules of evidence to limit or broaden the presentation of evidence. Different opponents may have theories or tactics which increase or limit their objections to evidence.

3. *Professional Responsibility.* Rules of professional responsibility and rules of decorum, along with local court rules or practices, may have an effect on the way in which the witness testifies, the lawyer behaves, and the evidence is presented.

4. *Witness Ability.* Each witness will have different capabilities. The attorney should explore and evaluate the witness' strengths and weaknesses in order to make the witness as effective as possible.

5. *The Facts.* The facts in a case include the objective information as well as the emotions and feelings involved. The facts will affect the extent and quality of the examination.

6. *The Law.* The burden of proof, the elements of the cause of action, and the defenses may restrict or expand the amount of permissible testimony.

B. Parts of a Direct Examination

1. *The Question.* Questions govern the structure of the direct examination. The attorney needs to consider how a question is asked and its wording, tone, and pacing. The attorney should also consider when the question will be asked and the likely or anticipated response.

2. *The Answer.* The witness' answer should be honest, concise, accurate, complete, and responsive. It should not be evasive, speculative, argumentative, or vague. An answer should not express an opinion unless the witness is an expert or the question involves an area in which a nonexpert can give an opinion.

C. Witness Selection and Preparation

The attorney must decide which facts are necessary to support the case and then which witnesses are most capable of presenting those facts.

1. *Which Witnesses to Call.* The lawyer should consider which witnesses can make the most effective presentation and corroborate critical information. The lawyer should also consider which witnesses will be persuasive, which will be the most cooperative, who are less inconvenienced, and who need not testify. Too much corroboration may be boring and confusing.

2. *Special Needs of Witnesses.* A witness may have special value to the case or need particular attention due to physical or mental

problems, difficulty in communication, nervousness, stubborness, hostility, anger or indifference.

3. *Sequence of Witnesses.* The attorney must decide whether a witness should be called at the beginning, middle or end of the case, and when during the day a witness should testify. The primacy/recency effect suggests that a strong witness is the most effective when called first or last. Often a strong witness will be called immediately before a recess. This is true whether the recess is for minutes, the evening, or for the weekend.

Most often, witnesses will be called in an order that supports a chronological presentation of the case. However, another order may be used, depending on the circumstances of the trial. Sometimes the order of witnesses can be arranged so that a strong witness will follow a weak witness to bolster the testimony of the weak witness.

4. *Preparing the Witness.* The preparation of the witness will begin at the initial interview, long before trial. Every contact with a witness should be viewed as an opportunity to cultivate that witness for trial.

D. Meeting the Witness

The attorney needs to consider several factors in analyzing a witness preparation meeting:

1. How will the meeting be structured?
2. Will the attorney structure the meeting or just let it happen?
3. What other ways are there to structure the meeting?
4. Is there a particular impression the attorney wants to convey to the witness?
5. How will the attorney prepare for the meeting?
6. Will the attorney know everything there is to know about the case or will more information be gathered?

See Form 6-1 Witness Information Worksheet.

E. Gathering Information

The attorney will want to know what the witness knows, does not know, and who this person is. To determine this information the attorney should consider whether:

1. To let the witness give a narrative description or lead the witness with questions.
2. To establish a mind-set with the witness by setting up the action or theme first.
3. To interrupt the witness, inquire about rumors or hearsay, or talk about matters not admissible at trial.
4. To show the witness statements made by other witnesses.
5. To explore any "skeletons" that may be hanging in the witness' closet.

6. To uncover any bias or prejudice the witness may have toward the client, other party, or case.
7. To take a signed or other statement from the witness.

F. Providing the Witness with Guidelines for Testifying

The best way to have a witness live up to the attorney's expectations is to inform the witness of what those expectations are. Some of the instructions given the witness should include:

1. The need to maintain some eye contact with the jury or judge.
2. The need to maintain eye contact with the examining attorney:
   a) Whom to look at during direct examination and cross examination; and
   b) The dangers of looking at the lawyer too much.
3. The attorney's role of protecting the witness from opposing counsel.
4. The dangers of becoming angry or losing control.
5. The importance of telling the truth and not exaggerating.
6. The benefits of appearing honest and sincere.
7. The necessity of not answering a question that is not understood.
8. The avoidance of speculation or inappropriate opinions when answering questions.
9. To decline to answer a question if the witness does not know.
10. The problems created by being nonresponsive or volunteering information.
11. How to explain technical terms during the trial.
12. The obligation of the attorney to control the case.
13. Appropriate dress.

G. Witness Dress

The credibility of a witness will be affected to some degree by the attire worn by that witness. It is difficult, if not impossible, to generalize about the type, color, and quality of clothing that should be worn. The essential principles that help guide individual decisions include:

1. The themes and theories of the case. The dress of a witness should be consistent with the role of that witness in establishing or reinforcing the themes and theories of the case.
2. The personality of the witness. A witness must portray himself or herself to be credible. Overdressing or underdressing may adversely affect the believability of a witness.
3. The expectations of the fact finder. The jurors or judge will have certain expectations based on community standards about how people should dress. Neatness is an example of such an expectation. Regardless of the type, color, or quality of clothing, if the witness dresses neatly the fact finder will be more comfortable listening to that witness.

H. Rehearsal   A well-prepared witness should be comfortable with the role to be played at trial before setting foot in the courtroom. Preliminary hearings and depositions serve as rehearsal vehicles. Some of the considerations in rehearsal include:

1. The witness should know which questions will be asked, and should not be asked "surprise" questions at trial.
2. The witness may need to understand the theories of the case and the purpose of the testimony.
3. The witness should not be coached to parrot answers.
4. The witness should realize that the examination at trial may differ because of changing trial strategies.
5. The rehearsal should take place far enough in advance of the trial that the witness will be able to incorporate the attorney's suggestions.
6. The witness should avoid the rehearsed look.
7. The witness should be comfortable with exhibits.

I. Order of Questions   The order of questions and the techniques used should help the witness communicate effectively. The lawyer should consider which kind of questions are best suited to each witness—narrative, specific, or a combination of each. Some questions should be avoided with some witnesses. See Form 6-2 Direct Examination Planning Worksheet.

J. Exhibit Management   After deciding which exhibits are necessary, including real and demonstrative evidence, it is a good idea to determine how the exhibit is to be prepared and presented and which witness will be used to present it. All the witnesses should understand the exhibit, and if they do not agree as to its accuracy the inconsistencies should be solved.

CASE LAW—LOCAL PRACTICE & PROCEDURE—IDEAS

Outline   Notes

6.3 Presentation &   See Form 6-3 Direct Examination Outline.
      Delivery

A. Portraying a Story   Generally, assuming that the judge and jury know nothing about the case is a good idea. The direct examination should start at the beginning and tell everything. The courtroom is a theater and the story is more than a still picture; it includes the sounds, smells, touches, and emotions of the case. The trial is like a play; the lawyer is the director and the witnesses are the characters. The lines must be persuasive, interesting, compelling and clear. The script and action must be prepared before "going on."

1. *A Simple Play.* The story should be told simply. People have only a limited ability to absorb and retain oral information. Most of what is learned comes through other senses besides hearing. The words should be chosen carefully. People do not understand "lawyer talk," jargon, technical descriptions, or expert terms.

2. *The Audience.* The attorney must pay careful attention to the audience in order to present the case effectively. The attorney should watch the jurors and make sure that they can see and hear what is going on. The attorney should be conscious of the witness' voice and of the attorney's own voice. The attorney should stand where the jury can observe the questioning. The audience must be able to hear. Both the attorney and witness must project their voices, however, neither needs to yell to be heard.

3. *The Scene, Then the Events.* Describing the parties and the scene before describing the action may be the most appropriate direct examination sequence. Action testimony is generally most effective and dramatic when presented in an uninterrupted manner. Flowing descriptions allow the jury to visualize the action.

4. *Chronological Presentation.* Chronological presentation is generally the easiest to present and to understand. However, any logical order of presentation may be appropriate. In some cases, for example, the witness might give the most dramatic or important testimony early when the jury is most alert. Sometimes, too, a witness is not available or an expert must be worked in around the expert's schedule.

5. *Detail and Repetition.* A witness who describes an event in vivid detail will be more persuasive and credible than a witness who testifies using general descriptions. Too much detail, however, particularly concerning minor events, may confuse the fact finder. Likewise, too much repetition may become boring.

B. Conduct of the   1. *Appearing Interested.* If the attorney does not appear to be in-
      Attorney   terested in what is going on, the judge and jury probably will not be interested either. The attorney should look at the witness during the examination. The attorney's posture, whether standing or

sitting, will indicate how important this witness or this testimony is.

2. *Tempo, Rhythm, Pacing, Timing, and Modulation.* Like music, a feeling can be developed through rhythm, tempo, and modulation, short or long questions, fast or slow questions, pauses between questions, or raised or lowered voices. A sense of kinetic energy through the tone of the questions, the pace, and the number asked will set and continue a mood for action sequences. The speed of words may also indicate intensity. Generally, effective direct examinations move quickly through general information and more slowly through the specifics of critical action.

3. *Listening.* The examiner must listen to and understand the witness' answers and react as if they were being heard for the first time. Reading or concentrating on other matters while the witness answers is not a good idea. The attorney should also be aware of the jury's and judge's responses to the witness' answers. Follow-up questions may be tailored to the witness' answers to create smooth flowing testimony.

4. *Relationship to the Witness.* The attorney should not appear too "chummy" with any of the witnesses. The attorney's credibility is enhanced by maintaining an interested, concerned, yet professional, profile during direct examination.

C. Enhancing the Credibility of the Witness

1. *Humanizing the Witness.* The jury is more likely to believe what the witness is saying if they view the witness as a likeable, nice person. How does the witness fit into the community? What is the witness' background? Does the witness have a family?

   A witness may also be humanized by using the witness' first name if permitted by local rule or custom. A progression of names from formal to personal may be used by referring to a witness first by full name, then by surname, and then by first name. This progressive familiarity may help the fact finder gradually become more comfortable with the witness.

2. *Background Information.* Initial questioning typically includes background questions to personalize the witness. Background information should be selected which may serve other purposes including:
   a) Allowing the witness to answer simple questions to relieve some of the initial anxiety.
   b) Identifying similarities the witness may have with the background of the jurors.
   c) Displaying the sincerity of a witness.
   d) Offering background traits or job experience which buttress the inferences of a case and the credibility of the witness.

3. *Demonstrating the Credibility of the Witness.* The credibility of the witness may be enhanced by eliciting certain details that corroborate the testimony: that the witness had a good opportunity to observe the incident; that the witness reported the incident; and, therefore, that the witness is a careful, caring person.

The witness' credibility is also enhanced by letting the witness tell the story in a way that appears natural. The attorney should not interrupt unless necessary; i.e., the witness is off track, rambling, or acting improperly. If inconsistencies arise, they should be explained.

D. The Questions

Questions should be prepared in advance in outlines or notes. Prepared questions should not be read unless they are technical and must be exact.

1. *Language.* Simple and brief language using everyday conversational words is generally the most effective unless it is snobbish, technical or vulgar. "After" should be used instead of "subsequent"; "how far" instead of "would you indicate the distance"; "did you" instead of "did you have occasion to"; "on April 1st" instead of "calling your attention to the date of April 1"; "car" instead of "motor vehicle." The lawyer should also avoid talking down to the jury or using double negatives, which can be confusing. Matters that do not make sense should be clarified and technical or unclear terms defined. Statutory language should be used in order to fulfill the exact requirements of the burden of proof; otherwise legalese is to be avoided.

2. *Impact Words.* The use of impact words such as "blown apart" rather than "exploded" or "shot in the back" rather than "wounded" may be very effective. The use of words that may influence the answer such as "how fast" rather than "how slow" may favorably affect the judge or jury.

3. *Respecting the Jury.* The witness should explain to "us" and avoid talking down to the jury. The jurors should not be embarrased or demeaned, and the lawyer should avoid any "tricks." The attorney is most persuasive by appearing polite and courteous.

4. *Leading Questions Generally Prohibited.* Generally, leading questions are not allowed during direct examination. See Fed. R. Evid. 611(c). Leading questions will often draw an objection from opposing counsel which interrupts the flow and slows the testimony. Leading questions do not give the witness an opportunity to testify and prevent the witness from appearing credible. The jurors may react negatively to what they perceive as the lawyer testifying.

5. *Leading Questions Sometimes Allowed.* Under Federal Rule of Evidence 611(c), leading questions may be permitted when necessary to develop testimony. They can be used in direct examination in the following instances:
   a) In preliminary matters;
   b) To elicit noncontroversial or undisputed facts;
   c) To establish inconsequential facts;
   d) To suggest a new topic;
   e) As a transition;
   f) To question a hostile witness or a witness predisposed against the case;
   g) To examine an adverse or reluctant witness;
   h) To lay foundation for certain exhibits;
   i) To examine a witness who has a difficult time communicating because of age or a handicap;
   j) To refresh a witness' recollection; and
   k) When asking a witness to contradict statements made by another.

   The careful use of leading questions mixed with non-leading questions may also help develop a variety in rhythm, tempo, and pacing.

6. *Open-Ended Questions.* Questions that are open-ended and call for a narrative response minimize the presence of the attorney and let the witness tell the story. Open-ended questions may cause problems if the witness adds improper or unnecessary information, is boring, needs help communicating, or is disorganized and has no ability to relate information.

7. *Concise Questions.* Specific, short questions make it easier for the lawyer to control the flow of evidence and result in more precise information. These questions do, however, tend to minimize the witness' role and may break the rhythm or prevent a good witness from testifying well.

8. *Double Direct.* An attorney will be able to emphasize testimony by repeating key words of a previous response in a preface to a follow-up question.

9. *Refreshing Recollection.* A witness who exhibits a memory lapse on the stand may be refreshed by having the attorney provide the witness with a previous statement or any other thing that would assist the witness to recall the answer. The lack of memory by a witness must be established before an attorney can attempt to refresh it. The document or thing used to refresh recollection may need to be marked as an exhibit, depending on the jurisdiction. The witness should not be permitted to keep the document while testifying but should return it to the attorney and testify independently. The cross-examiner will have access to the statement or thing used to refresh recollection.

10. *Handling Weaknesses.* Weaknesses in the witness' testimony may need to be presented during the direct examination to minimize the impact of the weakness and enhance the credibility of the witness and the attorney. Weaknesses that are exposed later during cross-examination by opposing counsel can be very damaging. The decision to admit weaknesses in the case is a major strategic decision. If a flaw or weakness cannot be protected by the rules of evidence or procedure and the cross-examiner will bring out the weakness or flaw, it should be exposed on direct examination (preferably somewhere during the middle of the examination). It may be left for re-direct if the witness has an effective response for cross-examination inquiries.

E. Order of Witnesses

The order of a particular witness will generally be determined by where that witness' testimony fits into the chronological presentation of the case. See Form 6-4 Witness List.

1. *First and Last Witnesses.* The first and last witnesses and those with the strongest personality characteristics have the greatest impact. The jury is more likely to remember what is heard first and last. Effective use of first and last witnesses requires daily preparation, review, and flexibility by the lawyer. The lawyer must try to anticipate recesses and adjournments and end on a high point to give the jurors a chance to think about what was said. However, before or after lunch might be a difficult time for jurors who are hungry or stuffed from a big meal; right before the end of the day when they are tired, or ready to go home, might also be a difficult time.

2. *Differing Testimony.* Every witness is an individual whose perceptions will not be identical to those of other witnesses. Sometimes the differences in witnesses' testimony are great enough to require explanation. The attorney must decide whether to call the witness at all, whether to elicit testimony concerning those differences, and anticipate how opposing counsel will use the differing testimony.

3. *Weak or Boring Witnesses.* Weak or boring witnesses can damage the case because they cause the jury to disbelieve their testimony by their demeanor, or they simply put the jury to sleep. The order of witnesses should be adjusted so that weak or boring witnesses are not presented consecutively.

4. *Rebuttal Witnesses.* Although the last witness is the most likely to be remembered, it is generally not a good idea to save a witness for rebuttal. The attorney may not get the opportunity to call the witness. Moreover, jurors may view "sandbagging" as unfair or "sly."

5. *Strong Finish.* The final witness that the attorney calls should be a strong witness. The witness should present important aspects of the case, have good style, and be able to withstand cross-examination.

CASE LAW—LOCAL PRACTICE & PROCEDURE—IDEAS

Outline   Notes

6.4 Types of Direct Examination

A. Adverse Examinations and Hostile Witnesses

A case may require that a witness who has an interest adverse or hostile to the attorney's client be called during the case in chief. The direct examination of this type of witness may be conducted by using leading questions as if the examination were a cross-examination. See Fed. R. Evid. 611(c).

B. Deposition Transcripts or Videotaped Depositions

Testimony may be offered in the form of a deposition transcript. Usually, the questions and answers are read to the jury in lieu of live testimony. A videotaped deposition may also be used to present the testimony of a witness. Both the transcript and the videotape may need to be edited because of objections made to inadmissable information.

C. Problems with Foundation

Foundation questions are preliminary questions which establish a basis for the introduction of further evidence. Foundation questions are necessary to show that certain evidence is admissible and to assist the fact finder in weighing the value of the evidence. There are several categories of evidence that require specific considerations regarding foundation.

1. *Qualifications of Witness.* Foundation questions must establish the personal knowledge of a witness for that witness to be competent to testify. Fed. R. Evid. 601–602.
2. *Sources of Information.* Foundation questions will be necessary to explain how, when, and where a witness saw an event first-hand.
3. *Conversations.* Foundation questions to establish the admissibility of a conversation include where and when the conversation took place and who was there. Telephone conversations will require further foundation that establishes how the witness identified the voice (prior conversations) or knew who the speaker was (by dialing a phone number).
4. *Opinions and Conclusions.* Foundation questions will be necessary to describe the basis for a witness' opinion. See Fed. R. Evid. 701. A witness can state that a person appeared drunk if they can testify to the person's glassy eyes, alcohol breath, slurred speech, staggered walk, and other observations which support such a conclusion.
5. *Documents.* Foundation questions which establish the authenticity of a document will be necessary. That is, before introducing a document it must be shown that the exhibit is what it purports to be.

D. Foundation Checklist

The specific foundation required will vary depending upon the type of evidence. A checklist of required points will make certain that a foundation has been established. The following factors will not apply to all foundations but if complied with will satisfy nearly all foundation requirements for direct examination:

1. Is the witness competent?
2. Is the witness qualified?
3. Is the evidence relevant?
4. Has the best evidence rule been complied with?
5. Is the exhibit authentic?
6. Is the evidence non-hearsay or a hearsay exception?
7. Are there any specific words that must be included in a question or answer?

E. Character Evidence

Character evidence is evidence of a trait or characteristic of a person offered to prove that the person acted in conformity with such character. Examples of character evidence range from a trait of violence to a characteristic of truthfulness. Character evidence is usually not involved in a case. Few civil cases place the character of a party or witness in issue. Criminal cases do not usually involve the character of the defendant or victim unless the defendant places such matters in issue. Civil cases that involve the character of a person include assault and battery (character for violence) and libel cases (damage to reputation). Criminal cases in which character evidence will arise include situations in which the defendant claims self-defense.

Character evidence, when allowable, is usually proved by reputation or opinion testimony. See Fed. R. Evid. 405(a). If character is an issue in a case it may also be proved by specific instances of conduct. See Fed. R. Evid. 405(b). Evidence that relates to the character of a person may be inadmissible to prove a matter, but the same evidence may be admissible to impeach a witness. These two conflicting rules create understandable confusion regarding when character evidence is or is not admissible. The following statements explain when character evidence will be admissible on direct examination.

1. A civil litigant may not place his or her character in issue by establishing on direct examination good character. See Fed. R. Evid. 404(a).
2. A criminal defendant may introduce good character evidence, may call a witness to testify to good reputation, and may place the pertinent character of a victim in issue. See Fed. R. Evid. 404(a)(1) & (2).
3. A civil litigant and a prosecutor may introduce character evidence to prove motive, opportunity, intent, plan, knowledge, identity, and related issues. See Fed. R. Evid. 404(b).

4. A civil litigant may offer adverse reputation or opinion evidence on direct to attack the truthfulness of a witness. See Fed. R. Evid. 608(a).

5. A prosecutor may introduce evidence on rebuttal to show the bad character of the defendant if the defendant has placed character in issue. See Fed. R. Evid. 404(a)(1).

6. A prosecutor may also introduce rebuttal direct testimony concerning the character of a victim. See Fed. R. Evid. 404(a)(2).

Sections 8.5(B)(5) and (E) describe situations when character evidence may be used to impeach a witness.

CASE LAW—LOCAL PRACTICE & PROCEDURE—IDEAS

Outline   Notes

6.5 Expert Witnesses   Although all witnesses share some characteristics, the expert witness requires some special considerations. See Form 6-5 Expert Testimony Planning Worksheet.

A. When to Use an Expert   The scientific, technical, or other specialized knowledge of an expert may assist the fact finder in understanding the evidence or determining a fact in issue. Certain fields of expertise are well recognized such as medicine, engineering, economics, ballistics, fingerprints, and accounting. See Fed. R. Evid. 702.

B. Who is an Expert?   A person who has some expert knowledge gained by skill, experience, training, or education may be qualified as an expert. A person experienced as a physician, engineer, economist, or accountant will qualify as an expert. A person experienced in mechanical repairs, laboratory analysis, and property assessment will also qualify as an expert. See Fed. R. Evid. 702.

C. Qualifying the Expert   The rules of evidence require that an expert witness be qualified in the area in which the expert will be testifying. See Fed. R. Evid. 702. The judge must determine whether a person is an expert based upon that individual's qualifications. The jury will want to hear the expert's qualifications to judge the expert's credibility. The expert may testify only in those areas in which qualified.

An opposing lawyer may offer to stipulate to an expert's qualifications. An attorney should not usually accept this stipulation because the jury will need to hear all of the background qualifications of the expert. However, a witness with marginal qualifications or lower qualifications than the other side's expert might be more credible with stipulated qualifications. In either case, the qualifications should be presented in an interesting, tasteful, and non-bragging fashion.

D. Knowing the Subject Area   The attorney should know the subject on which the expert will testify as well or better than the expert. The attorney will need to be educated, trained to read relevant materials and become throughly familiar with an area of expertise.

E. Preparing the Expert on the Law of the Case   The attorney should explain the law of the case to the expert. This will allow the expert to frame an opinion that meshes with the law of the case.

F. Preparing the Expert on the Facts of the Case   The attorney will often explain the facts of the case to an expert to establish a mind-set from which to proceed. This will include an opinion on how the attorney views the facts. The examination and opinion may then be prepared with an understanding as to how the attorney views the case. However, the attorney should remain open to the expert's ideas. Talking to the expert may provide new ideas and concepts, and correct mistaken ideas.

G. Opinion Testimony

An expert needs to testify to the sources of information supporting an opinion, to the opinion, and to the bases of the opinion.

H. Sources of Information

An expert may rely upon several sources of information including:
1. Personal firsthand information.
2. Data obtained from other experts, documents, treatises, files, persons, and other sources of hearsay as long as such data is the type reasonably relied upon by an expert. See Fed. R. Evid. 703.
3. Trial or deposition testimony.
4. Hypothetical questions.

I. Hypothetical Questions

Hypothetical questions should be prepared in advance. The attorney should prepare any hypotheticals with the assistance of the expert. Hypothetical questions should be written out so that no mistakes are made during the trial. They should be accurate, complete, simply phrased, and as short as possible.

J. Questions and Answers

Experts will often be permitted to testify in a narrative form with lengthy, explanatory answers. The attorney will also be permitted to ask questions which call for narrative responses.

K. Opinions

An expert will usually testify to a number of opinions. A case may involve a major opinion and several subordinate or minor opinions. Some judges may expect the attorney to elicit an opinion by asking the traditional questions: Do you have an opinion based upon a reasonable degree of expert certainty? What is that opinion?

L. Explaining Technical Terms

The examiner must understand and know how to pronounce all of the expert's technical terms and must learn how to explain the technical terms in plain English. If testing is involved, the expert must explain why the testing was done and the validity of the result.

CASE LAW—LOCAL PRACTICE & PROCEDURE—IDEAS

Outline   Notes

6.6 Redirect Examination

Redirect examination is the reexamination of a witness after the opposing attorney has finished cross-examining the witness. The purpose of redirect examination is to clarify any problems created during the cross-examination of the witness by the opponent. This would include clarifying and explaining contradictions, dismissing fallacies, and correcting any other problems created by the cross. The following guidelines are a summary of several areas in which the redirect examination will be different from the direct examination.

A. Question Forms

The same rules of evidence for direct examinations will apply to the redirect examination. Leading questions are not allowed on redirect examination. However, an opponent might not object to leading questions on redirect because the cross-examination tuned the opponent to leading questions. Moreover, many judges will allow a greater use of leading questions on redirect than on direct in order to focus the testimony on matters within the scope of the redirect examination. Further, because the witness has testified on direct and cross, an attorney may legitimately refer to previous answers by the witness.

B. Limited Scope

The scope of the redirect examination is limited to new matters covered during the cross-examination. Redirect examination may not be used to repeat matters covered on direct examination.

C. Reserving the Introduction of Evidence

The entire case should be presented during the direct examination and not saved for redirect examination. An attorney who reserves some evidence runs the risk of not being able to present an important or essential element of the case because the opposing attorney may not cover that area during the cross-examination. A strict judge could prevent that area from being covered during redirect examination. The same could be true if the opposing attorney decides not to conduct a cross-examination. Individual judges may be more or less willing to allow the attorney to cover new areas during the redirect examination. Some judges may allow the attorney to reopen the direct examination or allow the witness to be called again.

There may be an occasion when delaying the introduction of evidence for redirect is worth the risk. If the information to be "sandbagged" will have a significant impact on redirect, and the attorney knows or structures the case so that the opposing attorney *must* delve into that area during the cross-examination, "sandbagging" may be appropriate.

D. Refreshing the Witness' Recollection

Redirect examination may be used to refresh the witness' recollection if the witness has misstated or forgotten information during the cross-examination. See Fed. R. Evid. 612.

E. Forgoing Redirect   A well-prepared case and a good direct examination will often make redirect examination unnecessary. In making the decision whether to conduct a redirect examination, the following factors should be considered:

1. Having the last word is not necessarily that important.
2. Continuing with redirect examination may bore the jury, bother the court or accomplish very little.
3. Closing argument may be a better time to repeat the best parts of the case.
4. Cases can be lost by asking too many questions.

CASE LAW—LOCAL PRACTICE & PROCEDURE—IDEAS

Outline   Notes

6.7 Avoiding Mistrials and Reversals

A. Never Facilitate the Presentation of Perjured Testimony

The Code of Professional Responsibility prohibits the knowing use of fraudulent, false, or perjured testimony. See EC 7–26 and Model Rules 3.3–3.4. An attorney has a duty to prevent the mispresentation of testimony. DR 7–102(A)(4); Model Rules 3.3(a)(4), 3.4(b); *People v. Collier*, 105 Mich. App. 46, 306 N.W.2d 387 (1981). If the client in a civil case insists on testifying falsely, the attorney must inform the tribunal of the fraud in some manner. DR 7–102(B)(1) and Model Rule 3.3. This disclosure may occur by making a record of the fact that the client is taking the stand against the advice of counsel or by actually telling the judge about the perjury. If a client in a criminal case insists on presenting false testimony, the attorney has the same duty but may be limited by constitutional considerations in determining how or if the perjury may be revealed. A criminal defense lawyer may have to allow the defendant to testify but may not ask the witness questions nor argue the false testimony in closing. ABA Project on Standards for Criminal Justice, The Defense Funtion § 7.7(c) (1971).

In both civil and criminal cases, an attorney may request to withdraw, but the request may be denied. *People v. Schultheis*, 44 Colo. App. 452, 618 P.2d 710 (Colo. 1980). If an attorney knows that a witness who is not a client will offer perjured testimony, the lawyer may not call that witness to the stand.

B. Do Not Solicit Inadmissible Responses

The most common misconduct during direct examination is the solicitation of inadmissible responses. For example, misconduct will occur if plaintiff's counsel asks, "Did you ever take photographs of that automobile before the repairs were made?" and the witness responds, "The insurance company did." *Imparato v. Romez*, 95 Ill. App. 11, 419 N.E.2d 620 (1981).

Generally, questions which are immaterial or irrelevant to the issues in the case are objectionable. So, while certain information may bolster a witness' credibility with the jury, questions regarding relatives or friends may not be allowed and questions about religion will not be permitted unless germane to the issue at hand. *Tennis v. General Motors Corp.*, 625 S.W.2d 218 (Mo. 1981); *Albarran v. City of New York*, 80 A.D.2d 784, 437 N.Y.S.2d 4 (1981). While such questions are usually not reversable error, they may be if found to be prejudicial. See DR 7–106(C)(1) and Model Rule 3.4(e); *Christianson v. Kramer*, 257 Ia. 974, 135 N.W.2d 644 (1965).

C. Prepare the Witness

The inadvertent blurting out of inadmissible evidence by a witness can result in a mistrial or a reversal. *State v. Gegan*, 275 Minn. 568, 147 N.W.2d 925 (1967). A lawyer should control a witness, and this is best achieved by a preparation session prior to trial. Inadmissible evidence may be "cured" by an admonition from the presiding judge to the jury to disregard any improper statements or to forget what they heard. The adequacy of the curative admonition may become a question on appeal; however, a ruling upon an objection will seldom be disturbed unless a clear abuse of judicial discretion occurs.

D. Do Not Allow the Client or Witness to Disrupt the Trial

Allowing a client to disrupt a trial may bring disciplinary action against the lawyer. The most notorious case of client disruption prompted a number of studies on disruptions in criminal "political" trials. *In Re Dillinger*, 461 F.2d 389 (7th Cir. 1972) (trial of the "Chicago 7"). In civil cases, lawyers have received contempt citations and have been disciplined for standing by mute as their clients misbehave. One lawyer was jailed when his clients burst forth in song. *Kentucky Bar Association v. Taylor*, 482 S.W.2d 574 (Ky. 1972). Not only may the lawyer be punished, but a client can be cited for contempt also. *Eaton v. City of Tulsa*, 415 U.S. 697 (1974).

E. Honor Local Rules of Decorum

It is important to instruct a client or witness regarding decorum in the courtroom. Each jurisdiction has its own rules of decorum, adopted either by a local judges' association or perhaps the Supreme Court of that state. Some address the proper clothing to be worn or contain an admonition to attorneys to instruct their witnesses not to chew gum while testifying (i.e., Minnesota). Others may incorporate the Code of Professional Responsibility (New York and Texas) and may be more direct and emphatic regarding the attorneys' obligation to control their clients and witnesses. These rules are found in the rules of federal, state, and district courts. Failure to comply with these rules may be grounds for disciplinary action. DR 7–106(C)(5) and Model Rule 3.4(c), 3.5.

F. Do Not Hide Your Client

Deliberate substitution of someone other than a party at trial may warrant suspension from practice. *Matter of Weishoff*, 75 N.J. 326, 382 A.2d 632 (1978). DR 7–106(B)(2) states that an attorney must disclose to a tribunal the identities of the clients he represents. See also DR 7–102(A) and Model Rule 3.3–3.4. Thus, in a case in which identification is an issue, it may be unethical for a lawyer to seat someone other than the client at the counsel table at trial for the purpose of eliciting an erroneous identification or to test an eyewitness' identification. However, full disclosure of the tactic to the court and opposing counsel might permit its use. See Idaho State Bar Committee on Ethics Formal Opinion No. 106, August 14, 1981; see also *United States v. Thoreen*, 653 F.2d 1332 (9th Cir. 1981).

G. Follow Your Own Judgment

A lawyer is under no obligation to follow the dictates of the client regarding trial strategy. The lawyer, as a professional, is deemed to have the judgment and skills necessary to determine the most efficacious manner in which to present the case. Clients' suggestions may be rejected. *Frank v. Bloom*, 634 F.2d 1245 (10th Cir. 1980). However, if a client is damaged as a result of the lack of a reasonable degree of skill and care by a lawyer, then the lawyer will be held liable for those damages. *Frank v. Bloom*, 634 F.2d 1245 (10th Cir. 1980); see also *National Savings Bank of P.C. v. Ward*, 100 U.S. 196 (1880).

CASE LAW—LOCAL PRACTICE & PROCEDURE—IDEAS

Outline   Notes

6.8 Bibliography

TEXTS

G. Bellow & B. Moulton, *The Lawyering Process* 607–825 (Foundation Press, Mineola, NY, 1978).

P. Bergman, *Trial Advocacy in a Nutshell* 43–141, 357–62 (West Pub. Co., St. Paul, MN, 1979).

S. Goldberg, *The First Trial in a Nutshell* 103–45, 210–70, 355–60 (West Pub. Co., St. Paul, MN, 1982).

K. Hegland, *Trial and Practice Skills in a Nutshell* 7–36, 114–22 (West Pub. Co., St. Paul, MN, 1978).

J. Jeans, *Trial Advocacy* Chs. 9, 12 (West Pub. Co., St. Paul, MN, 1975).

R. Keeton, *Trial Tactics and Methods* 10–93 (Little, Brown & Co., Boston, MA, 1973).

J. Kelner & F. McGovern, *Successful Litigation Techniques* Chs. 8, 13, 15–16 (Matthew Bender, New York, 1981).

T. Mauet, *Fundamentals of Trial Techniques* 85–175 (Little, Brown & Co., Boston, MA, 1980).

J. McElhaney, *Effective Litigation* 8–15, 44–108 (West Pub. Co., St. Paul, MN, 1974).

A. Morrill, *Trial Diplomacy* 32–53, 127–32 (Court Practice Inst., Chicago, IL, 1972).

WITNESS INFORMATION WORKSHEET   Form 6-1

Case _____   File _____

Name of Case   Date of Incident

Name of Witness

Address

Phone: Home   Work/Office

Employer

Statement taken

Deposition taken

Subpeona/Duces tecum served

Witness given copy of Statement/
   Deposition to review

Witness Prepared

Trial Deposition   When

   Transcript Completed/Summarized:

Trial Appearance Date   Time

Purpose of Witness:

Type of Witness: Eye Witness   Expert

                  Exhibit/Chain of   Lay
                    Possession

                  Event — before —   Other
                    during — after

WITNESS INFORMATION
WORKSHEET

Form 6-1 (continued)

What will this witness prove

Key questions to ask this witness

What exhibits will be introduced through this witness

What demonstrative or real evidence can this witness use for better jury understanding

DIRECT EXAMINATION PLANNING WORKSHEET Form 6-2

Case _____   File _____

Name of Witness

| Key Facts to be Proved
by Witness | Rearrangement of Key Facts
Chronologically/Topically |

Exhibits to be introduced through witness

Important questions to ask during and to conclude witness testimony

DIRECT EXAMINATION OUTLINE   Form 6-3

Case _____   File _____

Name of Witness

Key Facts to be Proved by Witness	Key Phrases of Witness Testimony	Key Facts of Cross Examination

Conclusion

Exhibits to be introduced through witness

Exhibits introduced through witness by opponent

Key points to be covered in re-direct examination

WITNESS LIST

Case _____   File _____

Order to Be Called	Name	Address	Phone: Home/Work	Purpose

EXPERT TESTIMONY PLANNING WORKSHEET Form 6-5

Case _____   File _____

Name   Fees

How, when, where did expert become involved

Qualifications

Opinions

Basis of Opinion

Sources of Opinion

Exhibits

Probable cross-examination areas

Re-direct examination

Chapter 7
EXHIBITS

A pleasant illusion is better than a harsh reality.

—Christian Nestell Bovee

No matter how thin you slice it, it's still boloney [sic].

—Jean Jacques Rousseau

7.1 Description   There are three main types of exhibits that are covered in this chapter. They are real evidence, demonstrative evidence, and visual aids.

A. Real Evidence   Real evidence refers to those exhibits that are directly probative concerning one or more issues in the case. They are a "real" part of the event or transaction. Real evidence might include a gun, a contract, clothing, and other tangible items. Real evidence will usually be admitted into the jury room.

B. Demonstrative Evidence   Demonstrative evidence consists of those exhibits that are admitted for illustrative purposes only. Demonstrative evidence has no probative value in and of itself. Rather, its two primary purposes are to help a witness testify and to clarify the evidence for the jurors. Demonstrative evidence commonly includes diagrams, charts, graphs, and models. Demonstrative evidence may or may not be admitted into the jury room depending on the discretion of the trial judge.

C. Visual Aids   Visual aids refer to a group of exhibits that are used by the attorney during opening statement or closing argument. Visual aids help the attorney present and summarize the case in front of the jury. Visual aids are not admitted into evidence and do not go with the jury into the deliberation room. Commonly used visual aids include a chart summarizing a plaintiff's injuries or a pre-prepared outline of a summation written on a blackboard.

7.2 Purposes   People learn most of what they know through their sense of sight. Society, in general, has been transformed by modern media into a visual society. The predominance of listening and reading as the primary means of learning has passed. Attorneys must and have responded to these changes.

The use of exhibits helps attorneys present more persuasive cases. Exhibits give the jury and judge a focal point on which to center their attention. Exhibits also help the attorney gain and maintain the attention of both the jury and judge and focus that attention on the theme of the case. The use of exhibits also gives the impression that the attorney is prepared, serious about the case, familiar with the case, and has developed some expertise regarding the subject area.

CASE LAW—LOCAL PRACTICE & PROCEDURE—IDEAS

Outline   Notes

7.3 Relevancy Considerations

A. Threshold Test FRE 401 and 402

Exhibits meet the threshold relevancy test of FRE 401 if the exhibit has any tendency to make the existence of any fact that is of consequence to the determination of the action more or less probable. All relevant exhibits will be admissible, and, conversely, irrelevant exhibits will be inadmissible.

B. Balancing Test FRE 403

Relevant exhibits may be excluded if the probative value of the exhibit is substantially outweighed by the danger of its being unfairly prejudicial, confusing the issues, misleading the jury, causing undue delay, wasting time, or being needless, and cumulative.

C. Limited Admissibility FRE 105

When an exhibit that is admissible as to one party or for one purpose but not admissible as to another party or for another purpose is admitted, the court, upon request, will restrict the exhibit to its proper scope and instruct the jury accordingly.

7.4 Selecting Exhibits

A. Preparation

Careful consideration should be given prior to trial on when and how exhibits will be used. A prepared professional presentation of an exhibit can be a very persuasive part of a case. On the other hand, a sloppy, unprepared presentation of an exhibit can mislead or confuse the fact finder.

B. Choosing Exhibits

Every exhibit should be designed and chosen for maximum impact. When deciding whether to use a particular exhibit an attorney should consider:
1. The necessity of using the exhibit.
2. The degree to which the exhibit supports the case.
3. Whether the exhibit is relevant.
4. Whether the witness will be able to testify more effectively.
5. Whether there is adequate foundation.
6. Whether the exhibit will detract the jury's attention from the witness' testimony or from the case as a whole.
7. The possibility that the exhibit will confuse the jury.
8. Whether the exhibit is unnecessarily cumulative or repetitive.

C. Summary See From 7-1 Exhibit Selection Worksheet.

CASE LAW—LOCAL PRACTICE & PROCEDURE—IDEAS

Outline   Notes

7.5 The Elements of Foundation

A. Generally

The introduction of each exhibit must be supported with foundation questions. These questions vary from exhibit to exhibit but, in general, seek responses which establish the existence, identity, authenticity, and accuracy of the exhibit. An attorney needs to become familiar with the requisite foundation questions. A well developed technique of introducing exhibits will be invaluable during trial. A competent presentation will be necessary to meet the minimum grounds for admissibility. An effective presentation will enhance the weight afforded the exhibits by the jurors. A prepared list of foundation questions will prevent a step from being omitted and will overcome any possible objections. See Form 7-2 Exhibit Foundation Worksheet.

B. Types of Foundation

There are two levels of foundation that must be met during a trial. The first is the legal foundation and the second is the persuasive foundation. The judge will usually determine whether the legal foundation has been established and an exhibit is admissible. The jury will review the persuasive foundation and determine whether they believe the exhibit is what it purports to be.

7.6 Legal Foundation

Different types of exhibits have differing elements of foundation. The elements of foundation for several different types of evidence are presented below.

A. Tangible Objects and Properties (Including Products, Clothing, Appliances, and Weapons)

Elements to be proved through evidence:
1. The exhibit is relevant to the case.
2. The witness recognizes and can identify the exhibit.
3. The witness can recall what the exhibit looked like at the previous relevant time.
4. The exhibit is now in the same or substantially the same condition as when the witness saw it at the previous relevant time.

B. Chain of Custody (Including Liquids, Narcotics, Tobacco, Fluid, Dirt, and Other Such Properties)

A chain of custody may be required where an object is not unique or capable of identification through the senses to establish that it is the relevant exhibit. There are two primary ways of establishing an unbroken chain of custody:
1. The exhibit at all times has been in the safe, continuing, and sole possession of one or more individuals; or
2. The exhibit bears a unique mark, was distinctively marked, or was sealed and placed in a safe or other tamper-proof container.

C. Documents (Including Letters, Contracts, Leases, and Other Signed Writings)

Elements to be proved through evidence:
1. The document is relevant to the case.

2. The document contains a signature, was handwritten, or bears some other identifying characteristics.
3. The signature, handwriting, or characteristic belongs to or identifies a person.
4. The witness saw the person sign or write the document; or
   a) the witness knows, is familiar with, or can recognize the signature or handwriting; or
   b) the witness recognizes and can identify the characteristics of the document; or
   c) the witness is a party and admits signing, writing, or the contents of the document; or
   d) a handwriting expert states that the signature or writing is by a certain person or that the characteristics of the document identify it.
5. The document is authentic.
6. The document is an original or an admissible duplicate or other copy.
7. The document is now in the same condition as when it was made and has not been altered.

D. Business Correspondence (Including Letters, Memos, and Notes)

Business correspondence has the same foundation requirements as documents. Some correspondence may require additional foundation evidence to prove it was sent or received. In these instances, the elements that need to be proved in addition to those listed in Section 7.6(C) of this chapter include:

1. The correspondence was addressed to a certain person.
2. The witness saw or signed the original and any carbon or photocopy of the original.
3. The witness placed the correspondence in an accurately addressed delivery envelope; or the witness supervises a person who in the normal course of their business mails such correspondence.
4. The envelope was placed in a mailbox or given to another carrier; or the witness supervises a person who in the normal course of business mails such envelopes.
5. The photocopy or carbon of the original is an accurate copy.
6. The original correspondence was never returned to the sender or was received by the addressee.

E. Business Records (Including Any Memorandum, Report, Writing, or Data Compilation)

Records maintained in the ordinary course of business may be introduced through a witness who does not have personal knowledge of the recorded information but does have personal knowledge concerning the business recording process. Federal Rule of Evidence 803(6) allows the introduction of this information by establishing the foundation elements detailed in that rule. The term "business" includes any business, hospital, institution, organization, association, profession, occupation, and calling of every kind including non-profit agencies. The content of business records may include any facts, acts, events, conditions, opinions, or diagnosis that are relevant to the case. The elements to be proved under FRE 803(6) include:

1. The report must have been "made at or near the time" of the occurence of the information contained in it.
2. The record was made by "a person with knowledge" of the information or was made "from information transmitted by" a person with knowledge.
3. The record was kept "in the course of a regularly conducted business activity."
4. The record was made "in the regular practice of that business activity."
5. The witness is the "custodian or other qualified witness."

Computer printouts may or may not qualify as business records. When computer records will not qualify as business records additional foundational questions relating to the input, storage, and retrieval methods of the computer system and its reliability will be necessary.

F. Copies   Modern office equipment and practice create accurate copies of original documents and records. The original may be the most persuasive and should be offered to prove its content. See FRE 1002. A copy may be routinely admitted unless it is of questionable authenticity or it would be unfair to admit a copy. FRE 1003. A copy may also be admissible if the original has been lost or destroyed, is in the possession of the opponent, or is otherwise not obtainable. FRE 1004. The elements to establish the foundation for a copy include:

1. The copy is relevant to the case.
2. An original did once exist.
3. A copy was made from the original.
4. The copy is an authentic and accurate duplicate of the original.

G. Electronic Recordings (Including Audio and Video Recordings)   The elements to be proved by the evidence to establish a sufficient foundation for the introduction of recordings include:

1. The electronic recording is relevant to the case.
2. The operator of the equipment was qualified to run the equipment.
3. The recording equipment was checked before its use and operated normally.
4. The witness heard or saw the event being electronically recorded.
5. After the event had been recorded, the witness reviewed the tape and determined that it had accurately and completely recorded the event.

6. The witness can recognize and identify the sounds or images on the recording.
7. The recording is in the exact same condition at the time of trial as it was at the time of the taping.

H. Test Results (Including X-ray Films and Laboratory Analysis)

The results from tests, x-rays, and other procedures will require special foundation information to be introduced at trial. The elements to be proved include:
1. The exhibit is relevant to the case.
2. The witness is qualified to operate the equipment.
3. There exists a procedure which regulates the testing, x-ray, or analysis process.
4. The witness personally conducted or supervised an operator who conducted the testing, developed the x-rays, or completed the analysis.
5. The equipment was in normal operating condition.
6. The witness can recognize and identify the results, x-rays, or analysis.
7. The results, x-rays, or analysis are in the same condition as when they were completed.

I. Photographs (Including Prints, Slides, and Movies)

The elements to be proved by evidence include:
1. The photograph is relevant to the case.
2. The witness is familiar with the scene displayed in the photograph at the relevant time of the event.
3. The photograph fairly and accurately depicts the scene at the time of the event.

J. Diagrams (Including Charts, Models, Drawings, Overhead Transparencies and Similar Illustrative Aids)

Various types of demonstrative evidence will be useful during the presentation of a case. The elements to be proved to establish the foundation for the introduction of diagrams include:
1. The witness is familiar with the scene or event.
2. The witness recognizes the scene depicted in the diagram or is familiar with the exhibit.
3. The diagram will assist the witness in explaining testimony or will aid the jury in understanding the testimony.
4. The diagram is reasonably accurate (or is drawn to scale) and is not misleading.

K. Summary Exhibits

Summaries of evidence may be introduced as an efficient and effective means to explain evidence to the fact finder. Summary exhibits may include a chart detailing the testimony of one or more witnesses or may include a summary description of documents. Federal Rule of Evidence 1006 permits summaries of writings to be introduced as evidence. The elements for introduction of summaries include:

1. All the information summarized is relevant.
2. The witness has knowledge concerning the information contained in the summary.
3. The witness has verified that the exhibit is an accurate summary of the evidence.

L. Past Recollection Recorded

A witness who, at the time of trial, does not have a recollection of an event may have previously made a record of that event. Federal Rule of Evidence 803(5) permits a recorded recollection to be introduced at trial. The elements to establish the foundation of past recollection recorded exhibits include:

1. The witness has no present recollection of the relevant event.
2. The witness once had knowledge of the event.
3. The witness made a record of the event when the matter was fresh in the witness' memory.
4. The recorded recollection accurately reflects the knowledge of the witness.
5. The exhibit is in the same condition now as when it was made.

M. Stipulations

Any written stipulations the attorneys may have made need to be introduced during the trial. The attorney who wishes to introduce the evidence must request permission from the court to read or have someone read the content of the stipulation.

N. Pleadings, Admissions, and Discovery Information

Pleading and discovery documents will be part of the case but will not be considered as evidence by the fact finder unless or until an attorney affirmatively offers such information as evidence during the trial. The evidence may be offered during the direct or cross-examination of the witness who originally provided the information or it may be directly read to the jury during the offering party's case in chief or on cross-examination.

O. Self-Authenticating Documents

Extrinsic evidence of the authenticity of certain exhibits will be unnecessary pursuant to Federal Rule of Evidence 902. These self-authenticating exhibits include:

1. Domestic public documents under seal.
2. Domestic public documents not under seal.
3. Foreign public documents.
4. Certified copies of public documents.
5. Official publications issued by public authorities.
6. Newspapers and periodicals.
7. Trade inscriptions.

8. Acknowledged and notary public documents.

9. Commercial paper and related documents.

7.7 Persuasive Foundation

Persuasive foundation is testimony that enhances the credibility and weight of an exhibit. In a jury trial, the persuasive foundation will be as important as the legal foundation. The legal foundation for an exhibit may be quite simple to meet. However, the attorney may want to expand, simplify, or clarify the foundation to increase the weight that the jury will give that exhibit.

CASE LAW—LOCAL PRACTICE & PROCEDURE—IDEAS

Outline   Notes

7.8 Stipulations and Admissions

A. Stipulations

The legal foundation elements may be stipulated to by the attorneys thereby avoiding the need to ask detailed foundation questions. Stipulations will significantly reduce trial time and should be voluntarily entered into between counsel if there is no real dispute concerning the authenticity or accuracy of the exhibits. For example, hospital records will often be entered into evidence by stipulation because these records will usually be reliable. Judges will often suggest that the attorneys agree to the admissibility of reliable exhibits.

B. Civil Admissions

Rule 36 of the Federal Rules of Civil Procedure provides a means to secure admissions from the opposition regarding the genuineness of documents. See Section 3.8 Requests for Admissions.

7.9 Exhibit Systems

An adequate exhibit system should record exhibits offered by any party. The system should include the necessary foundation questions, a list of the witnesses needed to lay the foundation, and a chart showing exactly where each exhibit is in the process of introduction. See Form 7-1 Exhibit Worksheet. The exhibit system should keep track of opposing counsel's exhibits in order to prevent exhibits from being presented that have not been introduced into evidence. A good exhibit system will be very important where more than one witness must be used to lay the foundation for an exhibit. The exhibit tracking system should easily identify exactly where a particular exhibit is in the process of introduction. Has the exhibit been marked? Has it been offered? Has the exhibit been accepted? See Form 7-3 Trial Exhibits Chart.

CASE LAW—LOCAL PRACTICE & PROCEDURE—IDEAS

Outline   Notes

7.10 Planning Introductions

A. Preparing the Witness

The witness that will be used to introduce the evidence should be familiar with the questions and answers that will be necessary to introduce the exhibit and should be comfortable with handling or testifying about the exhibit. Exhibits that are introduced smoothly are perceived as more credible by the jury.

B. Preparing for Possible Objections

An objection, whether sustained or overruled, slows the presentation of the exhibit and the case. Delays caused by opposing counsel's objections may make the exhibit less effective. Preparation in advance to overcome potential objections to the use and introduction of exhibits will make the presentation more effective. Possible objections to exhibits include:

1. Prejudicial or gruesome. FRE 403.
2. Cumulative or repetitious. FRE 403.
3. Exhibit is not the same or similar to what it is claimed to be. FRE 901–03.
4. Lack of authentication and identification. FRE 1001–08.
5. Violation of best evidence rule. FRE 1002.
6. Misleading or inaccurate. FRE 403.
7. Waste of court's time or undue delay. FRE 403.
8. Exhibit does not assist the witness nor aid the jury. FRE 401.
9. Inadmissible hearsay. FRE 801–06.
10. Constitutional objections in criminal actions (i.e., denial of right to cross-examine).

Sometimes it will not be possible to overcome an objection. In these cases, it may be possible to offer the exhibit for illustrative purposes. The jury will then see the exhibit but may not be able to take the exhibit into the jury room. See FRE 105.

C. Supplementing Exhibits

The attorney will need to consider what other preparations will be necessary before the exhibit can be adequately presented during the trial. The considerations might include whether:

1. The exhibit will stand by itself.
2. The exhibit should be enlarged.
3. An overhead projector would be more effective.
4. Copies should be made of the exhibit.
5. The exhibit should be passed to the jury, and if so, when.
6. Questions should be asked while the exhibit is being passed among the jury.
7. The exhibit is too offensive to be passed.
8. The judge will require that questions be asked while exhibits are being passed.
9. The exhibit should be mounted.

10. The exhibit can be left in the presence of the jury or must be put away (i.e. will other witnesses be testifying about it later?).
11. An extension cord, screen, or easel is available.

CASE LAW—LOCAL PRACTICE & PROCEDURE—IDEAS

Outline   Notes

7.11 Presentation & Delivery

A. Professional Presentation

The attorney should develop confidence in the material to be presented. Style and delivery will be important when presenting exhibits. The judge and the jury will have certain expectations regarding the presentation of exhibits which should be satisfied. If the attorney cannot make a quality presentation that lives up to these expectations, the exhibits may be more damaging than helpful.

The attorney and the witness should be coordinated at the trial so that exhibits are marked appropriately, charts are flipped at the right time, the model works, and the overhead projector is plugged in. The attorney should know the courtroom, understand the limitations of the available space, and adapt accordingly.

B. Practical Problems

The attorney needs to be aware of the potential problems that can arise with exhibits during the trial. Most problems can be anticipated and prevented. Those that cannot will not be as disconcerting if the attorney has planned for that contingency. Below is a partial list of problems that may arise with the use of exhibits:

1. Visuals may be poorly drawn and confuse the judge or jury.
2. Exhibits may be too bulky.
3. The preservation of the exhibit for appeal may be difficult.
4. Exhibits may be offensive (i.e., using a real skeleton instead of a model).
5. The experiment or demonstration in court may malfunction or fail.
6. The attorney may lose the continuity of a presentation if the judge disallows the exhibit or cuts the demonstration off before it is finished.
7. The jury may perceive the case as a case of rich versus poor if only one side uses exhibits.
8. Exhibits that are bizarre, too numerous, waste time, clutter, or confuse the presentation may hurt the case.
9. Freehand drawings may be inaccurate and will tend to confuse the jury.

C. The Steps

There are several steps in the introduction of exhibits which must be memorized and mastered. The attorney will need to:

1. Qualify the witness by laying the foundation for the witness to identify the exhibit.
2. Have the item marked as an exhibit or make certain the exhibit has been pre-marked before the trial or witness.
3. Ask permission from the court to approach the witness. Many courts do not require this.
4. Request that the witness examine the object.

5. Have the witness identify the item.
6. Lay the necessary foundation for that particular exhibit.
7. Offer the exhibit into evidence by referring to its exhibit number or letter.
8. Provide opposing counsel the opportunity to review the exhibit. This opportunity may be provided earlier.
9. Respond to any objections opposing counsel may have to the exhibit.
10. Show the exhibit to the fact finder.

The order and content of each of these steps will vary from court to court. Likewise, the particular steps used to introduce a particular exhibit will vary depending on the characteristics of that exhibit. See Form 7-4 Exhibit Introduction Checklist.

D. Variation in Word Usage

The words used to introduce and describe an exhibit must be varied. "Boiler plate" terms that are repeated endlessly will bore the jury. Below are several ways of referring to exhibits:

1. This exhibit has been marked as Plaintiff's Exhibit 1. . . .
2. I am handing you. . . .
3. You have in your hands. . . .
4. I have just handed you. . . .
5. Here is. . . .
6. I am showing you. . . .

A varied style will hold the jury's attention longer than the use of monotonous "buzz" words. However, some judges require certain "buzz" words. In these circumstances, the attorney must use the phrases and words that the judge requires. Whatever description is used, the reference should include the exhibit number or letter to protect the record.

E. Leading Questions

Leading questions may be allowed when laying the foundation for some exhibits. Leading questions may be necessary to elicit the precise elements of foundation required for the introduction of an exhibit into evidence. For example, it is proper to lead a witness who identifies a photograph to say that the photo is a "fair and accurate" description. It will also be necessary to establish the foundation for a business record by asking leading questions which incorporate the specific language of the business record rule or statute. Without such leading questions, laying the foundation for exhibits might take forever. See FRE 611(c).

F. Finessing the Foundation

If there are a series of exhibits for which the foundations are similar, it may be possible to abbreviate the process of laying foundation after the first few exhibits have been introduced. The witness may be asked whether the response to the previous exhibit questions would be the same for additional exhibits. Once the judge and opposing attorney know that the attorney is prepared to present extensive foundation, the presentation of that foundation may not be necessary. This will speed up the process and reduce the potential for boredom.

G. *Location*   The attorney should stand in a position in the courtroom that maximizes the clarity and impact of the exhibit for the jury. The attorney should consider that each courtroom space provides many possibilities for movement, stance, and positioning. Repetitious and blocking movements and positions will diminish the effectiveness of the presentation. Where to place exhibits and where to stand will depend on a variety of factors including:

1. The ability of the attorney to stand without support from a table or lectern.
2. The ability of the witness to speak and be heard.
3. The size and impact of the exhibit.
4. The shape and acoustics of the courtroom.
5. Any constraints imposed by the trial judge.

H. *Voir Dire Examination*   Opposing counsel has the opportunity to examine the witness after an exhibit has been offered to determine if there is a basis for an objection. The questions that may be asked must seek to establish the lack of foundation required for an exhibit. The scope of this examination is very limited and usually only several questions may be asked. Voir dire examination should not be used unless the exhibit will most likely be excluded. Cross-examination will provide the opportunity to ask questions to reduce the evidentiary effect of an exhibit.

CASE LAW—LOCAL PRACTICE & PROCEDURE—IDEAS

Outline   Notes

7.12 Avoiding Mistrials and Reversals

The principal Disciplinary Rule dealing with exhibits is DR 7–102(A) which states:

In his representation of a client, a lawyer shall not:
* * *
(3) Conceal or knowingly fail to disclose that which he is required by law to reveal.
(4) Knowingly use perjured testimony or false evidence.
* * *
(6) Participate in the creation or preservation of evidence when he knows or it is obvious that the evidence is false.
(7) Counsel or assist his client in conduct that the lawyer knows to be illegal or fraudulent.

See also Model Rules 3.3 on Candor.

A. Obtain Court's Permission to Use Visual Aids

The attorney should always request the court's permission to use visual aids. Permission should be requested before bringing the exhibit into the courtroom and before the jury has seen it. Failing to get prior permission may not always result in a reversal on appeal, but will be embarrassing nonetheless. See, e.g., *Malik v. Johnson*, Minn., 219 N.W.2d 631 (1974) (attempted use of beer cans or paper representations of beer cans in closing argument improper).

B. Avoid Excessive Use of Exhibits

Although the trial court has broad discretion in admitting evidence of a prejudicial nature, once admitted that evidence should not be overused to inflame the jury. Potentially prejudicial evidence "should be introduced and displayed only in furtherance of a distinct purpose." *United States v. Cavell*, 284 F. Supp. 535 (E.D. Penn. 1968) (display of rape victim's undergarments six times during trial lasting one month was not "overuse" of exhibits).

C. Do Not Present Irrelevant Exhibits

Relevancy is defined by FRE 401. The introduction of an exhibit that is not relevant under the rules of evidence may warrant a new trial. See *Standafer v. First Nat'l Bank of Mpls.*, 236 Minn. 123, 52 N.W.2d 718 (1952). On the other hand, sometimes the irrelevant evidence is not viewed as so prejudicial that its introduction or presentation warrants a new trial. For example, in a case involving the drowning of a four-year-old boy, the attorney called the mother of the deceased. Her six-year-old daughter was sitting alongside her. Counsel showed the mother a photograph of her two children, the daughter and the boy who had drowned. She burst into tears, as did the daughter. The court held that although there was no legitimate reason for producing the photograph, it did not create such prejudice as to necessitate a new trial. *Harning v. City of Duluth*, 224 Minn. 299, 28 N.W.2d 659 (1947).

D. Obtain Pretrial Rulings on Gruesome Photographs

Gruesome photographs showing injured and deceased persons may be prejudicial. The attorney should present any potentially prejudicial or gruesome photographs to the trial judge and opposing counsel prior to trial. A favorable ruling will seldom be overturned. See, e.g., *United States v. Cannon*, 472 F.2d 144 (9th Cir. 1972); *Maxwell v. United States*, 368 F.2d 735 (9th Cir. 1966). Sometimes, however, the photograph may be of such a "gruesome and horrifying nature that its probative value is outweighed by the danger of inflaming the jury." *United States v. Brady*, 579 F.2d 1121, 1129 (9th Cir. 1978), citing, *Rivers v. United States*, 270 F.2d 435, 437–38 (9th Cir. 1959). Pretrial rulings on these types of photographs will prevent most reversals.

E. Do Not Create or Preserve False Exhibits

Creating or preserving false exhibits is absolutely forbidden. See Code DR 7–102(A) and Model Rules 3.3. The most comon infraction of this rule is the filing of false affidavits. See, e.g., *In re O'Hara*, 330 N.W.2d 863 (Minn. 1983); *In re Schiff*, 542 S.W.2d 771 (Mo. 1976).

Since depositions may become exhibits at trial, allowing a witness to commit perjury during a deposition has been found to violate this prohibition (among others). See *Commission on Professional Ethics v. Crary*, 245 N.W.2d 298 (Iowa 1976); *North Carolina State Bar v. DuMont*, 286 S.E.2d 89 (N.C. 1982). Other actions have also been found to violate the prohibition against creating or preserving false evidence. See *Florida Bar v. Willingham*, 386 So. 2d 553 (Fla. 1980) (creating forged documents); *Florida Bar v. Schonbrun*, 348 So. 2d 886 (Fla. 1977) (creation of post mortem will).

One court has held that the prohibition against creating false evidence does not apply to the attorney's own disciplinary proceedings. *Attorney Grievance Comm'n v. Leventhal*, 279 Md. 350, 369 A.2d 72 (1977).

F. Withholding Exhibits

The duty to disclose relevant evidence often conflicts with the attorney's responsibilities with respect to the attorney-client privilege. Sometimes the attorney-client privilege will warrant withholding an exhibit. See *In re Grand Jury Proceedings*, 473 F.2d 840 (8th Cir. 1973) (summaries of interviews protected by work product doctrine); *State v. Olwell*, 394 P.2d 681 (Wash. 1964) (withholding of suspected murder weapon). On the other hand, most courts require attorneys to produce all relevant exhibits, especially in criminal cases. See, e.g., *In re January 1976 Grand Jury*, 534 F.2d 719 (7th Cir. 1976) (money from bank robbery); *In re Ryder*, 381 F.2d 713 (4th Cir. 1967) (weapon and stolen money); *People v. Nash*, 313 N.W.2d 307 (Mich. Ct. App. 1981) (weapon and wallet); *Matter of Malloy*, 248 N.W.2d 43 (N.D. 1976) (secret contract).

CASE LAW—LOCAL PRACTICE & PROCEDURE—IDEAS

Outline   Notes

7.13 Bibliography   TEXTS

G. Bellow & B. Moulton, *The Lawyering Process* 346–48, 355–56 (Foundation Press, Mineola, NY, 1978).

P. Bergman, *Trial Advocacy in a Nutshell* 116–30 (West Pub. Co., St. Paul, MN, 1979).

M. Dombroff, *Dombroff on Demonstrative Evidence* (John Wiley & Sons, New York, 1983).

S. Goldberg, *The First Trial in a Nutshell* 26–43, 146–65 (West Pub. Co., St. Paul, MN, 1982).

K. Hegland, *Trial and Practice Skills in a Nutshell* 11–12 (West Pub. Co., St. Paul, MN, 1978).

E. Imwinkelried, Evidentiary Foundations (Bobbs-Merrill Co., Indianapolis, IN, 1980).

J. Jeans, *Trial Advocacy* Chs. 10–11, 15 (West Pub. Co., St. Paul, MN, 1975).

R. Keeton, *Trial Tactics and Methods* 79–89, 316–19 (Little, Brown & Co., Boston, MA, 1973).

J. Kelner & F. McGovern, *Successful Litigation Techniques* Ch. 12 (Matthew Bender, New York, 1981).

T. Mauet, *Fundamentals of Trial Techniques* 177–236 (Little, Brown & Co., Boston, MA, 1980).

A. Morrill, *Trial Diplomacy* 104–18, 226–34 (Court Practice Inst., Chicago, IL, 1972).

EXHIBIT SELECTION WORKSHEET

Form 7-1

Case _____   File _____

What Exhibits will be necessary or useful:

1. Tangible Objects: Clothing   Weapons   Products

   Appliances   Other

2. Documents: Letters   Memos   Correspondence

   Contracts   Leases   Bills   Checks   Other

3. Business Records

4. Computer Data

5. Audio/Visual Recordings

6. Test Results:
   X-rays   Laboratory Analysis

7. Photographs:
   Prints   Slides   Movies

8. Diagrams:
   Charts   Maps   Graphs   Drawings

9. Past Recollection Recorded

10. Exhibit Summaries

11. Demonstrations

12. Chain of Custody Problems

13. Other

EXHIBIT FOUNDATION WORKSHEET   Form 7-2

Case _____   File _____

Exhibit

Elements of Foundation	Which witness will provide	What witness will say
(1)		
(2)		
(3)		
(4)		
(5)		
(6)		
(7)		
(8)		
(9)		
(10)		

Exhibit marked (   )

Foundation completed (   )

Exhibit offered (   )   Accepted (   )   Rejected (   )

If rejected, offer of proof made (   )

Any pretrial rulings pertaining to this exhibit (   )

TRIAL EXHIBITS CHART

Form 7-3

Case _____   File _____

Court Exhibit Identification Number	Description of Exhibit	Offered By	Identified By	Introduced By	Received/ Denied	Offer of Proof Made

EXHIBIT INTRODUCTION CHECKLIST   Form 7-4

Case _____   File _____

_____ 1. Establish sufficient *foundation* for the witness to be able *to identify* the exhibit.

_____ 2. Have the exhibit *marked* or pre-marked before the trial.

_____ 3. Determine whether the judge requires permission to be obtained to *approach the witness.*

_____ 4. Request that the witness *examine* the exhibit.

_____ 5. Have the witness *identify* the exhibit.

_____ 6. Lay the necessary *foundation for the introduction* of the exhibit.

_____ 7. *Offer* the exhibit into evidence by referring to its exhibit number of letter.

_____ 8. Provide *opposing counsel* with an opportunity to *review* the exhibit (or provide this opportunity earlier.)

_____ 9. *Respond to* any *objections* made by opposing counsel regarding the exhibit.

_____ 10. *Show* the exhibit *to the fact finder.*

Chapter 8
CROSS-EXAMINATION

A witness between two lawyers is like a fish between two cats.
—Benjamin Franklin

A lie may live and even wiggle after it has been spiked, but not beyond the sundown.
—(Matthew) Heywood Campbell Broun

8.1 Purposes

Cross-examination is the process of questioning an adverse party or witness. Cross-examination questions should be limited to those which reveal information necessary to support statements made in the closing argument. Cross-examination usually consists of narrow, leading questions by the attorney, which call for "yes" or "no" or specific answers. There are exceptions to this generalization which are most likely to occur during supportive cross-examination. However, careful consideration must be given before open-ended questions are asked on cross-examination. See § 8.3.

Cross-examination serves two primary purposes:

Destructive Cross. Cross-examination can be used to discredit the testifying witness or another witness. This may be accomplished in several ways including attacking the credibility of the witness or testimony. Most of the questions asked on cross-examination will be designed to reduce the credibility or persuasive value of the opposition's evidence.

Supportive Cross. Cross-examination can be used to bolster evidence that supports the cross-examiner's theory of the case. Cross-examination may be used to independently develop favorable aspects of the case not developed on direct examination.

CASE LAW—LOCAL PRACTICE & PROCEDURE—IDEAS

Outline   Notes

270

8.2 Preparation and Organization

A. *Background*

Full preparation, including knowledge about the facts, evidence, law, opponent, and witness involved will facilitate cross-examination. All available discovery and investigation techniques should be used to find out everything there is to know about the case.

B. *Anticipation*

Anticipation of the opponent's side of the case is essential. Considerations include what all the witnesses will testify to, how the other side will try the case, how both sides of the case can be attacked, and what evidence can be kept out under the rules.

C. *Scope of Cross-Examination*

The scope of cross-examination will usually be limited to questions involving the subject matter of the direct examination or the credibility of a witness. See FRE 611. Most judges will provide cross-examiner reasonable latitude to explore relevant areas affecting the case or the credibility of a witness. The outside limits of cross-examination fall within the discretion of the trial judge.

If an area of inquiry extends beyond the scope of direct and does not involve credibility, then the cross-examiner has at least two options. The attorney can request that the judge in his or her discretion permit a broader inquiry, or the attorney can call the witness to testify as an adverse or hostile witness during the presentation of the case in chief or during rebuttal.

D. *Credibility*

Factors involved in evaluating and attacking the credibility of a witness include bias, interest, association with the other side, motive, experience, accuracy, memory, demeanor, candor, style, manner of speaking, background, and intelligence. See Section 8.5.

The following areas should be considered when weighing the credibility of the testimony:

1. Is the testimony consistent with common sense?
2. Is the testimony consistent within itself?
3. Is the testimony consistent with other testimony presented in the case?
4. Is the testimony consistent with the established facts of the case?

E. *Should There be a Cross-Examination?*

The most important decision in cross-examination is whether to cross-examine. The following should be weighed in making that determination:

1. Has the witness hurt the case?
2. Is the witness important to the other side?

3. Will the jury expect cross-examination? Will it affect the case if no cross-examination is done?
4. Was the witness credible?
5. Did the witness leave something out on direct examination that might get in if there is a cross-examination? Was the omission intentionally set up as a trap for the inexperienced cross-examiner?
6. Will cross-examination unavoidably bring out information that is harmful to the case?
7. Are questions being asked only for the sake of asking questions?
8. Does the witness know more than the attorney does about the case?
9. Will the witness be very difficult to control?
10. Has the witness been deposed or given statements?

F. Preparing Written Questions in Advance

Cross-examination is most effective when questions are prepared in advance. Most prepared questions will not need to be significantly altered during the trial, but an attorney must retain flexibility to adapt to new material or inconsistencies as they arise.

G. Structure

The areas selected for cross should be structured in a way that clearly shows their purpose and helps the fact finder remember that point. It is advisable to begin and end the cross with strong points. See Form 8-1 Cross Examination Outline.

H. Attention

Close attention to the witnesses on direct examination may reveal signs of deception, lack of assurance, or bluffing that can be explored on cross-examination. The attention shown by the jury or judge may also be a clue.

CASE LAW—LOCAL PRACTICE & PROCEDURE—IDEAS

Outline   Notes

8.3 Presentation and Delivery

A. Confidence

A confident attitude will assist in making the cross effective and persuasive.

B. Not Repeating Direct Examination

Generally, any repetition of the direct examination will only emphasize the opponent's case. However, repetition of any part of the direct that is supportive of the cross-examiner's case may be effective and with careful consideration may justify the use of an open-ended question or a question that requires an explanatory response.

C. Leading the Witness

Questions that suggest or contain the answer should be asked on cross. Questions that require "yes," "no," or short, anticipated answers help control the witness so the testimony develops as anticipated. The question "why" and questions which require explanations should be avoided because they call for open-ended answers which cannot be controlled.

D. Simple, Short Questions

Short, straightforward questions in simple, understandable language are most effective. Broad or confused questions may create problems of understanding for witnesses, attorneys, the jury and the judge.

E. Factual Questions

Questions which seek an opinion or conclusory response may permit the witness to balk or explain an answer. Questions which include fact words and accurate information will force the witness to admit the accuracy of the question.

F. Controlling the Witness

The most effective way to control a witness is to ask short factual questions. Some witnesses may need to be politely directed to respond; some witnesses may require the intervention and control of the judge.

G. Maintaining Composure

An attorney who displays a temper or argues with a witness may irritate the court and the jury, causing them to side with the witness or the opponent. In addition, such conduct makes thinking difficult and will draw objections.

H. Adopting Appropriate Approach

Some witnesses may deserve righteous indignation, others may be attacked, but most need to be carefully and courteously led. A cross-examiner can be very effective by being politely assertive and persistent without having to attack a witness.

I. Stopping When Finished

When the planned questions are asked and the desired information is obtained, the attorney should stop. It may hurt the case more by asking too many questions than by not asking enough.

J. Good Faith Basis

An attorney cannot ask a question on cross unless the attorney has proof of the underlying facts. An attorney cannot fabricate innuendos or inferences on cross-examination. The attorney must have a good faith basis which includes some proof of such facts. That proof may not be admitted as extrinsic evidence but the attorney must have available or access to a witness or document to support a fact.

K. Witnesses Requiring Special Consideration

Certain witnesses require special consideration in both the formulation and delivery of questions. These witnesses include children, relatives, spouses, experienced witnesses, investigators, experts, the aged, the handicapped, and those with communication problems. Outside resources may be used to assist in developing tactics to deal with special witnesses.

CASE LAW—LOCAL PRACTICE & PROCEDURE—IDEAS

Outline   Notes

8.4 Expert Witnesses   Areas for cross-examination of experts parallel areas for lay witnesses and permit additional areas of inquiry regarding:

1. Their fees;
2. The number of times they have testified before;
3. Whether they routinely testify for the plaintiff or defendant;
4. Their failure to conduct all possible tests,
5. The biased source of their information,
6. Their lack of information,
7. The existence of other possible causes or opinions,
8. The use of a treatise to impeach.

It is critical for a cross examiner to develop absolute mastery of the expert's field before examining the expert in a specific area. A well constructed concise hypothetical question may be effective cross-examination if it is clear, complete, and well presented and if it elicits an opinion contrary to the testimony on direct examination.

CASE LAW—LOCAL PRACTICE & PROCEDURE—IDEAS

Outline   Notes

8.5 Impeachment

A. *Factors*   Impeachment discredits the witness or the testimony. To evaluate whether impeachment is appropriate, the following should be considered:

1. How unfavorable is the testimony and how much did it hurt the case?
2. Will impeachment be successful?
3. Is there a sound basis for impeachment and can it be accomplished?
4. Is the impeachment material relevant to the facts or the credibility of the witness?
5. Is the impeachment material within the court's discretion and not too remote or collateral?

See Form 8-2 Cross Examination Planning Worksheet.

B. *Sources of Impeachment*   The credibility of a witness may be attacked in any number of ways. The following factors represent the more common and frequent matters employed to reduce the credibility of a witness. Many witnesses will not have obvious or apparent weaknesses in their testimony. The factors listed below and similar matters may raise implications and create inferences which reduce to varying degrees the credibility of a witness.

1. *Misunderstanding of Oath.* The witness may not understand the oath or know the difference between telling the truth and telling a lie. This situation will rarely arise.
2. *Lack of Perception.* The witness may not have actually observed the event, or the witness may have perceived something through the senses (sight, taste, hearing, smell, or touch) and it can be shown that conditions were not favorable to that perception.
3. *Lack of Memory.* The witness may not have a sound, independent memory of what was observed.
4. *Lack of Communication.* The witness may be unable to adequately communicate what was perceived.
5. *Bias, Prejudice, or Interest.* The witness may have a personal, financial, philosophical, or emotional stake in the trial.
6. *Prior Criminal Record.* The witness may have a prior criminal conviction which may be admissible. See FRE 609. Local law and practice may limit the use of this information.
7. *Prior Bad Acts.* Testimony concerning a witness' prior bad conduct may sometimes be used to impeach a witness if it is probative of untruthfulness.
8. *Character Evidence.* A witness may be impeached by a character witness who is familiar with the reputation of the witness for truth and veracity or who has an opinion regarding the truthfulness of the witness. See FRE 608(a).

9. *Prior Inconsistent Statements or Omissions.* The witness may have made former contradictory or inconsistent oral statements or may have omitted some facts during previous testimony or in a prior statement. If the witness denies these prior statements a copy of the statement or another witness may be needed to prove them.

Former contradictory or inconsistent written statements or admissions or omissions may be discovered in letters, entries in books or journals, business records, and signed or unsigned statements. Other sources include sworn statements or testimony from prior hearings, grand jury or coroner's inquests, administrative hearings or deposition transcripts. The witness may have previously failed to mention facts testified to on direct or may have made contradictory or inconsistent statements in the pleadings, affidavits, or other court documents in a case.

C. Extrinsic Evidence and Collateral Matters

An attorney may or may not be able to introduce extrinsic evidence if a witness denies a cross-examination impeachment question. Extrinsic evidence is evidence introduced through a source other than the witness, such as another witness or document. Whether extrinsic evidence is or is not admisable depends on whether the facts are "collateral" or "non-collateral" to the case. A matter is collateral and not admissable if it has no connection to the case. A matter is non-collateral and is admissable if it has a relationship to the case.

D. Use of Inconsistent Statements for Impeachment

The statements must be inconsistent or contradictory to be used. The document referred to must be available to prove the inconsistency. Federal Rule of Evidence 613 provides the attorney with the option of not showing the prior statement to the witness, but this option may be altered by tactical considerations or by local rule or practice.

The introduction of prior inconsistent statements or ommissions usually includes three stages:
1. The cross-examiner commits the witness to the direct examination testimony. This may be done by having the witness repeat such testimony to reaffirm the evidence.
2. The cross-examiner will usually then lead the witness through a series of questions which describe the circumstances and setting of the prior inconsistent statement.
3. The cross-examiner will then introduce the prior inconsistency. This may be done in several ways. The attorney may read from the prior statement or have the witness read it.

A fourth possible stage involves the attorney exploring both statements with the witness, but this may provide the witness with a chance to explain the discrepancy.

If the witness admits the prior statement, the impeachment process is concluded. If the witness denies the prior statement, the exhibit should be marked, identified, and offered as evidence. Proper foundation must be laid for its admission.

The opposing lawyer can request that other portions of the prior statement be introduced contemporaneously with the impeaching testimony to prevent a cross examiner from introducing selective facts out of context. FRE 106. The opposing lawyer on redirect will usually have the witness explain or clarify any discrepancy or rehabilitate the witness with a prior consistent statement, if available. See FRE 801(d)(1).

E. Cross-examination of Character Witness

Character witnesses may be impeached like any other witness. They may also be cross-examined regarding their knowledge of specific instances of bad conduct by the person whose character they praised. Some jurisdictions limit the specific acts to areas that are probative of the untruthfulness of the person. See FRE 608(b).

CASE LAW—LOCAL PRACTICE & PROCEDURE—IDEAS

Outline   Notes

8.6 Additional Considerations: The Ten Commandments

It is helpful to keep in mind Irving Younger's Ten Commandments for cross-examination:

1. Be brief.
2. Ask short questions and use plain words.
3. Never ask anything but a leading question.
4. Ask only questions to which you already know the answers.
5. Listen to the answer.
6. Do not quarrel with the witness.
7. Do not permit a witness on cross-examination to simply repeat what the witness said on direct examination.
8. Never permit the witness to explain anything.
9. Avoid one question too many.
10. Save it for summation.

These suggestions will not be applicable to all cases and all situations. The cross-examiner who has a legitimate reason for asking such questions—whether or not that reason "violates" one of the ten commandments—will conduct an effective cross-examination.

CASE LAW—LOCAL PRACTICE & PROCEDURE—IDEAS

Outline   Notes

8.7 Avoiding Mistrials and Reversals

A. *Do Not Harass or Embarrass the Witness*

Cross-examination unethical practice will occur through the use of accusatory questions which seek answers that would harass or embarrass witnesses, even though true, and which are irrelevant to the issues in the case. DR 7–106(c)(1) and (2) and Model Rule 3.4 forbid such questioning. See also FRE 611(a). An example would be where, in a motor vehicle accident case, the defense counsel brings out the fact that the plaintiff's child is illegitimate. *Jangula v. Klocek*, 284 Minn. 477, 170 N.W.2d 587 (1969).

B. *Avoid Innuendoes Based on Untrue Facts*

Since the lawyer is allowed to use leading questions during cross-examination, there is a great opportunity for abuse. Questions might be asked which discredit a witness before the witness even answers. This can be accomplished by sneers and innuendoes as well as by asking questions that the lawyer knows cannot be proved by any evidence. *State v. Flowers*, 262 Minn. 164, 114 N.W.2d 78 (1962).

C. *Do Not Elicit Irrelevant and Prejudicial Responses*

Other questioning may not be harrassing or damaging to a particular witness, but may be irrelevant and so prejudicial as to warrant a new trial. For example, in a wrongful death action, it is unethical for the plaintiff's attorney to ask the defendant's expert witness if he didn't say to the plaintiff's attorney, off the record during the deposition, that plaintiff's attorney "had a good case and knew it." *County of Maricopa, Arizona v. Mayberry*, 555 F.2d 207 (9th Cir. 1977).

CASE LAW—LOCAL PRACTICE & PROCEDURE—IDEAS

Outline   Notes

8.8 Bibliography   TEXTS

G. Bellow & B. Moulton, *The Lawyering Process* 607–825 (Foundation Press, Mineola, NY, 1978).

P. Bergman, *Trial Advocacy in a Nutshell* 142–245 (West Pub. Co., St. Paul, MN, 1979).

S. Goldberg, *The First Trial in a Nutshell* 128–33, 271–354 (West Pub. Co., St. Paul, MN, 1982).

K. Hegland, *Trial and Practice Skills in a Nutshell* 50–82 (West Pub. Co., St. Paul, MN, 1978).

J. Jeans, *Trial Advocacy* Ch. 13 (West Pub. Co., St. Paul, MN, 1975).

R. Keeton, *Trial Tactics and Methods* 94–165 (Little, Brown & Co., Boston, MA, 1973).

J. Kelner & F. McGovern, *Successful Litigation Techniques* Chs. 8, 14–15 (Matthew Bender, New York, 1981).

T. Mauet, *Fundamentals of Trial Techniques* 237–94 (Little, Brown & Co., Boston, MA, 1980).

J. McElhaney, *Effective Litigation* 24–43 (West Pub. Co., St. Paul, MN, 1974).

A. Morrill, *Trial Diplomacy* 54–85, 134–47 (Court Practice Inst., Chicago, IL, 1972).

CROSS-EXAMINATION OUTLINE   Form 8-1

Case _____   Witness _____   File _____

Key Facts of Anticipated Direct Examination	Key Areas for Cross-Examination	Sources of Information

CROSS-EXAMINATION PLANNING WORKSHEET Form 8-2

Case _____   Witness _____   File _____

Supportive Cross: Facts which support case   Prior Statement/Probable Testimony

Destructive Cross: Sources of impeachment

  Poor Perception

  Poor Memory

  Poor Communication

  Testimony inconsistent with common sense

  Testimony inconsistent with other facts

  Bias/Prejudice/Interest

  Prior Criminal Record

  Bad Reputation/Bad Acts

  Character Evidence

  Prior Inconsistent Statements

Other Areas for Cross

Chapter 9

OBJECTIONS

One unerring mark of love of the truth is not entertaining any proposition with greater assurance than the proofs it is built upon will warrant.

—John Locke

Whoever wrestles with us, strengthens our nerves and sharpens our skill. Our antagonist is our helper.

—Edmund Burke

9.1 Purposes   An objection is the procedure used to oppose the introduction of improper evidence, testimony, and argument or to oppose inappropriate behavior and procedure during the trial. An objection is both a strategic and tactical tool for the attorney. Both the use of objections and the knowledge of when to use them are crucial to winning a case. Objections are one tool which, when used properly, enhance the attorney's control, credibility, and persuasiveness in the courtroom.

The main purpose of making evidentiary objections is to prevent damaging evidence or testimony, which is not admissible under the rules of evidence, from being introduced. Objections are also used to control the form of questions and to protect witnesses from harassment by the opposing attorney. Another important purpose of objections is to make a record. A complete trial record is necessary to preserve objections for potential appeal. Sometimes objections can be used strategically to help a witness, to respond to a suggestion by the judge, to intimidate an inexperienced opponent, or for other tactical reasons. Whatever strategy the attorney uses, the overall effect should be consistent with the theories of the case.

9.2 Preparation and Organization
A. Opposing Lawyer   As with every other aspect of the case, a thorough understanding of the facts and issues is necessary in order to make and anticipate objections. Many objections may be dealt with by a motion in limine brought, heard, and decided before the trial. In addition to the particular circumstances surrounding the case, the attorney should be familiar with the various types of objections. A list of possible objections is included in Form 9-1 Common Legal Objections.

The attorney will also want to consider when it is proper to object. Although much of the skill of objecting involves quick thinking and instant decision making at the trial itself, a more consistent strategy can be developed by considering when it is that the attorney will object to evidence.

An objection should seldom, if ever, be made when the testimony will be favorable or neutral to the case. The attorney should also consider how the objections impact on the jury. Jurors often think that lawyers who object are hiding something from them. Also, an objection calls the jury's attention to the evidence that the attorney is attempting to exclude, tending to emphasize its significance.

Objections are best reserved for testimony or evidence that the attorney is reasonably certain will harm the case. The likelihood of the objection being sustained is also an important factor to consider before making an objection. An objection may unnecessarily highlight a problem, and objections should only be made when there is a good chance of the objection being sustained. The attorney will, regardless of the ruling on the objection, want to preserve the record in case of an appeal.

B. Examining Attorney

The examining attorney in preparing and presenting evidence must recognize and understand possible objections that can be asserted against its introduction. The attorney can then alter the question or restrict the evidence to avoid the objectionable matter. It should be the goal of an examining attorney to present evidence that is not objectionable. Skilled advocates will often conduct examinations with few or no objections.

C. Anticipating Evidentiary Problems

It is important for an attorney to anticipate evidentiary problems in a case and to plan how to handle them. Certain evidence the attorney wants to introduce may have some evidentiary infirmities. The attorney will need to consider how the evidence may be made admissable or alternative ways to introduce other evidence. Certain evidence the opponent will probably introduce may be inadmissible. The attorney needs to prepare objections to such evidence. See Form 9-2 Objection Planning Worksheet.

A motion in limine may be brought before the trial begins or before a witness testifies to obtain a court ruling on the admissability of evidence before it is introduced.

CASE LAW—LOCAL PRACTICE & PROCEDURE—IDEAS

Outline   Notes

9.3 Common Objections

The Rules of Evidence create the grounds for objections. See Form 9-1 Common Legal Objections. Additional objections may be based on the rules of trial practice, civil or criminal procedure, case law, common sense, or fairness. The judge is the final determiner whether an objection is proper. Not all judges recognize all objections. An attorney may have to assert those objections which the judge does recognize rather than argue the accuracy of other discretionary objections.

A. Relevance (FRE 401–402)

Evidence must be relevant in order to be admissible. Testimony and evidence is relevant if it has probative value, which is defined as the tendency to make more or less probable any facts of consequence to the outcome of the case. A piece of evidence may be relevant to prove something, but it may not have any probative value in the case being tried. Generally, the majority of relevancy objections arise with the introduction of circumstantial evidence. This is because the probative value of circumstantial evidence requires the drawing of inferences that may be weak or remote. Also, relevant evidence may be excluded when the probative value of that evidence is outweighed by its prejudicial effects (FRE 403).

B. Materiality (FRE 401–402)

Evidence is material if it has some logical relationship to the case. Materiality has been subsumed by FRE 401–402, and is included in an objection based on irrelevancy.

C. Prejudicial (FRE 403)

Relevant evidence may be objectionable when its prejudicial effect outweighs its probative value. This objection is most often made against photographs, videotapes, and other visual exhibits that graphically display injuries or a scene. A prompt, if not a pretrial, objection is necessary when this type of evidence is presented because once the jury has seen it the evidence will be etched in their memories. This objection also applies to testimony and persons wishing to display their injuries in the courtroom.

Additional types of inadmissible prejudicial evidence includes:
1. Improper Character Evidence. FRE 404 and 405.
2. Improper Habit Evidence. FRE 406.
3. Subsequent Remedial Measures. FRE 407.
4. Offers of Compromise. FRE 408.
5. Payment of Medical Expenses. FRE 409.
6. Plea Bargains. FRE 410.
7. Liability Insurance. FRE 411.

D. Privileged Communication (FRE 501)

Privileged communications are defined mostly by local statutes. A privileged communication usually consists of a communication between persons having a certain relationship. A valid objection based on privilege will bar the underlying communication from being disclosed. In order to raise this objection the attorney must first answer several questions: Was the discussion or matter subject to a privilege? Was the communication made under confidential circumstances? Is the privilege absolute or qualified? Has there been a waiver of the privilege? Who holds the privilege and has it been asserted by the proper party? Local statutes and case law should be referred to in order to resolve these issues.

Typical privileges include: attorney/client, physician/patient, spousal testimony, interspousal marital communications, clergy/penitent, trade/business secrets, informant indentity, governmental information, and news sources.

E. Competence *(FRE 601–602)*	The witness must be competent to give testimony. Competency may be defined by state statutes. Generally, in order to be competent the witness must have firsthand knowledge of the facts with which the testimony deals. In order to testify witnesses must take an oath and then recall and communicate what they observed and perceived.

E. Competence
(FRE 601–602)

The witness must be competent to give testimony. Competency may be defined by state statutes. Generally, in order to be competent the witness must have firsthand knowledge of the facts with which the testimony deals. In order to testify witnesses must take an oath and then recall and communicate what they observed and perceived.

F. Lack of Foundation
(FRE 901–903)

This objection is used to prevent the introduction of evidence or simply to force the opposing attorney to provide the missing element of foundation. If the objection does not keep the evidence out but forces the opposing attorney to establish the missing element of foundation, it may be strategically inappropriate to object because the evidence may appear more credible in the jurors' minds. Sometimes, the better tactical approach, where the missing element can be established, is to not object and argue the missing element in summation.

G. Questioning by the
Court (FRE 614)

Although Rule 614 allows the court to call and interrogate witnesses, the court is not permitted try the case. The purpose of this objection is to prevent the judge from "taking over" or unduly influencing the jury by questioning a witness. Rule 614(c) allows this objection to be made either at the time of the judge's questioning or at the next available time when the jury is absent. If during questioning by a judge, the court asks an objectionable question, a lawyer may object on any evidentiary ground and request the court to rule on the propriety of the question.

H. Opinion
(FRE 701–705)

There are two types of opinion testimony: by an expert and by a lay person. Experts can give opinion testimony only after the expert has been qualified regarding the area of the opinion. FRE 702. An objection to expert opinion testimony may be made when the expert has not established expertise in the area for which the opinion is requested or when the supporting data, opinion, or bases of the opinion is inappropriate. FRE 703–705.

Non-experts may give opinions in many circumstances. A lay witness must first demonstrate competence and personal knowledge of the facts leading to the opinion and must hold an opinion that is based on the rational perception of the witness and that will assist the jury in understanding the case. FRE 701. Examples of permissible lay opinions include speed, time, distance, emotions, feelings, age, health, reasonable estimates, and sobriety. Many lay opinions will be objectionable. The lay person should only be allowed to tell what was observed and not give editorial comment concerning those observations.

I. Conclusions (FRE 701)	Witnesses are generally permitted only to testify to facts and opinions. Conclusions and inferences are left to the jury. This is basically the same objection as opinion testimony.
J. Speculation (FRE 602, 701)	Any question that asks the witness to guess or engage in conjecture is objectionable. Words like if, should, could, and similar phrases in a question may render a question susceptible to this objection.
K. Best Evidence Rule (FRE 1001–1007)	The traditional best evidence rule requires that the original of a document or other writing be introduced at trial when the original is available. The modern rule (FRE 1003) permits duplicates to be introduced absent any question of authenticity or unfairness. The original rule dealt only with writings. Today, the rule includes recordings and photographs as well. The best evidence rule does not apply to testimony.
L. Lack of Authentication (FRE 901–902)	Writings and conversations must be authenticated to be admissible; that is, they are what they purport to be. This is a foundation-type objection.
M. Parol Evidence Rule	The parol evidence rule provides that a written agreement cannot be contradicted by oral testimony. This objection is best raised in limine. Local statutes and case law need to be researched to determine when this objection may be raised successfully.
N. Hearsay (FRE 801)	1. *Definition.* Hearsay is an out-of-court statement offered to "prove the truth of the matter asserted." A "statement" is an oral or written assertion or nonverbal conduct intended to be an assertion. Hearsay is excluded because at the time the statement was made the person was not under oath, there is no way for the fact finder to observe the credibility of the person when the statement

was made, and it is not possible to cross-examine the person who made the statement. The attorney should always ask, "What is the proponent trying to prove?" The statement is only hearsay if the statement is introduced to prove the truth of the statement. There are many exceptions to the rule excluding hearsay. The exceptions are based on two variables: (1) the likelihood that the hearsay is reliable, and (2) the need to receive the hearsay. Much of the evidence admitted during a trial will constitute hearsay information rendered admissible by rule, statute, or case law.

2. *Non-Hearsay Assertions.* A common form of out-of-court assertions admitted are statements made by a party opponent. The federal rules (801(d)(2)) define these statements as non-hearsay which renders them admissible. Any statement made by an opposing party or the party's agent, employee, or representative will be admissible (subject only to other objections). Another prior statement that will be deemed admissible in most circumstances is a prior statement by a witness under oath and subject to cross-examination offered as a prior inconsistent statement on cross-examination or as a prior consistent statement on rebuttal. FRE 801(d)(1).

3. *FRE 803 Exceptions.* Hearsay exceptions which render prior statements admissible regardless of whether the declarant is available to testify at the trial include:

   a) *Present sense impressions, excited utterances, and state-of-mind exceptions.* These three exceptions render many statements admissible. These statements usually appear to be reliable because they are made in response to an event, usually in a spontaneous fashion, and without time or a need to be fabricated:

      i) *Present Sense Impression.* 803(1). These include statements describing or explaining an event made while the declarant perceived the event or immediately after the event. This is a broad exception and covers many statements made by persons involved in or who observed an event.

      ii) *Excited Utterances.* 803(2). Statements made by the declarant while under stress or excitement caused by a startling situation or condition fall within this exception.

      iii) *Existing Mental, Emotional, or Physical Condition.* 803(3). A statement made by a person involving that individual's state of mind, emotion, sensation, or physical condition (such as intent, plan, motive, design, mental feeling, pain, and bodily harm) will be admissible.

   b) *Medical Diagnosis Statements.* 803(4). Statements made by a person who describes medical history or past or present pains and symptoms for purposes of medical diagnosis will be reliable because that person has little or no incentive to distort the truth.

c) *Past Recollection Recorded.* 803(5). Records concerning a matter which a witness no longer recollects but which a witness once knew and accurately recorded at a time when the matter was fresh will be admissible evidence.

d) *Records and public entries.* These records will typically be admissible because such information is usually entered and maintained in a reliable fashion:

   i) *Business Records.* 803(6). Records kept in the ordinary course of a business or other organization will be admissible. These records need to be entered as a regular business practice and be made at or near the time of the event by a person with knowledge of the information.

   ii) *Public Records.* 803(8). Records maintained by a government office or agency fall within this exception.

   iii) *Vital Statistics.* 803(9). Records of births, deaths, and marriages will also be admissible.

   iv) *Absent Entries.* 803(7) and (10). The absence of business and public records may prove the non-existence of a fact.

   v) *Market Reports and Commercial Data.* 803(17). Market quotations, lists, directories, and other compilations will be admissible.

   vi) *Land Records* 803(14) *and Property Documents* 803(15). These entries constitute reliable, admissible information.

   vii) *Records of Religious Organizations* 803(11) *and Marriage and Baptismal Certificates* 803(12). These records also constitute exceptions.

   viii) *Family Records.* 803(13). Facts concerning personal or family history contained in family records will be admissible.

   ix) *Ancient Documents.* 803(16). Statements in an authentic document in existence for twenty years or more constitute a hearsay exception.

e) *Learned Treatises.* 803(18). Statements contained in established publications may be admitted in cases involving expert witnesses.

f) *Judgments.* Civil or criminal judgments may include admissible information:

        i) *Judgment of Previous Conviction* 803(22). These judgments will be admissible in certain situations.

        ii) *Judgment Involving Personal, Family, History, or Boundaries.* 803(23). Judgments which resolve proofs of these matters will be admissible.

    g) *Reputation.* Evidence of reputation and character may be admissible:

        i) *Character Reputation.* 803(21). This testimony will be admissible based upon the reputation of a person in a community. Also see FRE 404, 405, and 608.

        ii) *Personal and Family Reputation.* 803(19). Information about family status and relations will be admissible.

        iii) *General History and Boundaries Reputation.* 803(20). This type of information in the form of reputation testimony constitutes a hearsay exception.

4. *FRE 804 Exceptions.* Hearsay exceptions which render prior statements admissible only when the declarant is not available to testify because of privilege, death, refusal, absence, or unavailability include:

    a) *Previous Testimony.* 804(b)(1). Testimony by a witness at a former proceeding will be admissible.

    b) *Dying Declaration.* 804(b)(2). A statement made by a declarant who believes death is imminent and which concerns the cause or circumstances of death will be admissible in most cases.

    c) *Statement Against Interest.* 804(b)(3). A statement made by a person contrary to that person's interest will be an exception to the hearsay rule. If the person is an opposing party or agent, the statement will be admissible under 801(d)(2) regardless of whether it is a statement against interest.

    d) *Statement of Personal or Family History.* A statement by a declarant concerning that person's personal or family status will be admissible. 804(b)(4).

5. *Other Trustworthy Statements.* 803(25) and 804(b)(5). Hearsay statements which do not fall within the stated exceptions may be admissible if (a) the statement is a material fact, (b) no other more probative evidence exists, and (c) its admission will serve the interests of justice.

O. Leading (FRE 611)

Generally, it is improper to ask leading questions during direct examination. FRE 611. Leading questions are questions that are suggestive of the answer. For example, "And then Mr. Jones hit you, didn't he?" Leading questions are permitted during direct examination in certain circumstances. These circumstances include: preliminary matters (FRE 611(c)); noncontroversial, undisputed or inconsequential facts; topic transition; examination of an adverse or hostile witness; when the witness has poor communication skills; refreshing a witness' recollection; and when asking a witness to contradict earlier testimony by a different witness.

P. *Narrative (FRE 611)*   An objection may be made to a question that calls for a narrative answer or to an answer that turns into a narrative. A narrative question is a question that allows the witness to tell a long uncontrolled story. For example, "In your own words, Ms. Smith, tell the jury everything that happened to you on July 1." A narrative question is objectionable because it allows the witness to interject inadmissible testimony without giving the opposing attorney a reasonable opportunity to object. Sometimes a witness will give a narrative response to an otherwise permissible question. A narrative answer may be objected to as being a narrative answer or as being non-responsive.

Q. *Non-responsive,*   A non-responsive or volunteered answer occurs when a witness
Volunteered (FRE 611)   provides information not required by the attorney's question. Any response that extends beyond the specific information required would be objectionable. Depending on the nature of the volunteered testimony, the attorney may request the court to admonish the witness to answer only the questions asked.

R. *Repetitious*   If the question has been "asked and answered," the attorney may
(FRE 403 & 611)   object to the question as repetitious. The purpose of this objection is to prevent the opposing attorney from gaining undue advantage by repeating favorable testimony in front of the jury. The form of the questions do not have to be absolutely identical in order to raise this objection. If the new question calls for an answer previously given the question is objectionable as repetitious.

S. *Cumulative*   Cumulative evidence is a form of repetitious evidence. The trial
(FRE 403 & 611)   court has the discretion to control cumulative and repetitive evidence. Cumulative witnesses commonly occur when testimony regarding character and reputation is involved. Cumulative exhibits are most often photographs. Cumulative evidence is objectionable because it is repetitive, unnecessary, and a waste of time.

T. *Vague, Ambiguous,*   A question must be reasonable, clear, and specific so that the
Misleading, Confusing   witness knows what is being asked.
or Unintelligible
(FRE 401–403)
U. *Multiple or*   A multiple or compound question presents two or more ques-
Compound Questions   tions within a single question. These types of questions are objec-
(FRE 611)   tionable because the answer will usually be ambiguous. An example

of a compound question is, "Was the defendant wearing brown shoes and was he driving?" Answers to multiple or compound questions, which sometimes seem straightforward and understandable in the courtroom, can become extremely confusing when reviewed upon the record.

V. Assuming Facts not in Evidence (FRE 611, 701–704)

This objection is often used to object to questions on cross-examination that include statements of facts which are in dispute or facts that are not in evidence. This objection is also used to object to hypothetical questions that assume facts not in evidence. A direct examiner who faces this objection, may revise the question to eliminate the assumption of fact or may tell the court that the assumed fact will be proved later. If the latter course is taken, the assumed fact must be proved. If that fact is not proved later, the opposing attorney may request that the judge advise the jury to disregard such evidence. The cross-examiner who faces this objection may argue that one of the purposes of cross is to test the memory and credibility of a witness and that the witness can deny the asserted facts if the witness disagrees with the assertion.

W. Misstatement or Mischaracterization of Testimony or Evidence (FRE 611)

Misstatement or mischaracterization of evidence and testimony is objectionable because it inaccurately describes evidence or draws inferences that are reserved for the jury's determination. This objection may be used to object to testimony as well as questions. A misstatement or mischaracterization of evidence or testimony is usually, but not always, done inadvertently. The opposing attorney may not remember exactly what was said in previous testimony. Likewise, the mistake may be accidental where a piece of evidence may reasonably be described by more than one term. For example, a letter opener may arguably be referred to as a knife. Of course, in this example, the opposing attorney could also be acting intentionally. In either case, an objection should be asserted and the court requested to instruct the opposing attorney to make proper reference to the evidence or testimony.

X. Argumentative (FRE 611)

Any question that is essentially an argument to the jury is improper. The role of the attorney is to question and not to testify. An argumentative question is recognized either by the fact that it elicits no new information or that it is a form of harassment of the witness. Argumentative questions often assume a sarcastic tenor, "Do you mean to tell me," or "Doesn't it seem preposterous that."

Y. Improper Impeachment (FRE 613)

Improper impeachment is an impermissible attempt to discredit a witness. Improper impeachment may occur in a variety of ways. A cross-examiner may attempt to impeach the witness on a collateral matter. Or the cross-examiner may attempt to impeach the witness with a prior statement that is not materially inconsistent. In considering whether to object in these situations, the attorney should weight the consequences of the impeachment testimony against the damage the other attorney is causing by appearing picayunish.

Z. Beyond the Scope (FRE 611)   Cross-examination, redirect examination, rebuttal testimony, and rebuttal closing arguments are each limited in scope. Any questions or argument that goes beyond the permissible scope is objectionable. Cross-examination is limited to the subject matter of the direct examination and other matters relating to the witness' credibility. If the cross-examiner wishes to go beyond the scope of the direct, the cross-examiner must usually recall the witness. The cross-examiner may, however, raise new matters in a non-leading way if the court permits. See FRE 611(b).

The scope of many examinations will usually be broad enough to permit inquiries on cross or re-direct that do not go beyond the scope of the examination. The issue of credibility may be sufficient in itself to justify most cross-examination questions. Usually judges view the scope of an examination liberally and permit wide ranging examinations as long as the questions are relevant to the case.

Redirect questions should be limited in scope to those matters raised in cross-examination. Rebuttal testimony will be permitted to rebut evidence introduced during the opponent's case in chief. Rebuttal closing argument will be limited to new matters raised by the opponent's summation.

CASE LAW—LOCAL PRACTICE & PROCEDURE—IDEAS

Outline   Notes

9.4 Objections to Demonstrative Evidence

A. Prejudicial or Gruesome (FRE 403)

See Section 9.3(C) Prejudicial.

B. Misleading, Inaccurate or Distorting (FRE 403)

Demonstrative evidence has the potential to clarify evidence and aid the jury in understanding the case. On the other hand, demonstrative evidence may also mislead, confuse or distort the facts. Drawings that are not drawn to scale, photographs taken of a scene at a time far removed from the time of the incident, and other differences, can be misleading. The attorney should request to see demonstrative evidence prior to trial so that objections can be made before the jury is exposed to the evidence.

C. Lack of Foundation (FRE 901–903)

See Section 9.3(F) Lack of Foundation.

D. Waste of Court's Time/Undue Delay (FRE 403)

Sometimes the presentation of demonstrative evidence may be time consuming or require extensive preparation. In these instances, the value of the demonstrative evidence must be weighed against the cost of court time and delay. Demonstrative evidence that does not significantly add to the case will be rejected more frequently when it will take a long time to prepare or present the evidence than demonstrative evidence that is crucial to the case.

E. Evidence Does Not Aid or Assist Jury (FRE 401)

Even demonstrative evidence must meet the relevancy requirement of Rule 401. Demonstrative evidence that does not aid or assist the jury is objectionable.

F. Sixth Amendment/ Denial of Right To Cross-examine

In criminal actions, the introduction of demonstrative evidence may be objectionable as a violation of the defendant's sixth amendment right to cross-examine witnesses. The defendant may not be able to cross-examine the person who made the drawing or took the photograph. This objection is best used in conjunction with another ground supporting an objection.

CASE LAW—LOCAL PRACTICE & PROCEDURE—IDEAS

Outline   Notes

9.5 Objections During Jury Selection

A. Mentioning Insurance (FRE 411)

As a general rule it is improper to mention the existence or nonexistence of insurance coverage during jury selection. However, some jurisdictions permit inquiries on voir dire to determine bias, prejudice, or interest in insurance matters.

B. Arguing the Law

Voir dire may not be used to argue the law. However, most judges will permit some general questions concerning the law.

C. Arguing Facts

Jury selection may not be used to argue the facts. An attempt to present the facts of the case during jury selection is objectionable.

CASE LAW—LOCAL PRACTICE & PROCEDURE—IDEAS

Outline   Notes

9.6 Objections During Opening Statement

A. Explaining the Law or Instructions

Opening statement is intended to allow each party an opportunity to present their version of the case and what they expect to prove. Explaining the law or instructions is considered premature and is objectionable in most courts. Most judges, however, will permit some limited explanations if related to the facts.

B. Argumentative

The opening statement should consist of a synopsis of the facts to be presented. The opening statement is usually confined, therefore, to a discussion of what will be proved. Argument is appropriate only in closing argument.

C. Mentioning Inadmissible Evidence

One of the main purposes of excluding certain evidence is to prevent the prejudicial effects of that evidence. Consequently, it would be improper to attempt to discuss excluded or questionably admissable evidence during opening statements. This would include any evidence excluded by pretrial rulings, or likely to be excluded by the rules of evidence.

D. Mentioning Unprovable Evidence

Mentioning unprovable evidence is tantamount to using fiction to prove a case. The attorney may only discuss evidence that can be proved. The test in these instances is one of good faith.

E. Personal Opinions

Phrases such as "I think" or "I believe" are objectionable. The jury should be left to decide the case on the evidence.

F. Discussing the Other Side's Case

This objection is generally used only in criminal cases where the prosecutor suggests what the defense will prove.

CASE LAW—LOCAL PRACTICE & PROCEDURE—IDEAS

Outline   Notes

9.7 Objections During Closing Arguments

A. Misstating Evidence

Misstating or mischaracterizing the evidence is objectionable. If a description or characterization does not reflect the testimony and evidence given during the trial it is objectionable.

B. Misstating Law and Quoting Instructions

Misstating the law, like misstating the evidence, is objectionable. A misstatement of law may be equally, and possibly more, prejudicial than a misstatement of facts. Courts allow attorneys to highlight, comment on, and explain instructions during closing argument. However, it is improper in many jurisdictions to read the instructions verbatim.

C. Per Diem Damages Argument

A per diem request for damages is objectionable in personal injury cases for pain and suffering in many jurisdictions. For example, a plaintiff may not request $25 per day for a life expectancy of 40 years to yield $365,000 for pain and suffering.

D. Personal Opinions

Personal opinions are not appropriate in closing argument. An attorney may not use phrases such as "I think" or "I believe" during closing argument.

E. Appealing to Jury's Bias, Prejudice or Pecuniary Interests

Suggesting, even indirectly, that a verdict may personally affect the jury is improper. This can happen whenever a government agency or insurance company is a defendant, for example.

F. Personal Attacks on Parties and Counsel

A trial should be a reasoned and rational decision-making process. Personal attacks in the courtroom do nothing to further this objective.

G. Prejudicial Arguments

Comments that have little or nothing to do with the facts are objectionable. An attorney may not ask the jury if they would "take $500,000 if they were offered it for their arm." Nor may an attorney say that if the defendant is not found guilty "he will continue to commit crimes."

CASE LAW—LOCAL PRACTICE & PROCEDURE—IDEAS

Outline   Notes

9.8 Presentation and Delivery

A. How to Object

1. It is best to rise when making an objection. Most judges will expect an attorney to stand and the extra second gained may help in framing an objection. Some judges may allow an attorney to remain seated or an attorney may request to remain seated.

2. In order for an objection to be effective it must be timely. The objection must be made before the jury hears the testimony or sees the evidence. Also, a timely objection is necessary to preserve the objection for appeal.

3. If a question is improper, the objection should be made before an answer is given. If an answer is improper, an objection should be asserted as soon as the problem becomes apparent.

4. The proper way to object is simply to say "Objection" and then state the specific, precise legal grounds in one or a few words. FRE 103(a)(1). If the grounds for the objection are clear, it may be sustained without further explanation. If an explanation is requested, a further statement may be made.

5. An objection may be sustained by the judge even if the attorney does not advance a specific reason if the ground for the objection is apparent from the content of the evidence. FRE 103(a)(1).

6. Usually the reason supporting an objection will be obvious from the judge's ruling. If the attorney is uncertain about the ground for an objection the attorney may ask the judge to explain the ruling. In some jurisdictions the attorney has a right to such an explanation. In other courts, the judge may refuse to explain a ruling and expect the attorney to determine the basis of the decision.

7. If an attorney wishes to argue an objection, the attorney should ask the court to be heard on the matter and approach the bench in a jury trial. Arguments or comments about the evidence should occur outside of the hearing of the jury. If an attorney engages in such conduct, the court should be requested to admonish that attorney.

8. It may be necessary to insist on a ruling to the objection. The attorney has a right to it. If the objection is sustained, the attorney may request a curative instruction. If the objection is overruled, the attorney should make sure that the legal basis for the objection is on the record to preserve the issue for appeal. See also FRE 103(a)(1).

B. Continuing Objection

If an objection has been overruled and subsequent questions are asked on the same topic and will also be overruled the attorney may note on the record a continuing or running objection to a line of testimony. this device eliminates the need for the attorney to object like a jack rabbit to every question.

C. Curative Instructions   After an objection has been sustained, the attorney may ask the judge to instruct the jurors to disregard the response or the question. Whether this instruction emphasizes the damaging evidence or is effective is a matter of debate. A motion to strike may also be made, although it is an archaic request because nothing is ever stricken from the record.

D. Offers of Proof (FRE 103)   When an objection is made and sustained to questioning or testimony, it may be necessary to make an offer of proof. There are two types of offers of proof. The first involves the attorney summarizing the proposed testimony on the record outside the hearing of the jury. Another method of making an offer of proof is to examine the witness in question and answer dialogue out of the jury's presence. This method is time-consuming, but has the advantage of completeness and accuracy. This method should only be used for a crucial part of the case. Offers of proof must conform to the usual rules of evidence. Opposing counsel may make other objections during an offer.

CASE LAW—LOCAL PRACTICE & PROCEDURE—IDEAS

Outline   Notes

9.9 Avoiding Mistrials and Reversals

A. Assert your Point on the Record as Efficiently and Courteously as Possible

In order to preserve an issue for appeal, it must be placed on the record. If opposing counsel's questioning or argument violates the rules of evidence or seriously breaches a rule of professional responsibility or decorum or if the judge makes an incorrect ruling or commits error, a timely objection should be made. Objections not made are deemed waived unless a substantial right of a party is affected. See FRE 103 and e.g., *Falconer v. Salliotte*, 103 Mich. App. 234, 303 N.W.2d 11 (1981).

B. Do Not Use Objections to Attack or Harass Opposing Counsel

There are serious considerations to be given to the style and number of objections made during the course of a trial. Generally, permissible objections are derived from the rules of evidence and have a legal basis. Objections made merely to interrupt or attack opposing counsel may be unethical. Ethical Consideration 7-37 admonishes against haranguing and offensive tactics, and advises that even though the litigants may have ill feelings toward each other, such animosity should not influence the lawyers. Section 7-1(a) of the ABA Standards Relating to the Defense Function and Section 5-2(a) of the Prosecution Function advise that the lawyer should manifest an attitude of professional respect toward opposing counsel (as well as all members of the tribunal). See Model Rule 2.4 on Fairness.

Overly zealous objecting which is permeated with antagonistic personalizations may cause a lawyer to suffer reversal of a verdict and can be grounds for suspension as well. *State v. Turner*, 217 Kan. 574, 538 P.2d 966 (1975). Even in a case where there is a question of real provocation, the lawyer's behavior will not be justified.

C. Zealous Advocacy or Obstructionist Tactics?

It is incumbent upon the lawyer not only to watch an adversary for abuses of the trial system, but to watch his or her own manner in doing so. Many breaches of decorum and other questionable outbursts may be attributed to the "heat of trial." *Nelson v. Gyestrum*, 118 Minn. 284, 136 N.W. 858 (1912). Increased adoption by the courts of the Code of Professional Responsibility, the Model Rules, and evolving case law provides more ammunition to an adversary's attack on appeal of an opponent's behavior during trial. See, e.g., *United States v. Thoreen*, 653 F.2d 1332 (9th Cir. 1981); *Corti v. Fleisher*, 93 Ill. App. 3d 517, 417 N.E.2d 764 (1981); *State v. York*, 632 P.2d 1261 (Ore. 1981).

While zeal may involve "histrionics and voracity," there exists a line whereby behavior, even though zealous, is no longer acceptable. *In the Matter of Friedland*, 268 Ind. 536, 376 N.E.2d 1126 (1978). Seemingly less zealous behavior such as throat clearing, paper shuffling, and other distracting noises from counsel may produce such a state of disorder or disturbance as to warrant a new trial. *Smilges v. City of Chicago*, 97 Ill. App. 3d 1127, 423 N.E.2d 1288 (1981). Such jury-distracting tactics are frowned upon and are sufficient cause in themselves for reversal.

Case law reveals that in close cases where a line needs to be drawn betwen vigorous advocacy and actual obstruction, doubts will be resolved in favor of vigorous advocacy. However, an attorney may be polite, respectful, and even subdued in his perserverance to make the record and still be found in contempt. *Commonwealth of Pennsylvania v. Local Union 542, Int'l Union of Operating Engineers*, 552 F.2d 498 (3rd Cir. 1977); *United States v. Thoreen*, 653 F.2d 1332. Overt physical disorder is not necessary to obstruct the administration of justice. A lawyer has a right to press a claim, even if it appears to be farfetched and untenable. However, once a lawyer receives an adverse ruling, the attorney may only state briefly what is necessary to preserve the point for appeal. *Sacher v. United States*, 343 U.S. 1 (1952).

A lawyer should refrain from conduct that may be labeled "vituperous," "pettifoggery," or "chicanery." Such labels attach when conduct is seen to cause an actual material obstruction of justice. The conduct crosses over the line when it impedes the court's search for truth and results in delays. Words or conduct which personally insult or affront a judge may be insufficient to support a finding of contempt. Yet "if mere words are so offensive and so unnecessary that their very utterance creates a delay" which obstructs justice, then a contempt citation, as well as disciplinary action, may be supported. *United States v. Thoreen*, 653 F.2d 1332. The challenge, for an attorney, is to determine which words, in what manner, under what circumstances, and before which judge will constitute a problem.

CASE LAW—LOCAL PRACTICE & PROCEDURE—IDEAS

Outline   Notes

9.10 Bibliography   TEXTS

P. Bergman, *Trial Advocacy in a Nutshell* 346–56 (West Pub. Co., St. Paul, MN, 1979).

K. Hegland, *Trial and Practice Skills in a Nutshell* 123–32 (West Pub. Co., St. Paul, MN, 1978).

J. Jeans, *Trial Advocacy* Ch. 14 (West Pub. Co., St. Paul, MN, 1975).

R. Keeton, *Trial Tactics and Methods* 166–215 (Little, Brown & Co., Boston, MA, 1973).

J. Kelner & F. McGovern, *Successful Litigation Techniques* Ch. 19 (Matthew Bender, New York, 1981).

T. Mauet, *Fundamentals of Trial Techniques* 362–97 (Little, Brown & Co., Boston, MA, 1980).

J. McElhaney, *Effective Litigation* 16–23 (West Pub. Co., St. Paul, MN, 1974).

A. Morrill, *Trial Diplomacy* 119–126 (Court Practice Inst., Chicago, IL, 1972).

COMMON LEGAL OBJECTIONS

Form 9-1

Exclusionary Rules of Evidence

Relevancy

FRE 401–411

Irrelevant
No Probative Value
Prejudicial
Improper Character
Improper Habit
Subsequent Remedial Measures
Offers of Compromise
Plea Bargains
Payment of Medical Expenses
Liability Insurance

Privileges

FRE 501

Attorney/Client
Physician/Patient
Spousal Testimony
Marital Communications
Clergy/Penitent
Trade/Business Secrets
Informer Identity
Governmental Information
News Sources

Competence

FRE 601–602

Incompetent
Lack of Personal Knowledge
Lack of Memory

Foundation

FRE 601–602
Lack of Foundation

Lay Opinion

FRE 701

Impermissable Opinion
Impermissable Conclusion
Speculation

Expert Opinion

FRE 702–705

Unqualified Witness
Impermissable Opinion

Authentication

FRE 901–902

Lack of Authenticity

Best Evidence

FRE 1001–1007

Unauthentic Copy
Non-genuine Original

Parole Evidence

Statutory or Case Law

Hearsay

Declarant
Not Under Oath
Not Subject to Cross
Credibility Not Observable

COMMON LEGAL OBJECTIONS
IMPROPER FORM OF QUESTION Form 9-1 (continued)

Leading

    FRE 611

        Lawyer Testifying

Narrative

    FRE 611

        No Question Before Witness

Non-Responsive

    FRE 611

        Volunteered

Repetitious

    FRE 403 & 611

        Asked and Answered
        Cumulative

Vague

    FRE 401–403

        Ambiguous
        Confusing
        Misleading
        Unintelligible

Multiple Questions

    FRE 611

        Compound Questions

Assuming Facts Not in Evidence

    FRE 611 & 701–704

        Inaccurate Hypothetical

Mischaracterization of Testimony

    FRE 611

        Misstatement of Evidence

Argumentative

    FRE 611

        Badgering

Beyond Scope

    FRE 611

        Direct or Cross

COMMON LEGAL OBJECTIONS
SUMMARY HEARSAY ANALYSIS Form 9-1 (continued)

Definition FRE 801

    Out of court statement?
    Assertive or non-assertive?
    Offered to prove truth of
        statement?

Non-Hearsay 801(d)

    Party Admissions
    Prior Statements

Hearsay Exceptions:

Sense Impressions

    Present Sense Impression 803(1)
    Excited Utterance 803(2)
    State of Mind 803(3)

Medical Diagnosis 803(4)

Past Recollection Recorded 803(5)

Records

    Business Records 803(6)
    Public Records 803(8)
    Vital Statistics 803(9)
    Absent Entries 803(7) & (10)
    Commercial Data 803(17)
    Property Records 803(14) & (15)
    Official Certificates 803(11) & (12)
    Family Records 803(13)
    Ancient Documents 803(16)

Learned Treatises 803(18)

Judgments

    Previous Convictions 803(22)
    Other Judgements 803(23)

Reputation

    Character 803(21)
    Family 803(19)
    General History 803(26)

Declarant Not Available

    Previous Testimony 804(b)(1)
    Dying Declaration 804(b)(2)
    Statement Against
        Interest 804(b)(3)
    Personal History 804(b)(4)

Reliable Hearsay 803(25) & 804(b)(5)

1. Material Fact
2. No Other Probative
    Evidence
3. Serve Interests of Justice

OBJECTION PLANNING WORKSHEET   **Form 9-2**

Case _____   File _____

Anticipated major evidentiary problems and objections

Objections to be asserted against the adversary's case:

Evidence	Rule of Evidence	Statute	Case Law

Probable objections to be asserted by adversary:

Evidence	Rule of Evidence	Statute	Case Law

Relevant pretrial evidentiary rulings

Chapter 10
CLOSING ARGUMENT

Facts, as such, never settle anything. They are working tools only. It is the implications that can be drawn from facts that count. . . .
—Clarence Beldon Randall

Insist on yourself; never imitate. Your own gift you can present every moment with the cumulative force of a whole life's cultivation; but of the adopted talent of another, you have only an extemporaneous half-possession. That which each can do best none but his Maker can teach.
—Ralph Waldo Emerson

10.1 Purposes

Following the presentation of evidence, the closing argument is made to either a judge sitting without a jury or to a jury. Usually the party with the burden of proof argues last or has an opportunity for a rebuttal. During closing argument, the attorney attempts to convince the judge or jury that the evidence presented requires a finding of certain conclusions that necessitate a particular verdict or decision in light of the applicable law. The closing argument permits both attorneys to argue the merits of their case in a light most favorable to their client, thus assisting the trier of fact in determining a just and fair verdict.

Final argument can never be a substitute for the facts and the law. Lawsuits are won by what happens during an entire trial. Rarely will an attorney be able to convince the judge or jury of the legitimacy of the attorney's cause in summation if the attorney was not able to do so during the presentation of the evidence. A recent study found a strong correlation for many jurors between their opinion after opening statements and their decision at the end of the trial.

The value of closing argument, however, should not be minimized. It is important for several reasons.

1. The closing argument, prepared in advance of trial, provides the focus, structure, and themes for the entire trial process including preparation. The entire case points to the final argument and should be prepared and presented to be consistent with the closing. The focus, structure, and themes of the final argument will be those used in preparation, voir dire, opening, direct, and cross examination.

2. Final argument is the attorney's last opportunity to summarize for the fact finder what the evidence has shown the facts to be in the case.
3. Summation is the most effective occasion in the trial to explain to the jury or judge the significance of the evidence.
4. The closing is the time when the creative trial lawyer can draw inferences, argue conclusions, comment on credibility, refer to common sense, and explain implications which the fact finder may not perceive.
5. Final argument is the only chance the attorney will have to explain and comment on the judges instructions on the law and to weave the facts and law together.
6. Summation is the attorney's last opportunity to urge the fact finder to take a specific course of action.

The materials in the section address concerns relating to the presentation of a closing argument to a jury. Many of these considerations will apply to a court trial, but not all. See Section 1.14 Court or Jury Trial.

CASE LAW—LOCAL PRACTICE & PROCEDURE—IDEAS

Outline	Notes

10.2 What Can be Argued

A. Facts

Facts and opinions presented by any side of the case which are a part of the record, even those in dispute, may be part of the closing argument and may be persuasively woven into the presentation.

B. Inferences

Inferences are conclusions drawn from the evidence presented. Standards controlling which specific inferences, conclusions, and implications may be drawn vary from jurisdiction to jurisdiction, but generally the attorney may draw all permissible inferences from any of the facts on the record so long as the inferences are logically related to the evidence presented.

C. No Requirement to Discuss All Facts

The attorney is not required to summarize or comment upon any facts whether supportive or contrary to the theories of the case. However, at a minimum, closing argument should summarize and emphasize the major points the attorney attempted to establish through the presentation of evidence. A failure to comment on and refute a credible position or defense developed by the opposing counsel may prove fatal. A decision not to address an issue, an opponent's theory, or a particular fact should be based on an analysis of the importance of that item, and the ability of the attorney and the opponent to deal with it and to present the point persuasively.

D. Urging a Result

The closing argument permits the attorney to explain the specific result the attorney wants. A closing argument is the time to convince the jury that the facts and the law support a verdict in favor of the client, that the verdict will result in justice having been done, and with that verdict the jury will have met their responsibility as jurors. It is also the time in a court trial to persuade the judge that certain findings of fact and conclusions of law have been established.

CASE LAW—LOCAL PRACTICE & PROCEDURE—IDEAS

Outline   Notes

10.3 Preparation and Organization

A. Early Preparation

See Form 10-1 Closing Argument Worksheet.

The preparation of a case for trial should include the planning of the closing argument. See Section 1.15 Planning the Closing Argument. The final argument provides the focus for the entire case. Throughout all facets of the trial, the attorney should be preparing the jury or judge for what will be heard during the closing argument. A closing argument should reemphasize the central theme and major points repeatedly presented to the jury in voir dire, opening statement and case presentation. The factual and legal foundation that supports the closing argument must be laid throughout the entire case presentation. The preparation of a closing argument will resemble in part preparation efforts for an opening statement. Portions of this and other sections will parallel some comments in Chapter 5 Opening Statement.

B. Refining the Issues and Theme for the Case

The issues, themes and theories of a case that were selected when the case preparation began will provide a framework of ideas for the closing argument. These concepts may need to be refined or expanded depending on how the evidence was developed during the trial.

C. Jury Instructions

Prior to the closing argument the judge will inform the attorneys of the exact instructions of law to be provided to the jury. Section 11.2 describes the need and procedures for attorneys to submit proposed jury instructions to the judge. It is vital that the attorney review these final instructions and make certain that the evidence explained in the final argument supports the elements of law as explained by the judge.

Any statement of the law by the attorney must be accurate. The attorney should know what the judge will say and define the law exactly as the judge does. The judge will tell the jury that if the attorney has defined the law differently than the judge the jury must ignore the attorney's statement. If there is a misstatement on the law the attorney will lose credibility and diminish the impact of an otherwise good closing. If the attorney states the law correctly, even using the same words as the judge, the result can raise the credibility of the attorney and positively reinforce the attorney's argument.

J. Anticipating the Opponent's Position

The preparation of the case requires an attorney to anticipate the various issues, themes, and theories of the opposing lawyer. The presentation of the case makes clear the exact positions taken by the opposing lawyer. By the close of the evidence, an attorney should know what the opposing attorney will argue in closing argument.

These positions need to be analyzed and taken into consideration when an attorney refines the final argument.

E. Selecting Visual Aids and Exhibits

The attorney must decide whether to use any visual aids or trial exhibits during the closing argument. Consideration should be given to the impact the visual aid or exhibit may have on the jury, the importance of the exhibit in the trial, and whether the attorney is capable of being comfortable and effective using these tools.

Real evidence, demonstrative evidence, visual aids, deposition transcripts, witness statements, discovery responses, and any other evidence exhibit that has been introduced may be used during closing argument. Visual aids may also be created which highlight summation. A visual aid may take a variety of forms including posters, foam core boards, an overhead transparency, or a blackboard. An attorney may use any one of these forms for a variety of purposes.

F. Written Outline and Detailed Script

The final argument outline that was prepared during trial preparation may need to be revised. This final outline should include all facets of the closing argument to make certain that the attorney has included every matter that needs to be addressed.

Some lawyers may prefer to write or dictate a complete closing argument. This draft may then be reviewed and improved. This approach may help the attorney in finalizing the contents of the closing argument and in determining whether some matter has been omitted. This script should not be used during the presentation of the closing argument to the jury. Reading a script of a closing argument will quickly bore the jurors and will significantly diminish the persuasive power of the attorney because the presentation will appear dry and impersonal. The attorney should prepare a key word outline from the script. With practice and preparation the outline should be all that is needed during final argument. When notes or outlines are used they should be used in a candid forthright fashion.

G. Practice

The closing argument should be rehearsed by the attorney before presentation to the jury. Verbally practicing the closing argument will permit the attorney to improve both its content and the style of delivery. It is a worthwhile idea to rehearse the closing argument before colleagues or others, in front of a mirror, or on videotape for later review and critique. The attorney should practice rehearsing the summation until it can be done in as persuasive a manner as possible. A non-memorized but thorough understanding of the argument comes through practice. A sincere, flowing, and persuasive argument can only be presented when the attorney is comfortable with the material and the delivery.

H. *Local Requirements*

The attorney needs to ascertain before summation whether the trial judge has any special requirements or limitations regarding the argument. This determination will avoid having the closing argument interrupted by the trial judge or by the opposing counsel making objections. Local practice and procedures, such as the prohibition of the use of some trial exhibits during closing argument, may limit what can be done during summation.

I. *Timing*

Which party argues first and which argues last depends upon the procedures of a jurisdiction. Usually, the party with the burden of proof will argue last to the jury, which means that the defense argues first followed by the plaintiff's summation. Many jurisdictions permit rebuttal, which means that the plaintiff will argue first, followed by a summation by the defense, and concluded with a short rebuttal argument by the plaintiff. In criminal cases, the prosecutor has the burden of proof and will either argue last or argue first and last with a rebuttal, except in those jurisdictions where the prosecutor argues first without a rebuttal opportunity. In civil cases, both parties may carry a burden of proof and in these situations usually the plaintiff has the opportunity to have the final argument before the jury.

Many lawyers believe that which attorney has the last opportunity to argue to the jury has a significant advantage over the other side. The attorney who argues last usually does have an advantage the significance of which depends upon how effective the initial lawyer has been with the closing argument and how accurate the opposing lawyer has been in anticipating the final summation.

CASE LAW—LOCAL PRACTICE & PROCEDURE—IDEAS

Outline   Notes

10.4 Preparing the Jury For Final Argument

A. Voir Dire

The first opportunity to present a case to a jury is during voir dire. The attorney is prohibited from directly arguing the case on voir dire but may indirectly inform the potential jurors about the theories and themes of the case. The attorney, through questions, will be preparing the jurors for what they will hear during the trial. In addition, the attorney may attempt to persuade the jurors to find a favorable verdict by asking a question and later during closing argument referring back to the answer, promise, or committment the jurors gave. This technique creates a psychological inducement for the jurors to act consistently.

B. Opening Statement

The first formal opportunity to lay the foundation for closing argument is during opening statement. During opening statement, the attorney will explain what the evidence will show the facts to be and the attorney's position on the issues. At this point, the attorney is laying the foundation upon which to later build the case for closing argument. Opening statement is the first opportunity to summarize what the evidence will show and what verdict the trier of fact should render as a result of the evidence. The themes and theories of the opening statement should be consistent with the themes and theories of the final argument.

C. Presenting the Evidence

Direct and cross-examination testimony develops the facts that were initially explained during the opening statement. Unless the facts are fully presented in a case, the closing argument will be very difficult to present because the jury will realize that the attorney has failed to provide information that was promised during the opening statement. Complete and accurate factual presentation is the last step in preparing the jury for final argument.

CASE LAW—LOCAL PRACTICE & PROCEDURE—IDEAS

Outline   Notes

10.5 Structure of a Closing Argument

A closing argument must be presented in a structured, ordered fashion. The closing argument must be planned and shaped to conform to the theory, facts, themes and circumstances of the case and to the most effective presentation of the information. Any structure will be appropriate as long as it is simple and clear. The structure must be designed so the entire case can be framed within it and so that the jury can relate the facts and the issues to the structure clearly and easily.

While a chronological story is one effective way of structuring a closing argument other structures can be equally effective depending on the circumstances. The facts can be presented in the order in which the witnesses testified. The evidence could be explained first by describing the undisputed facts and then summarizing the disputed facts. A flashback technique can be used by explaining the end of the story and flashing back to earlier events. Injuries and damages could be described first and then the facts surrounding liability could be described. The story could be presented in topical or emotional clusters. A criminal defense lawyer may structure a closing by listing the number of reasonable doubts which exist. Any number of other structural approaches may be appropriate depending on the circumstances of the case. An effective technique to determine the most effective structure is for the attorney to review the initial outline of the proposed closing argument and then move the segments around experimenting with different presentation patterns keeping an open mind until the most clear and persuasive structure appears.

A. Introduction

Summation should begin with an introduction that draws the jurors' attention and interest to the presentation and the case. The jury's attention level will usually be high at the beginning of the opening statement as they realize the trial draws near to a close. Full advantage should be taken of this opportunity.

The introduction should be designed to have the highest impact on the jurors concerning the information, facts, and themes that the attorney wants the jury to remember. The introduction will set the tone for the rest of the presentation.

Some attorneys may begin summation by indicating that the trial is about over and by thanking the jurors. This courteous explanation, if done with sincerity, may be necessary and effective, but it can be stated at a later stage of summation, preserving the introduction for more important purposes.

B. Explanation of Purpose

Some attorneys will begin a closing argument with an explanation of the purpose of summation. The advantage of these preliminary remarks is that the jurors may better understand the value and import of the closing arguments. The disadvantage of these remarks is that they may not be the most effective and persuasive way to begin summation.

Introductory "boiler plate" remarks are used often because the attorney needs something comfortable to say to reduce nervousness, is unprepared, does not know how to structure a final argument, or has heard someone else say the same thing and has never thought about the need to begin the presentation in a more persuasive way. If the attorney believes this "boiler plate" information is necessary, it may be best placed in the body of the argument.

C. Argument   The closing argument allows an attorney to say most anything that falls within the broad definition of argument. An attorney may:
1. Draw reasonable inferences from direct or circumstantial evidence,
2. Suggest that certain evidence implies a reasonable conclusion,
3. Present conclusions based upon the circumstances of the case,
4. Use analogies and metaphors to explain the import of certain situations,
5. Suggest that the jurors apply their common sense and life experiences in determining a fact,
6. Comment on the credibility of witnesses.

One of the primary tasks of the attorney in closing argument is to be creative and innovative and explain to the jury the significance of inferences. The direct and circumstantial evidence may lead jurors to clear and obvious conclusions. It will be the task of the attorney to explain to the jurors the less obvious conclusions. The advocate will need to highlight for the jury the subtleties and nuances of the facts presented.

D. Explanation of the   A substantial part of a closing argument will consist of the attor-
Evidence   ney summarizing and explaining the evidence to the jury. This description should be consistent both with the facts described in the opening statement and with the evidence produced during the trial. The attorney should be careful not to exaggerate the nature of the evidence presented during the trial because the jurors will easily recognize such overstatements and will lose faith in the credibility of the attorney. Some attorneys will be tempted to take closing argument to an extreme and try to argue that certain evidence has more value than a reasonable juror would ascribe to that evidence. This approach will generally fail because the jury has or will understand that they are to be the finders of fact and not the attorney.
1. *The Story.* The explanation of the facts may be told in a story form which includes descriptions of the scene, the characters, and the event. The goal of the attorney should be to summarize such facts in a way that is reasonable and consistent with the

recollection and memory of the jurors. The attorney should keep in mind that the jurors have heard the evidence and need to be accurately reminded of the facts and not misled by inaccurate argument.

2. *Reference to Actual Testimony.* The factual explanation should employ the words used by the witnesses or supported by the contents of documents. The attorney should neither overstate the facts nor understate them. Quoting the testimony of a witness and mixing that quote with a factual summary may be an effective approach. Reading testimony from a transcript of the case is permissible and may also be persuasive. The evidence should be explained in as dramatic a fashion as appropriate and with a persuasive, interesting style. The elements that make a story very believable and very interesting appear in the great works of literature, art, and theater.

3. *Detail and Corroboration.* The amount of detailed facts the attorney should include in a closing argument depends upon the circumstances of the case. A very detailed factual explanation has the advantage of refreshing the recollection of the jury and explaining the relationship between various types of evidence that may not have been obvious or made clear during the trial. A detailed presentation has the disadvantage of increasing the risk that the jury's memory of the evidence differs from that of the attorney's explanation. A detailed explanation will be more effective if the attorney accurately and consistently summarizes the details.

Summation permits the attorney to explain the primary source of the facts and to describe sources of circumstantial evidence and corroborating facts. This explanation will increase the persuasiveness of the evidence by explaining the connection between facts which the jurors may have missed.

E. Explanation of Law

The judge will explain to the jurors final jury instructions after closing argument. An attorney may and should summarize and explain pivotal instructions. The attorney must be cautious with such explanations and make certain that the description of the law parallels the content of the instructions to be provided. The attorney may believe that some instructions do not adequately or clearly explain part of the law. In these situations the attorney may comment on the instructions and provide an expanded description of the language of an instruction or of its meaning.

An attorney may rely on a variety of sources for legal explanations. It is usually permissible for an attorney to read to the jurors from an accurate, reliable source such as a case, a treatise, or other book. It will often be difficult to discover quotations that will be understandable to the jury. Some judicial opinions will be a good source. To avoid any problem with the use of a case, the judge should be advised before summation of the intended use.

A case may involve special interrogatories which compel the jury to make specific findings of fact during deliberations. These interrogatories may accompany a general or special verdict. The attorney may read special interrogatories to the jury and urge the jurors to answer in a specific way. Local rules and case law will determine whether an attorney can inform the jury that their answers to any one of the interrogatories may determine the outcome of the case. In most cases, the attorney can comment upon the effect of special interrogatories. In some cases, particularly comparative fault situations, an attorney may not be permitted to make such comments.

F. Conclusion

Summation should conclude with a climactic ending. The attorney should review the facts, the themes, and the law and create a conclusion that leaves the jury believing that the verdict requested is the only fair and just verdict. There is a strong likelihood that the final remarks of a presentation will be remembered by an audience. Even if there has been some problems in the argument and the attorney gets flustered or lost, a strong conclusion will help offset these problems. The conclusion of the argument should be well thought out, well prepared, and should make it clear that it is the end of the argument.

The conclusion will also be an opportunity for an attorney to politely and sincerely thank the jurors for their time and attention. Most jurors will appreciate this courtesy if done appropriately.

G. Jury Participation

A closing argument should be designed to actively involve the jurors in the presentation. The conclusions the attorney suggests during closing argument should not be the attorney's position but rather should be a position that the jurors have reached and adopted as their own. Most of the statements an attorney makes during summation should reaffirm for the jurors conclusions and positions they have already adopted by having listened to the voir dire, opening statement, and presentation of the evidence. The inferences the attorney explains during summation should parallel many of the inferences the jurors have already made.

The more the jurors mentally participate in the trial the stronger their conviction will be during deliberation. An attorney should not approach summation with the idea that all the jurors need to be persuaded by all of the arguments. Many of the jurors have made decisions regarding certain facts, inferences, and arguments. An attorney needs to recognize this phenomenon and to employ techniques that take advantage of it. One technique is to advise the jurors that much of what will be said during closing argument will only reaffirm what they have been thinking already. Other techniques may be useful in attempting to have the jurors actively participate with their thoughts, memories, attitudes, and feelings.

H. Length

Summation should be long enough to cover the essential arguments of the case, yet short enough to maintain the jurors' attention. The optimum length for a closing argument will vary depending upon the circumstances and complexity of the case and the speaking ability of the attorney. Many closing arguments will extend between twenty to forty minutes. The longer a closing argument is the more difficult it is to maintain the interest of the jurors.

I. A Final Argument Test

After constructing the closing argument, the attorney can reflect on the following test to determine if the argument is adequate:

1. Does the closing argument tell the jury why to find for the client?
2. Does the closing argument make the jury want to find for the client?
3. Does the closing argument tell the jury how to find for the client?
4. Does the closing argument have a structure that is clear and simple?
5. Is the closing argument reasonable and consistent with the opening statement, the facts, and the law?

CASE LAW—LOCAL PRACTICE & PROCEDURE—IDEAS

Outline   Notes

10.6 Content of Closing Argument

A. Analogies/ Anecdotes

The jury may base their verdict upon common sense and life experiences in addition to the facts and law presented during the trial. The attorney may wish to refer the jury to analogous situations or anecdotal stories to make a point during summation. The concrete images described by an attorney through an analogy or anecdote may assist the jury in understanding the point of law or application of fact to law. An effective story will command the jurors' attention and will provide them with a comparison to determine the appropriateness of a point made during argument. An example of an anecdote to bolster circumstantial evidence is the story of Robinson Crusoe who knows there is someone else on the island because of a discovered footprint. An example of an analogy to explain discrepancies in a case is the comparison of the case to a coin which always has two sides but is one amount.

While a carefully drawn, common sense anecdote or analogy may assist the jury in understanding a concept, careful consideration should be given before one is used. If the analogy or anecdote is too simple or does not make sense the point will not be made with impact. If there is an opportunity to argue following the presentation of an analogy or anecdote, the opponent could use the analogy or anecdote as a part of the opponent's case or may make the use of these tools appear foolish or simplistic. An opposing attorney may comment that the comparison to Robinson Crusoe or a coin diverts the jury's attention away from the facts. Before either an analogy or anecdote is used the attorney should consider whether they need to be employed, whether they are fillers for not taking the time to explain the point without a crutch, and what can an opponent do with either of them by turning them around or by making the argument look silly.

B. Credibility of Witnesses

An attorney may comment on the credibility of a witness, may demonstrate how an observation or statement is inaccurate, or may attempt to show a witness is biased or prejudiced in testifying. These and other impeachment techniques may be used during the trial to establish facts to reduce that witness's credibility. During closing the attorney can summarize those different facts and inferences that have been established and argue that a witness should not be believed or that a witness' perceptions are unlikely or improbable. The attorney may also refer to the instruction on credibility that the judge will provide and explain to the jury how the facts in the trial match the factors of that instruction in reducing the credibility of a witness.

C. Contradictions

It will be obvious to the jury that there exists a dispute between the parties. However, it will not always be obvious what the specific factual contradictions are that exist in the case. Many cases do not involve major factual differences but rather involve contrary inferences and conclusions. The attorney in summation may need to highlight the inconsistencies between witnesses, to point out the contradictions in testimony, and to make certain the jury understands the factual disputes.

D. The Use of Exhibits

Section 10.3(E) described the matters that need to be addressed in selecting visual aids and exhibits to be used in closing argument. The design, placement, and use in the presentation are as important as the visual aid or exhibit itself. The impact words and colors on visual aids, the importance of the exhibit in the trial, the location in the room for clear viewing and easy access, the placement in the structure of the presentation, and the style of the lawyer in the use of and reference to the exhibit are important considerations in determining whether the exhibit will aid or interfere with the final argument presentation.

E. Criminal Case: Burden of Proof and Lesser Included Offenses

Two areas regarding closing arguments in criminal cases that require special consideration include the burden of proof and lesser included offenses. Both the prosecution and the defense may explain the nature of the "beyond a reasonable doubt" standard. It may be difficult to fully comprehend the meaning of this standard and consideration should be given to a clear and simple explanation that will place the meaning of the standard in perspective.

Another difficult area involves the matter of lesser included offenses. A prosecutor has to decide how to deliver an argument seeking a premeditated murder conviction and in the same argument explain the elements of manslaughter. The defense must consider how to reduce the chances that the jury will find a defendant guilty of premeditated murder and at the same time not concede a conviction based on manslaughter. These and other areas need to be carefully and delicately presented to the jury during summation.

F. Civil Case: Burden of Proof, Liability and Damages

Two areas in civil cases that will require special consideration include the burden of proof and liability/damages. The burden of proof must be explained. Consideration must be given as to whether the judge's instructions defining preponderance of the evidence are sufficient and need only to be repeated, emphasized, and related to the facts or whether examples and more detailed definitions must be given. Many jurors may confuse the burden of proof in a civil case and think that the phrase "beyond a reasonable doubt" which they have heard countless times in movies, books, and television should apply. The plaintiff's attorney should make certain the jury does not confuse the required burden of proof.

A plaintiff in a civil case may prefer to argue damages after explaining the basis for liability in a closing argument. This tactic may leave the jurors at the conclusion of an argument at an emotional peak with a lasting impression of the damages the plaintiff has suffered. A defense attorney may prefer to argue against damages initially in the closing argument and then argue the lack of liability on the part of the defense. This approach reduces the awkwardness of having to explain the possibility of damages after arguing that the plaintiff has no right to recovery.

G. Case Weaknesses

Every case will have some weak points which the attorney must address in closing argument. If an attorney can think of a reasonable interpretation that reduces the obvious weakness of a point, then that explanation should be provided the jury. If the attorney cannot think of any mitigating explanation, then the weakness should be conceded in a candid and forthright manner. This disclosure may enhance the credibility of the attorney and reduce the impact of the opposition's focus on such weakness.

H. Attacking Opposition's Positions

An effective technique may be to attack the logic and reasonableness of the opponent's contentions. An attorney may select one or more specific arguments of the opponent, demonstrate the weakness of the evidence or contentions, and explain how this information must be reconciled in favor of the attorney's client.

It is not wise to spend significant portions of the closing argument responding to the opponent's issues, positions, and argument. The jury may perceive an attorney who does this as an advocate without any substantial positions. Arguments which attack the opponent's case must be balanced with arguments that support the attorney's case.

I. Broken Promises

During opening statement the opposing attorney may have described some facts to the jury regarding which no evidence has been introduced during the trial or may have made some promise to the jury which has not been met. An attorney during closing argument should review statements made during the opening and inform the jury that the opposing counsel has failed to do what was described or promised.

J. Non-Facts

During closing argument an attorney may comment on the facts that have not been introduced as well as the facts that have been introduced in the case. If the opposition has failed to have a witness testify, if a witness fails to attend a trial and testify, or if a witness is unable to recall and testify to certain important points, an attorney may comment on the significance of that non-evidence. Some situations may prohibit comments about the lack of certain evidence. For example, it is unconstitutional for a prosecutor to comment on the criminal defendant's failure to testify. It may also be improper for a party to comment on the lack of certain evidence if that information is protected by a privilege.

K. Lie vs. Mistake

Every trial will involve contradictory evidence pitting the testimony of one witness against another. Few witness will deserve to be called and classified as a liar. The more effective tactic will be for an attorney during closing to describe a witness as mistaken about a fact rather than denigrating that individual by suggesting a lie was committed. It may be sufficient to point out that everyone sees an event from different perspectives and how the witness has perceived an event may be a mistaken observation based on an incorrect initial perspective.

In claiming that a witness has lied or is mistaken an attorney should provide a reason to the jury why that person is lying or is mistaken. It will not be enough just to say that a witness has made an intentional or negligent mistake. The facts established on the cross-examination of that witness must be summarized to demonstrate to the jury that witness' lack of credibility.

L. Rhetorical Questions

The rhetorical question can be an effective tool of persuasion because it involves the jurors in the presentation. The essential aspect of a rhetorical question is that, after the question has been asked, the answer should be obvious. A second important aspect is to never answer the question. The jurors should answer it silently to themselves, thereby directly involving them in the opening statement. When a juror has answered a rhetorical question, the thought then becomes that of the juror and not just another part of the closing.

However, rhetorical questions may diminish the positive force of summation. In addition, the jurors may not answer the rhetorical question in the same way the attorney would, and the attorney would not know if the jurors had the correct impression of the facts.

M. Emotion v. Logic

Whether an attorney relies upon emotion or logic or both for part or all of an argument depends upon the circumstances of a case. With some cases it will be more effective for the attorney to present a rational, logical explanation of the evidence and the law. In other cases, it will be more effective for the attorney to rely on the emotions and feelings created by the facts. Often a mixture of both approaches will be the most effective. An attorney must carefully balance the use of emotion in a case. An attorney may more dramatically present an argument by relying upon its emotional aspects but must be cautious not to play to the passion and prejudice of the jurors in reaching a verdict.

N. Avoiding Improper Comments   Section 10.9 describes in detail types of comments that will be inappropriate during closing argument. Some comments may not fall within the category of unethical or legally improper statements but may offend the jury. Comments that denounce the opposing counsel, party, or witnesses may reduce rather than enhance the image of fairness of the attorney unless evidence has been produced during the trial to support such comments.

O. Requests for Verdict   A closing argument must include an explanation of the specific verdict the attorney wants for a client. This explanation should be clear and understandable so the jurors understand what conclusion they must reach to find for a party. In most cases, the request will be a specific request for a verdict of guilty or not guilty or for a verdict for the plaintiff or defendant. The argument may contain a request for a specific amount of damages to be awarded with supporting documentation for this amount of money. In other cases, the attorney for a plaintiff may not wish to be specific regarding an amount of damages, particularly for pain and suffering, and may request a general amount of damages as part of the final verdict.

P. Rebuttal   In many jurisdictions the party who has the burden of proof and the opportunity to begin the closing argument may also conclude summation with a rebuttal. It may be necessary for the attorney to reserve time for rebuttal by requesting permission from the judge. The points made during a rebuttal should counter points by the opposition made during that closing argument. A rebuttal argument should be planned in advance and be coordinated with the initial closing; revisions and additions can be made during and after the opposition's summation.

CASE LAW—LOCAL PRACTICE & PROCEDURE—IDEAS

Outline   Notes

10.7 Presentation and Delivery

The manner in which the attorney delivers a closing argument will effect the jurors' understanding of the evidence, significantly influence many of their conclusions about the case, and shape their deliberations and verdict. The more effective and persuasive an attorney can be in presenting a closing argument the greater the chance that a favorable verdict will be reached by a jury. If the evidence presented in a case is weak, then the attorney will have little or no chance in convincing the jury in closing argument to return a verdict for that client. If the evidence presented during the trial by the attorney is strong, statements made by the attorney during summation will most likely match the conclusions the jury has already reached. If, however, the evidence presented by both sides is balanced, then the closing argument becomes vitally important and may make a difference in which verdict the jury returns.

Many of the same factors that influence the presentation of an opening statement affect summation. The following factors relating to presentation and delivery parallel most of the considerations that have been discussed in Section 5.5 regarding opening statements.

A. Confidence

The attorney during final argument should appear confident and should have command and control of the case. Jurors will usually be impressed by attorneys who are forceful yet tactful, candid yet not condescending, and positive yet realistic.

B. Sincerity

An attorney needs to appear sincere and to believe in the merits of the client's cause to be effective during summation. The failure to be sincere will invariably cause the jury to think that if the attorney does not believe in or care about the case the jury need not care.

C. Interest

An argument made in an interesting manner will hold the jury's attention and sound more persuasive than an argument made in an uninteresting or boring fashion. Interest may be established and maintained in any number of ways. The attorney must first appear to be interested in the case. An argument made in a compelling, energetic, and professionally enthusiastic manner will be a more effective approach than a dull, listless monotone approach.

D. Integrity

Throughout the trial the attorney must have appeared to be fair and honest in the eyes of the attorney. An attorney needs to establish such credibility with the jury if the jury is to accept inferences and conclusions the attorney suggests during summation. The attorney can maintain this appearance during final argument by being straightforward and candid about the case and evidence. The attorney must not oversell or overstate the case. A statement of the law and facts must be reasonable and accurate. The emotional content of the argument must parallel the emotional impact of the evidence.

E. Attitude   The attorney must continue to approach and treat the jurors with respect. The jurors should be treated as equals and not demeaned. Any different treatment will only insult and alienate them. An effective approach with most jurors is to remind them of the serious nature of their duties as jurors and the social responsibility they bear as important members of the justice system.

F. Stance   It will usually be more effective for an attorney to stand in front of the jury box and not behind a lectern or table during summation. This stance will usually hold the juror's attention more than if the attorney hides behind a lectern. This is not to say that an effective closing argument cannot be presented using a lectern, but a lectern may unnecessarily interfere with an attorney establishing an effective presence with the jury.

The attorney must maintain an appropriate distance from the jury. This distance should not be too far away so that personal contact is lost nor too close so that the jurors feel uncomfortable. The exact distance will depend upon the number of jurors, the size, energy, and presence of the attorney, the size, shape, and acoustics of the courtroom, and the content of the statement being made. A distance of between five and eight feet can be used as an appropriate guide, but the distance should be flexible and vary in different circumstances. An attorney can approach closer or move farther away to make a point more effectively.

G. Posture   The attorney's body language must match what is being said to prevent the jurors from being adversely affected by the inconsistency. Good posture is essential for an advocate. Good posture does not require that the attorney stand stock still and straight as a rod during summation. A comfortable, nonslouching posture should be appropriate.

Movement and gestures are important, particularly if the closing argument is long. Movement, stance, pacing, and timing should be orchestrated so as not to be distracting. The attorney may employ movement as a transition during the argument or to make a point more effectively and should avoid movement that appears to be purposeless.

H. Dress   The attorney's appearance is an important consideration in closing argument as well as throughout the trial. An attorney who is tastefully dressed and well groomed will usually appear more professional and credible to the jury.

I. Gestures Effective speakers usually employ gestures to make a presentation more interesting. An attorney needs to incorporate appropriate gestures into the summation. The lack of any gestures and the use of awkward hand movements or wild gesticulations need to be avoided. Gestures should be natural, firm, and purposeful.

J. Eye Contact Establishing eye contact with jurors will help the attorney in creating a sincere and courteous relationship with the jury. Looking jurors in the eye while talking will substantially increase the impact of what is being said. However, staring at a juror will undoubtedly make the juror uncomfortable and adversely affect the attorney's rapport with that juror. It is vital for the attorney to periodically make eye contact with each individual juror.

K. Voice Control and Pace The tone, volume, modulation, and pace of an attorney's voice will affect the listening abilities of the jurors. A dull, monotone presentation will be as ineffective as ranting and raving. A balanced and well modulated approach will usually be most effective.

Sometimes the best thing an attorney can say is nothing. Silence can be an effective way to highlight a point, to gain attention, or to create a transition. An attorney needs to learn to tolerate appropriate silence during closing and to use it constructively.

L. Word Choice
1. *Simple language.* Clarity of expression is important. The words the attorney choses to use will effect the understanding of the jury. Simple and clear language is preferable to complex legalese. Using large words just to show vocabulary skill will turn off the jury. Overly simplistic words may give the jury the impression of being talked down to. The attorney must balance the need for simple language against the danger of appearing condescending.
2. *Word selection.* The factual words chosen must parallel the evidence. Conclusory words must be selected which match the reasonableness of the position asserted. Often an attorney will employ adjectives that exaggerate a position hoping to convince the jury by such an argument. For example, an attorney may state that a specific event is "obvious" or that the evidence is "extremely clear" in situations where a reasonable juror may have some doubt about the event or evidence. This type of overstatement may weaken the impact of the argument and reduce the credibility of the attorney on that point.
3. *Impact phrases.* Descriptive words will be useful in emphasizing the important facets of the case, will portray a more vivid image for the jury, and will more easily be remembered by the jury during deliberation. Impact words that graphically describe a situation may have been employed by a witness during testimony

or may be a reasonable inference derived from some evidence. Descriptive words should be selected which accurately reflect the facts of what happened and care must be taken not to misuse such language. Words that emphasize the theory or theme of the case and that produce some emotional response from the jurors may make a closing argument sound more persuasive.

M. Transitions

The closing argument will be more effective if the attorney employs transitions in the presentation. Prefatory remarks, silence, a louder voice, a softer voice, movement, gestures, emotion, and logic are all devices which can signal a transition.

N. Drama

To the extent possible and appropriate, the presentation of an argument should be made in a serious, dramatic manner. The attorney should deliver a final argument taking full advantage of the theater of the courtroom. The closing argument provides the attorney with substantial freedom to present an argument. An attorney should employ as many varied communication techniques as will be appropriate and persuasive.

O. Developing Own Style

An attorney must deliver the final argument in a style that reflects that attorney's abilities. An attorney should avoid copying and mimicking another lawyer's style but should be open to adapting and reworking what someone else has done if it appears effective. Many parts of a closing argument will be plagiarized from a previous argument because of the similarity of the cases and issues. This form of plagiarism can be most effective as long as the attorney appears to be presenting it in a spontaneous, fresh manner.

P. Observing the Jury's Reaction

The attorney should observe the juror's reaction during the closing argument and mold the presentation to the reactions of the jurors. The facial expressions, body language, and eye contact displayed by individual jurors will usually communicate some information about a juror's attitude or position. These perceptions may not always be accurate and an attorney must cautiously attempt to read the jury. Because it is difficult to accurately determine what a person is thinking just by watching them during a presentation, care must be taken not to overreact, not to completely change an approach because of a perceived reaction, and not to focus on one or two jurors because they seem to be responding positively. An attorney who remains conscious of the reaction of the jury will more easily maintain the interest and attention of the panel.

Q. Notes and Outlines

It will be necessary in many cases for an attorney to rely upon notes or an outline during closing argument to make certain that all the important points have been covered. A final argument may be presented more effectively if an attorney does not need to refer to written preparation. The longer the closing argument the more likely it is for an attorney to need to rely on notes. An attorney should never read a prepared closing argument to the jury or follow the notes so closely that minimal eye contact is established with the jury. Reading the argument will lead to a very boring and uninteresting presentation. Occasional references to notes will be appropriate as long as such references do not unreasonably interfere with or detract from the presentation. Often notes are only available as a crutch which an attorney does not need. A persuasive, flowing argument will usually be more effective even if one or two points are omitted. Continuous use of notes to make sure that every detail is included often will lead to a flat and ineffective presentation.

Prepared outlines can be effectively used in summation if combined with the use of visual aids. An overhead transparency, a pre-prepared diagram, or a blackboard may contain an outline of part or all of the closing which will highlight important matters for the jurors and assist the attorney in explaining the argument.

CASE LAW—LOCAL PRACTICE & PROCEDURE—IDEAS

Outline   Notes

10.8 Objections   Section 9.3 lists common objections that may be asserted during closing argument. If an attorney has an opportunity for a closing argument or rebuttal after the opposition that attorney may prefer not to object but later comment on the inappropriate statement made by the opposing lawyer. If an attorney has no further summation, then an objection and a curative instruction may be necessary to repair any damage. An objection and a request for a curative instruction may be necessary in any case to preserve a matter for appeal.

Most attorneys will not object during final argument unless the opponent is saying or doing something that is clearly improper and damaging to the case. Attorneys usually extend a courtesy to each other so that the final arguments are uninterrupted. Zealous, and effective, but not bizarre, behavior is usually accepted without objection.

CASE LAW—LOCAL PRACTICE & PROCEDURE—IDEAS

Outline   Notes

10.9 Avoiding Mistrials and Reversals

A. Do Not Misstate the Evidence

Since the closing argument is the time when the lawyer sums up all of the evidence and argues interpretations of law and inferences as convincingly as possible, this phase of the trial is subject to abuses. Much of the misconduct during closing involves misstating the evidence or arguing facts not in evidence. DR 7–106(C)(1) expressly forbids this, but the "strictures of DR 7–106 are not infrequently overlooked in oral argument." *In Re Conduct of Rudie*, 290 Or. 471, 622 P.2d 1098 (1981). See also Model Rule 3.3 on Candor. Illogical inferences may not necessarily be wrong. *Alabama Power Co. v. Goodwin*, 210 Ala. 657, 99 So. 158 (1923). Exaggeration of the facts may not be necessarily improper. *Nashville Ry. & Light Co. v. Owen*, 11 Tenn. App. 19 (1929). A new trial will be granted for attorney misconduct not as a disciplinary measure, but to prevent a miscarriage of justice. *Nadeau v. County of Ramsey*, 277 N.W.2d 520 (Minn. 1979).

B. Do Not Interject New Evidence into the Argument

The lawyer is generally allowed wide latitude in discussing the evidence and presenting theories. *State v. Burris*, 198 Ia. 1156, 198 N.W. 82 (1924); *Cherry Creek Nat'l Bank v. Fidelity & Cas. Co.*, 202 A.D. 787, 202 N.Y.S. 611 (1924). All the tools of oratory are at the lawyer's disposal, and tactics calculated to convince or engage sympathy can be used to their fullest. *Mitchell v. Mystic Coal Co.*, 189 Ia. 1018, 179 N.W. 428 (1920). However, no tactics are allowed that are not based on evidence and serve only to inflame the passions or prejudices of the jury. *People v. Dukes*, 12 Ill. 2d 334, 146 N.E.2d 14 (1957). Just what differentiates sympathy from passion or prejudice is a gray area. *See* Gaudineer, *Ethics: The Zealous Advocate*, 24 Drake L. Rev. 79, 89 n.107 (1974). One example is arguing to the jury that a claim for personal injury is fraudulent stating, "a foul odor of greed" permeated the trial, when there was no basis in the evidence for such an allegation. *Delott v. Roraback*, 179 Conn. 406, 426 A.2d 791 (1980).

Arguing facts not in evidence or misstating evidence is always improper. EC 7–25, DR 7–106(C)(1). The final argument should help the jurors determine the issues based only upon the evidence presented at trial. The closing argument is not a time to inject new evidence even if only by way of demonstrating a point. It is improper to introduce information about similar cases decided by different juries. *Salgo v. Leland Stanford Jr. University Bd. of Trustees*, 154 Cal. App. 560, 317 P.2d 170 (1957). It is also improper for an attorney to interject new evidence in a tax evasion case by using a blowup of a political cartoon showing various disreputable characters passing the blame. *United States v. Singer*, 482 F.2d 394 (6th Cir., 1973).

Allowing an inadmissible newspaper clipping to fall at an opposing counsel's feet during final arguments would be unacceptable. *Maker v. Roisner*, 239 Minn. 115, 57 N.W.2d 810 (1952). This does not mean that charts, models, or graphs explaining the evidence already admitted are improper. The concern is whether the demonstrated device adds anything to the merits which is prejudicial to the case. *Edwards v. Sears, Roebuck & Co.*, 512 F.2d 276 (5th Cir. 1975).

C. Do Not Use Tactics Calculated to Arouse the Passions or Prejudices of Jurors

A jury may be aroused to prejudicial or passionate feelings when they are asked to put themselves in the place of the victim or personal injury plaintiff in what is called the "golden rule" argument. *Colgan v. Raymond*, 275 Minn. 219, 146 N.W.2d 530 (1966). Another manner of arousing prejudice might be the tear-jerking recounting of a child crying at the father's grave in arguing a wrongful death suit. In *Edwards v. Sears, Roebuck & Co.*, 512 F.2d 276, the appeals court found the tactic, as calculated to prejudice the defendant, improper. However, if an aggrieved widow faces the jury and weeps while her lawyer argues that her judgment creditors are "leeches and oppressors of poor women and widows," the court may be reluctant to interfere with this "kind of stage performance" which appeals to the "sympathy" of the jury. *Dowdell v. Wilcox*, 64 Ia. 721, 21 N.W. 147 (1884). Telling the jury that awarding a mother compensation for her negligently killed son was tantamount to "selling beef" is an example of a highly inflammatory and prejudicial remark. *Martin v. State Farm*, 392 So.2d 11 (Fla. 1980).

It is improper to single out a juror by name and appeal to him or her during summation. *Peters v. Hoisington*, 72 S.D. 542, 37 N.W.2d 410 (1949); *In re Maier's Estate*, 236 Iowa 960, 20 N.W.2d 425 (1945). Implying to the jury that they, as taxpayers, would be ultimately responsible for a damage award to a plaintiff who sued the state is clearly improper. *Rollo v. State of Vermont*, 421 A.2d 1298 (Vt. 1980) (citing EC 7–25 and DR 7–106(C)(1)). Conversely, telling the jury that this present case would not be the first time litigants had asked for and received large punitive damages is improper. *Carroll Kenworth Truck Sales, Inc. v. Leach*, 396 S.W.2d 1044 (Ala. 1981) ("Right here in Montgomery County it has happened very recently.") It may also be improper to refer to a large corporate plaintiff as "Goliath" suing the defendant "David." *Norlin Music, Inc. v. Keyboard "88" Inc., of Warwick*, 425 A.2d 74 (R.I. 1981). In civil cases, the deliberate mention of insurance usually leads to prejudice in one way or another and, if not at issue in the case, is not permitted. *Laguna v. Provtz*, 300 N.W.2d 98 (Ia. 1981). It is, of course, far more serious to allude to insurance falsely than to let the truth slip out.

Comments may be of a type usually termed prejudicial; however, if they are born out by the evidence, they will be allowed. A Georgia court has remarked:

As to appellant's contention that he was denied a fair trial because the appellee's attorney in closing argument described appellant as a cheapskate, a scheming low-down pup, cheating and swindling, stealing and waiting like a snake in the grass, and further described the case as 'the stinkingest case,' we have studied the attorney's argument in light of all of the evidence, and we do not find that the argument was based on matters not in evidence. . . .

Dudar v. Ferris, 158 Ga. 724, 282 S.E.2d 194 (1981).

An attorney may also be able to legitimately invoke the emotions in a case. It is permissible to read poetry in summation to make a point. *Colorado & S. Ry. Co. v. Chiles*, 50 Colo. 191, 141 P. 661 (1911). Tears may naturally result from the changed atmosphere of the courtroom and case and be appropriate. *Furguson v. Moore*, 98 Tenn. 342, 39 S.W. 341 (1897).

D. A Prosecutor has a Higher Standard

In criminal cases, it is often the prosecutor who must guard against overstepping the bounds of fair argument. Under EC 7–13, the prosecutor is bound by a higher standard than the attorney appearing on behalf of an individual client. The prosecutor must seek justice, not just a verdict. Thus, accusing a rape defendant of "burning with hellish lust," when the disputed issue is who is the aggressor, is improper. *State v. Morgan*, 235 Minn. 388, 51 N.W.2d 61 (1952). *See also United States v. Drummond*, 481 F.2d 62 (2d Cir. 1973); *United States v. White*, 486 F.2d 204 (2d Cir. 1973). As the appellate judge stated in the latter case, "a few injudicious words uttered in the heat of battle by an assistant United States Attorney may undo months of preparation by police, prosecutorial and judicial officers . . . . His excess zeal may be so egregious that it taints a conviction, requiring . . . a new trial." Telling the jury that the defendant is in the palm of their hands and they would waste taxpayers' money if they don't bring in a conviction will require a new trial. *State v. Perry*, 274 Minn. 1, 142 N.W.2d 573 (1966). So will telling the jury that they are naive in drug matters and, therefore, must rely on the state's expertise. *State v. Davis*, 305 Minn. 539, 233 N.W.2d 561 (1975).

E. Argue Facts, Not the Law

The summation is intended to be an argument on the facts of the case and not an argument on the lawyer's view of existing laws. The jury receives the law from the judge, not the lawyers, although control in this area remains at the discretion of the trial judge. *McCullough v. L & N. Ry. Co.*, 396 So.2d 683 (Ala. 1981); *Stephen W. Brown Radiology Assoc. v. Gowers*, 157 Ga. 770, 278 S.E.2d 653 (Ga. 1981).

F. Do Not Argue from a Personal Viewpoint

Personal remarks or personal viewpoints have no place in the final argument, although slipping into an occasional "I believe" will not seriously prejudice a case. State v. Miller, 271 N.C. 646, 157 S.E.2d 335 (1962). The lawyer's remarks are not evidence and the judge usually warns the jury to ignore them. The concern here, again, is whether the remarks will so seriously prejudice a jury creating the need for a reversal and a new trial. *Sanders v. Wheaton*, 273 Ark. 416, 619 S.W.2d 674 (1981); *Funk v. Venture Stores*, 94 Ill. App. 3d 115, 418 N.E.2d 498 (1981). DR 7–106(C)(3)–(4). A lengthy comparison between the size and wealth of the opposing counsel's law firm, and the lack of such resources in an attorney's firm may be inappropriate comments requiring a new trial. *Anderson v. Hawthorne Fuel Co.*, 201 Minn. 580, 277 N.W. 259 (1938).

G. Do Not Place the Jurors in the Position of a Party

It is improper to ask the jurors to put themselves in the place of either party. See Annot. 70 A.L.R.2d 935. Such a plea diverts the jurors attention from the facts of a case and focuses attention on sympathy and pity. An argument such as "would any of you accept $250,000 for your right hand" plays to the passion and prejudice of the jury. Smith v. Merzolf, 59 Ill. App.3d 635, 375 N.E.2d 995 (1978).

H. Do Not Interrupt An Opponent

Finally, objecting to a logical and effective argument merely to interrupt and distract the jury is viewed with disfavor by some courts (and may be a clear breach of DR 7–106(C)(6) and Model Rule 3.4 which call for courteous conduct). *Stroncek v. Berkshire Life Insurance Co.*, 292 Minn. 57, 193 N.W.2d 286 (1971). It will be necessary to interrupt to make a prompt objection to preserve a matter for appeal. *Thomson v. Boles*, 128 F.2d 487 (8th Cir. 1941) cert. denied, 315 U.S. 804 (1942). On the one hand, it is not improper to criticize opposing counsel during summation. See *Missouri-K-T.R. Co. v. Ridgway*, 191 F.2d 363 (8th Cir. 1951). On the other hand, it is also not improper to compliment the opposing lawyer during closing. See *Commercial Standard Ins. Co. v. Noack*, 45 S.W.2d 798 (Tex. Civ. App. 1932).

CASE LAW—LOCAL PRACTICE & PROCEDURE—IDEAS

Outline   Notes

10.10 Bibliography

TEXTS

G. Bellow & B. Moulton, *The Lawyering Process* 826–965 (Foundation Press, Mineola, NY, 1978).

P. Bergman, *Trial Advocacy in a Nutshell* 259–332 (West Pub. Co., St. Paul, MN, 1979).

S. Goldberg, *The First Trial in a Nutshell* 88–94, 390–96 (West Pub. Co., St. Paul, MN, 1982).

K. Hegland, *Trial and Practice Skills in a Nutshell* 37–49 (West Pub. Co., St. Paul, MN, 1978).

J. Jeans, *Trial Advocacy* Ch. 16 (West Pub. Co., St. Paul, MN, 1975).

R. Keeton, *Trial Tactics and Methods* 237–44 (Little, Brown & Co., Boston, MA, 1973).

J. Kelner & F. McGovern, *Successful Litigation Techniques* Chs. 17–18 (Matthew Bender, New York, 1981).

T. Mauet, *Fundamentals of Trial Techniques* 295–360 (Little, Brown & Co., Boston, MA, 1980).

J. McElhaney, *Effective Litigation* 123–269 (West Pub. Co., St. Paul, MN, 1974).

A. Morrill, *Trial Diplomacy* 86–103 (Court Practice Inst., Chicago, IL, 1972).

CLOSING ARGUMENT WORKSHEET   Form 10-1

Case _____   File _____

Themes/Theories

Introduction

Facts

Inferences

Credibility of Witnesses

CLOSING ARGUMENT
WORKSHEET

Form 10-1 (continued)

Analogies/Anecdotes

Exhibits/Visual Aids

Case Weaknesses

Opposing Argument

CLOSING ARGUMENT
WORKSHEET

Facts not Proved/Promises not Kept

Jury Instructions

Legal Elements

CLOSING ARGUMENT
WORKSHEET

Emotional Aspects of Case

Request for Verdict

Conclusion

Rebuttal

Chapter 11

VERDICT AND APPEAL

Whereof you are a well deserving pillar, proceed to judgment.
Shakespeare, Merchant of Venice, Act IV, Scene 1

Four things belong to a judge: to hear courteously, to answer wisely, to consider soberly, and to decide impartially.

Socrates

11.1 Scope   This chapter covers matters occuring after the close of final argument. Jury instructions, jury deliberations, announcing the verdict, post-trial motions, stays of proceedings, completing the record, appeals, and execution are all addressed.

11.2 Jury Instructions   The preparation of jury instructions will often begin early in the case. An instruction explains the law on a matter, and provides, in effect, an outline of the elements of law that need to be proved. Jury instructions will often be considered early in the planning stages of a case because they comprise a major element of the closing argument. See Form 11-1 Jury Instruction Worksheet.

A. Understandable Jury Instructions   Jury instructions should be clear, understandable, and legally correct. The jury must be able to understand the instructions. This is as important as ensuring that the instructions reflect the proper law. Jury instructions that use plain English to explain the law are more likely to be understood by the jurors.

B. Sources of Instructions   Instructions must be based upon the substantive and procedural law of the jurisdiction. Case law, statutes, and other legal authorities will provide the bases for the content of instructions. Jury Instruction Guides (JIGs) will be a common source for standardized instructions. These form instructions should be reviewed to ensure they are clear and correct.

C. Submitting Instructions   Jury instructions must be submitted in accordance with the rules of civil or criminal procedure. See Fed. R. Civ. P. 51; Fed. R. Crim. P. 30. Usually an attorney seeking an instruction must submit a copy of that instruction with supporting authorities. An attorney may submit shorthand requests for instructions by providing the judge with a list of the appropriate numbers from the standard JIGs.

D. Verdict Forms

There are three major verdict forms:

1. *General Verdict.* A jury may return a general verdict form, which is signed by the foreperson or by the entire jury finding for the plaintiff or the defendant or finding a person guilty or not guilty.
2. *Special Verdict Form.* The judge may submit a special verdict form to a jury which requires the jury to make special written findings upon specific issues of fact.
3. *Written Interrogatories.* The court may submit a general verdict form with written interrogatories concerning one or more issues of fact, the decision of which will be necessary to the verdict.

In addition to providing the verdict form, the judge will also give procedural instructions to the jury on how to complete the form, make their findings, and answer any interrogatories. The rules of civil or criminal procedure may regulate the use of verdict forms. See Fed. R. Civ. P. 49.

E. Court Trial

In a civil court trial, the judge decides the case by making findings of fact and conclusions of law. The attorneys typically submit proposed findings of fact and conclusions of law which are consistent with the relief sought. See Fed. R. Civ. P. 52.

In a criminal court trial, the judge may declare the defendant guilty or not guilty. In some jurisdictions, the judge may have to prepare written findings. In other cases, the judge may wish to explain the decision on the record or in writing.

F. Jury Instruction Conference

Before final argument and after the attorneys have submitted proposed jury instructions and verdict forms to the judge, the judge will hold a conference with the attorneys to determine various matters, including:

1. The appropriateness of the proposed instructions.
2. Revisions, modifications, or deletions of proposed instructions.
3. The inclusion of other instructions or verdict forms.

After this conference, the judge will usually issue an order on the record specifying the instructions and verdict forms the court plans to give, proposed instructions or verdict forms which the court has refused to give, and modified instructions. The attorneys must make certain that objections to instructions and verdict forms are made on the record for purposes of appeal. See Fed. R. Civ. P. 51.

CASE LAW—LOCAL PRACTICE & PROCEDURE—IDEAS

Outline   Notes

11.3 Jury Deliberation Procedures

After the judge has instructed the jury, the jurors will be sworn to render a true verdict and led to the deliberation room by the bailiff.

A. Stipulations

Before the case is submitted to the jury, the judge may request that the attorneys consider stipulating to the following:

1. That the court may, upon request of the jury, and in the absence of counsel read to the jury any instruction previously given.
2. That a stay of entry of judgment for an agreed upon number of days shall be granted after a verdict.
3. That a sealed verdict may be returned.
4. That the parties waive the right to have the clerk and reporter present when the jury returns the verdict.
5. That the parties waive their right to poll the jury and will have the verdict immediately recorded and filed in open court.

B. Use of Jury Instructions

A judge may order or an attorney may request that the jury instructions be sent to the jury room for use by the jurors during deliberations. Some portions of the instructions may need to be removed, such as the number, caption, citations of authority, and other comments.

C. Use of Exhibits and Notes

The trial judge will decide which exhibits are allowed in the jury room during deliberations. Real evidence is usually allowed in the jury room. Demonstrative evidence is usually not allowed to go to the jury. A judge may decide not to submit real evidence because the jury will place undue emphasis on it or because it may be dangerous. If a piece of demonstrative evidence would help the jury in making its decision, the trial judge may decide to allow it in the jury room. Although jurors will often be allowed to take notes during the course of the trial, many judges will not allow the jurors to bring these notes into the deliberation room. The exclusion of jurors' notes avoids the problems of notes being considered evidence and prevents those jurors from exercising undue influence over other jurors.

D. Questions by Jurors

If a jury has questions regarding the case during deliberations, the foreperson will reduce it to writing and submit it through the bailiff to the judge. The judge will prepare an answer, consult with the attorneys by telephone, and then announce the question and answer in open court. The parties may waive their right to consult with the judge or to be present when the question and answer are presented to the jury.

CASE LAW—LOCAL PRACTICE & PROCEDURE—IDEAS

Outline   Notes

11.4 Announcing the Verdict

After the jury has reached a verdict, the jurors return to the courtroom where the foreperson delivers the completed verdict form to the bailiff, clerk, or judge. The verdict will be read in open court unless the parties have agreed on some other procedure or waived their right to be present.

A. Polling the Jury

An attorney may request that the jury be polled after the return of a verdict. The trial judge or clerk usually polls the jury by asking each individual juror whether they support the verdict.

B. Discharging the Jury

After the verdict has been read, the judge will discharge the jurors and advise them that they may, but need not, speak to anyone about the case. The attorneys may wish to speak with members of the jury to determine what influenced their verdict and gain their impressions about how the attorneys presented the case. Many jurisdictions restrict the scope of questions attorneys may ask the jurors.

CASE LAW—LOCAL PRACTICE & PROCEDURE—IDEAS

Outline   Notes

11.5 Motion for Directed Verdict

A motion for a directed verdict will be made during the trial at the close of the opponent's evidence, the close of all the evidence, or on both occasions. This motion, outside the hearing of the jury, requests the judge to review the evidence and rule the evidence that has been admitted is insufficient to sustain a verdict for the opponent. See Fed. R. Civ. P. 50(a); Fed. R. Crim. P. 29(a) & (b). The judge must determine that there exists no question of fact supported by the evidence upon which the jury could render a verdict for the opposing party. Most judges will be disinclined to grant a directed verdict motion. These judges prefer to allow the case to go the jury and then grant a judgment notwithstanding the verdict to correct any problem with the verdict. See Section 11.6(A).

If a motion brought by the defendant after the plaintiff has rested is granted, the defendant need not introduce any evidence and judgment will be granted for the defendant. If a motion brought by either party after both sides have rested is granted, then there is no need for closing argument or jury deliberations and a judgment will be entered by the court for the prevailing party.

A. Specific Grounds

A motion for a directed verdict should not be automatically made unless a party has sufficient and specific grounds to support such a motion. A party who brings a motion for a directed verdict must state the specific grounds which support the motion. This means that a party must point out either that the evidence presented supports a judgment for the moving party or must argue that the lack of certain evidence fails to support a judgment for the opposing party. This information discloses the deficiencies in a case to the opponent.

B. Motion for Leave to Reopen a Case

A party who opposes a motion for a directed verdict and realizes that some evidence has been overlooked and not introduced may bring a motion requesting the court for leave to reopen the case and introduce additional evidence. Courts usually grant this motion if the evidence is readily available and substantial enough to raise a question of fact sufficient to deny the directed verdict motion.

CASE LAW—LOCAL PRACTICE & PROCEDURE—IDEAS

Outline   Notes

11.6 Post-Trial Motions

After a verdict one or both parties may submit post-trial motions requesting the court to review the verdict. These motions will often be required to preserve the right to appeal. See Form 11-2 Post-Trial Motions Worksheet.

A. Motion for Judgment Notwithstanding the Verdict

1. A motion for judgment notwithstanding the verdict (judgment n.o.v.) may be made after the verdict has been returned by the jury. The basis for determining whether to grant or deny this motion is identical to a motion for directed verdict. The judge must find that as a matter of law the only reasonable conclusion that can be reached from the evidence is that one party or another is entitled to judgment. See Fed. R. Civ. P. 50(b). If the judgment n.o.v. is overturned on appeal, the jury's verdict will become the final verdict in the case. Consequently, many courts are more inclined to grant a motion for judgment n.o.v. than a motion for directed verdict because the potential of having to retry the case is lessened.

B. Motion for New Trial

A party may seek a second trial if some irregularity regarding the law, facts, rules, or procedure occurred during the first trial. The bases for a new trial may raise both questions of law and fact. The exact grounds will vary from jurisdiction to jurisdiction, but generally, a new trial may be granted if:
1. A party was deprived of a fair trial because of irregularities in the proceedings caused by the court, referee, jury, or prevailing party.
2. The jury or prevailing party committed misconduct.
3. The trial was prejudiced by an accident or surprise which could not have been prevented by using ordinary care.
4. Material evidence has been newly discovered which, with reasonable diligence, could not have been found and produced at the trial.
5. Excessive or insufficient damages were awarded by the jury apparently under the influence of passion or prejudice.
6. Errors of law occurred at the trial.
7. The verdict is not justified by the evidence or is contrary to the law.
8. A verdict is otherwise fatally defective.
See Fed. R. Civ. P. 59; Fed. R. Crim. P. 33.

In some jurisdictions, the appellate courts will limit their scope of review on appeal if a motion for new trial is not made. If a motion for new trial is not made to the trial court, the appellate court will only review the case to determine if the evidence and law support the verdict. Other issues, including procedural and evidentiary objections, may not be reviewed unless the attorney has made a motion for a new trial. See, e.g., *Gruenhagen v. Larson*, 310 Minn. 454, 246 N.W. 565 (1976).

C. Motion to Amend Court Findings and Conclusions

In a court trial after a judge has reached a decision and completed findings of fact and conclusions of law, a party may move the court to amend the judgment. The motion will explain which findings are not supported by the evidence, which conclusions are not supported by the law, and suggest revised findings and conclusions.

D. Timing

When a post-trial motion can or must be made depends upon the rules of the court, which will vary from jurisdiction to jurisdiction. The time available to submit post-trial motions will usually be limited to no more than 10 or 15 days after a verdict or after a party has been notified of the filing of the decision. See, e.g., Fed. R. Civ. P. 59; Fed. R. Crim. P. 29, 33, 34, & 45.

E. Supportive Memorandum

The submission of a supportive memorandum explaining the factual and legal grounds for the motion may increase the chances of obtaining a favorable ruling from the judge. In some cases, supportive affidavits will be necessary to establish the grounds for a motion.

F. Stay of Entry of Judgment or Proceeding to Enforce Judgment

A court may order a stay of entry of judgment or any proceeding to enforce a judgment while the attorneys are proceeding with post-trial motions. If a stay is imposed, the court may attach appropriate conditions for the security of the adverse party. See Fed. R. Civ. P. 58 & 62; Fed. R. Crim. P. 34.

CASE LAW—LOCAL PRACTICE & PROCEDURE—IDEAS

Outline   Notes

11.7 Making a Record   The primary purpose of making a trial record is to establish and preserve grounds for appeal. The trial record usually consists of a transcript of the proceedings, exhibits, jury instructions, the jury's completed verdict form, pleadings, discovery requests, motions, memoranda, orders, the judgment, the notice of appeal, and any other filed documents. See Fed. R. App. P. 10. The attorney must continually be aware of the need to make the record for possible appellate review.

A. Preserving the   Most appellate courts require compliance with certain proce-
Grounds for Appeal   dures to properly raise an issue for appeal. Typically, the trial record must reflect the following:

1. A record of the ruling, order, conduct, or event creating the ground for appeal.
2. An objection by the attorney to an error in the trial.
3. A request for a curative instruction by the judge to the jury if the error occurred within the hearing of the jury.
4. An offer of proof if an evidentiary objection has been sustained.
5. The submission of a post-trial motion to the judge.

These requirements are intended to prevent appeals unless the attorney has properly objected thereby providing the trial judge an opportunity to correct or reduce the impact of the error. Some issues, such as the sufficiency of the evidence to support the findings, will be appealable even if an objection was not made at trial. If manifest injustice could result from the denial of an appeal, some courts will allow an appeal where issues have not been preserved for appeal.

CASE LAW—LOCAL PRACTICE & PROCEDURE—IDEAS

Outline   Notes

11.8 Appeals   The subject of appellate procedure and practice is beyond the scope of this *Trialbook*. The publications listed in the bibliography provide information regarding appellate rules and practice.

The trial lawyer will be involved in the decision whether to appeal. This decision must be taken in consultation with the client. The degree of error committed, the substantial rights of the party affected, the economic resources of the client, and the chances of success on appeal are important decisional factors to be considered. Further, the reality that only a very small percentage of cases will be reversed on appeal may be the most important factor of all. Once the decision to appeal is made, many trial lawyers will refer the appeal to another lawyer who specializes in appellate practice. See Form 11-3 Appeal Planning Worksheet.

A. Harmless Error   Any error at the trial level in either the admission or exclusion of evidence or a defect in a ruling or order or anything done or omitted by a court or any of the parties will not be sufficient grounds for reversing a judgment unless the substantial rights of the parties have been affected. Any matter short of depriving a party of substantial justice will usually be deemed harmless error and insufficient to overturn the verdict. See Fed. R. Civ. P. 61; Fed. R. Crim. P. 52.

B. Appeallable Orders and Judgment   A final judgment or an order must be entered by the trial court before an appeal will be allowed. Rules and procedure vary from jurisdiction to jurisdiction, but the requirement of finality is almost universal. See Fed. R. App. P. 4; Fed. R. Civ. P. 58, 79; see also 28 U.S.C. 1291. Some orders which are interlocutory in nature may be appealable depending upon their importance and impact. Orders which grant or deny preliminary motions will ordinarily not be appealable. Appellate courts will grant writs of certiorari if they decide to hear a discretionary appeal. See generally Fed. R. App. P. 5; see also 28 U.S.C. 1292.

C. Notice of Appeal   To initiate an appeal, the attorney must submit a notice of appeal to either the trial or appellate court. See, e.g., Fed. R. App. P. 3 & 5. Additional required documents may include a statement of the case, a petition, or similar documents.

D. Stay or Injunction Pending Appeal   When an appeal is taken, the appellant may obtain a stay or injunction while the appeal is proceeding. Often the rules of appellate procedure will require that the request for an injunction or stay have first been brought in the trial court. An appeal may need to be accompanied by a supersedeas bond which conditions the allowance of the appeal on the posting of security for the appellee. See Fed. R. App. P. 8; Fed. R. Civ. P. 62; Fed. R. Crim. P. 38.

CASE LAW—LOCAL PRACTICE & PROCEDURE—IDEAS

Outline   Notes

11.9 Judgment and Execution

If a general verdict form is used, the clerk will automatically enter the judgment unless the court orders otherwise. If a special verdict form or general verdict form with interrogatories is used, the clerk will enter judgment only upon the direction of the court. A judgment is not effective until entered by the clerk of court. See Fed. R. Civ. P. 58; Fed. R. Crim. P. 32.

A. Taxation of Costs

The prevailing party in a civil case is entitled to receive reimbursement for the expenses incurred during the trial unless the court orders otherwise. See Fed. R. Civ. P. 54. These costs typically include witness fees, deposition expenses and the transcripts if used during the trial, reasonable expert witness' fees, service fees, filing fees, and related expenses. These expenses do not include attorney's fees unless a statute or contract between the parties permits such recovery. The attorney should provide the necessary expense information to the court clerk who will include those costs in the entered judgment.

Interest will also be recoverable on the judgment until it is satisfied. A specific statute or rule will usually govern the amount of interest and when it begins to accrue.

B. Satisfaction of Judgment

A judgment becomes a satisfied judgment when a losing party pays the judgment. In some cases a judgment may be satisfied upon partial payment if consideration exists for the payment, such as a waiver of a party's right to appeal.

C. Execution

Execution, garnishment, attachment, replevin, and other forms of statutory or judicially enforced collection may be necessary if the losing party in a case fails to voluntarily abide by a judgment.

CASE LAW—LOCAL PRACTICE & PROCEDURE—IDEAS

Outline   Notes

11.10 Bibliography

TEXTS

G. Bellow & B. Moulton, *The Lawyering Process*, 855–69, 898–99, (Foundation Press, Mineola, NY, 1978).

P. Bergman, *Trial Advocacy in a Nutshell*, 293–98, (West Publishing Co., St. Paul, MN, 1979).

S. Goldberg, *The First Trial in a Nutshell*, 95–98, (West Publishing Co., St. Paul, MN, 1982).

I. Goldstein & F. Lane, *Goldstein Trial Technique*, (Callaghan & Co. Wilmette, IL, 1969 & 1981 supp.).

K. Hegland, *Trial Practice Skills in a Nutshell*, (West Publishing Co., St. Paul, MN, 1978).

J. Jeans, *Trial Advocacy*, 32, 72, (West Publishing Co., St. Paul, MN, 1975).

R. Keeton, *Trial Tactics and Methods*, 221–23, 237–44, (Little, Brown & Co., Boston, MA, 1973).

J. Kelner & F. McGovern, *Successful Litigation Techniques*, Chs. 18–19, (Matthew Bender, New York, 1981).

T. Mauet, *Fundamentals of Trial Techniques*, 317–318, (Little, Brown & Co., Boston, MA, 1980).

C. Kunz, R. Haydock, & J. Sonsteng, *Appellate Advocacy Videotape Manual*, (Nat'l Inst. for Trial Advocacy, St. Paul, MN, 1981).

J. McElhaney, *Effective Litigation*, 6, (West Publishing Co., St. Paul, MN, 1974).

A. Morrill, *Trial Diplomacy*, 125–126, 221–223, 235–239, (Court Practice Institute, Chicago, IL, 1972).

J. Nolan, *Trial Practice*, 148–151, 159–164 (West Publishing Co., St. Paul, MN, 1981).

JURY INSTRUCTION WORKSHEET

Form 11-1

Case _____   File _____

Jury Instruction	Source/JIG	Submitted to Judge	Accepted	Rejected	Modified

POST TRIAL MOTION WORKSHEET   Form 11-2

Case _____   File _____

1. Motion for Directed Verdict Grounds:

2. Motion for Judgment Notwithstanding the Verdict Grounds:

POST TRIAL MOTION
WORKSHEET   **Form 11-2 (continued)**

3. Motion for New Trial Grounds:

   A. Irregularity in proceedings by court, referee, jury, or prevailing party

   B. Irregularity in order or abuse of discretion resulting in deprivation of fair trial

   C. Misconduct of jury or prevailing party

   D. Accident or surprise

   E. Newly discovered material evidence

   F. Excessive or insufficient damages due to passion or prejudice

   G. Errors of law

   H. Verdict not justified by evidence or contrary to law

APPEAL PLANNING WORKSHEET   Form 11-3

Client _____   File _____

1. Issues for appeal:

2. What substantial rights of the party have been affected?

3. What are the chances of success?

Statutes and Rules

FEDERAL RULES OF CIVIL PROCEDURE

FEDERAL RULES OF CRIMINAL PROCEDURE

FEDERAL RULES OF APPELLATE PROCEDURE

*

General Index

†